Flyfishing Adventures™
MONTANA

John E Holt

Fishing Titles Available from Wilderness Adventures Press, Inc.™

Flyfishers Guide to™

Flyfisher's Guide to Alaska

Flyfisher's Guide to Arizona

Flyfisher's Guide to Chesapeake Bay

Flyfisher's Guide to Colorado

Flyfisher's Guide to the Florida Keys

Flyfisher's Guide to Freshwater Florida

Flyfisher's Guide to Idaho

Flyfisher's Guide to Montana

Flyfisher's Guide to Michigan

Flyfisher's Guide to Minnesota

Flyfisher's Guide to Missouri & Arkansas

Flyfisher's Guide to Nevada

Flyfisher's Guide to the New England Coast

Flyfisher's Guide to New Mexico

Flyfisher's Guide to New York

Flyfisher's Guide to the Northeast Coast

Flyfisher's Guide to Northern California

Flyfisher's Guide to Northern New England

Flyfisher's Guide to Oregon

Flyfisher's Guide to Pennsylvania

Flyfisher's Guide to Saltwater Florida

Flyfisher's Guide to Texas

Flyfisher's Guide to the Texas Gulf Coast

Flyfisher's Guide to Utah

Flyfisher's Guide to Virginia

Flyfisher's Guide to Washington

Flyfisher's Guide to Wisconsin & Iowa

Flyfisher's Guide to Wyoming

Flyfisher's Guide to Yellowstone National Park

Best Fishing Waters™

California's Best Fishing Waters

Colorado's Best Fishing Waters

Idaho's Best Fishing Waters

Montana's Best Fishing Waters

Oregon's Best Fishing Waters

Washington's Best Fishing Waters

On the Fly Guide to™

On the Fly Guide to the Northwest

On the Fly Guide to the Northern Rockies

Anglers Guide to™

Complete Anglers Guide to Oregon

Saltwater Angler's Guide to the Southeast

Saltwater Angler's Guide to Southern California

Field Guide to™

Field Guide to Fishing Knots

Fly Tying

Go-To Flies™

11"x17" Tri-fold River Maps
Montana:

Bear Trap Canyon	Madison River
Big Hole River	Middle Fork Flathead River
Big Horn River	Rock Creek
Blackfoot River	South Fork Flathead River
Clark Fork River	Upper Missouri River
Flathead River System	Yellowstone River
Gallatin River	

Flyfishing Adventures™
MONTANA

John Holt

Wilderness
Adventures
Press, Inc.™

Belgrade, Montana

Flyfishing Adventures" Series

Published by Wilderness Adventures Press, Inc."
45 Buckskin Road
Belgrade, MT 59714
866-400-2012
Website: www.wildadvpress.com
email: books@wildadvpress.com

First Edition 2010

Printed in Canada.

ISBN 978 -1-932098-80-8 (8-09206-98808-8)

Twenty-five percent of the royalties earned by this book will be given to the Alliance for the Wild Rockies.

I have fished for trout since I was a boy and I admit I still know little or nothing about them. Indeed this is one of the special fascinations of pursuing them. Perhaps it is also the beginning of trout wisdom.

Trout Madness – Robert Traver

Table of Contents

Foreword

It's early September and Blanche, John Holt, and I are deep in the middle of the Blackfoot Reservation. There are no paved roads on the Rez, only primitive dusty tracks. We drop John off at a no-name lake with his fly rod. We are going farther up the road with our German wirehaired pointers to hunt Hungarian partridge.

John looks at the sky and says, "There are storm clouds in the west. If it starts to rain get back here as fast as you can. These dirt roads will turn to gumbo and we could be stuck here for days!"

We travel about a mile up the road and stop to let our dogs out and begin to hunt the prairie for Huns. In an hour we make a sweep over the prairie with no luck. On our way back to the rig the clouds open up and it begins to pour. We throw our gear into the truck, load our dogs, and drive down the road to get John. Soon the road turns to mud and the rig careens from side to side. When we get to the lake John is standing by the muddy road with his rod broken down. We slow down and John opens the door and jumps in. It's a wild half hour ride to the paved road. John tells us he caught two 18-inch rainbows and had an even larger one on when the rain started and he broke the fish off.

When we get to our motel the rain has turned to snow. We unpack, set up the small barbeque, and grill some steaks and spuds while we have a scotch. It has been another day of adventure in Big Sky Country.

Over the years the blue ribbon trout streams of Montana have seen increasing pressure. The fishing is still great but the overall experience is not what it was 20 years ago. There are a number of streams and lakes in Montana that provide the angler with the opportunity for a quality fishing adventure without the crowds.

John and his wife Ginny spend most of their fishing time seeking out these unknown gems. When I decided to start a new series about great fishing waters that are often off the beaten path, with little or no fishing pressure, majestic views, and quality fishing I knew that John was the one person to write *Flyfishing Adventures: Montana.* John is one of a few writers who can entertain you with his stories while imparting solid information on the waters.

John shares 21 of his favorite waters and takes you with him and Ginny as they explore and fish for trout, pike, and bass in Montana. John weaves a story about each water while giving you tips on when to go, his favorite fly for each water, and tying instructions. He also describes some special places to stay, camp, and eat.

I know that you will enjoy John's book and, hopefully, you will come to Montana to one of these waters for your own Montana adventure.

CHUCK JOHNSON, PUBLISHER

Introduction

WHERE'S THE FIRST TEE AND WHAT'S THE COURSE RECORD?

Flyfishing has been a passion and essential part of my life ever since I first cast a Royal Coachman to brook trout in the remote and black-fly-and-mosquito-infested Sand River flowage of central Ontario 47 years ago. Had I known that these first, primitive attempts would lead me down a winding backroad or even lesser thoroughfare toward and beyond horizons of joy, wonder, frustration, and discovery filled with fantastic landscapes, eccentric individuals much like myself, and wild, free-form fish, I would have dropped out of school and hitched my way to Montana well before I reached full-blown puberty, saving myself and others much embarrassment and misery – "How many colleges does that make that he's quit or been kicked out of?"

This book is a distillation of what fishing in Montana has become for me. The adventure of the unknown and the return to the familiar that create a strong sense of security within the natural rhythms of seasons, good country, and my true companion on this often esoteric ride, my wife and photographer, Ginny. This is not about numbers or size. Where the country is still good – healthy, relatively pristine, often remote, few or no other humans – that's where we bounce and lurch. A trickle of bubbling water, a few wild rainbows and brookies, coyotes and nighthawks riffing natural jazz, thunderstorms blasting counterpoint, a sky filled with whirling stars, galaxies, planets, and a crescent moon rising – that's more than enough. We'll take all of it to go, please.

When I say, "Where's the first tee and what's the course record?" this is not offered in a competitive sense, but rather as an attitude of optimism, adventure, and a challenge to make the most out of each day. I fish to catch fish but that's only part of the deal. The adventure of finding new waters or re-visiting old ones and finding out that they're as good as they've always been keeps flyfishing fresh. Gone are the 200-days-per-year 12-hour outings of my youth. I take things easier; having little desire to drive myself as I once did. I catch more large fish than I used to and I gain

more enjoyment from savoring the fewer hours spent wading and casting, because I'm moving at a pace that is in tune with the land and its waters. Spending days and nights that blend into weeks in good country is probably what draws me the most to catching trout, bass, northerns, carp, whitefish, and so on. Camping, hiking, photographing, reading one of Charles Willeford's fine novels in the afternoon or just sitting on a log and taking in the surroundings is more than enough, and only serves to enrich the time I spend chasing fish.

In the trip information section at the end of each chapter, directions for finding the waters, the best times of the year, gear and patterns are included, as are places to eat and to stay. These are merely suggestions. Go your own way and live dangerously. I left out the dwindling number of old roadside motels that feature black-and-white TV, magic fingers, velvet paintings, and old furniture circa the movie, *A Touch of Evil,* or better yet, *Fool For Love* with Kim Bassinger, Sam Shepard, and the one and only Harry Dean Stanton. The mood of the latter is what Ginny and I search for when we're out and about. Maybe you'll tumble onto one of these frozen-in-time gems. That's part of this chase, too.

As I said earlier, the size of the quarry has never mattered. A seven-inch native redband taken from a tiny trickle in the mountains or a two-foot brown beneath an overhanging cottonwood along a wide river – all the same to me. Each has its own attractions. I prefer to fish where there are no others, and that takes effort these days as more and more people populate the planet and, in turn, rightfully take up flyfishing to escape the madness of overcrowding. I do enjoy fishing with friends, especially my best friend, Ginny.

All of the chapters are in this book because, while they share the mystery, excitement, and beauty of classics like the Madison, the Bitterroot, and the Missouri, each offers at least one small esoteric variation on the theme of flyfishing. And mixed in on a few occasions, as is my nature, are a few minor rants or opinions on subjects related to flyfishing. Can't help myself here. Some of the waters are difficult to find, let alone get to. Others feature small, and I mean small, water. Still others feature wild horses in the surrounding hills or slightly crazed packs of coyotes barking jazz riffs beneath the night sky. All of them have brought a great amount of joy and necessary peace in my life over the decades and I'm grateful that these places still hold their arcane magic.

I hope they give the same to you. As my dear friend and tremendous writer, the late Robert F. Jones, would say when we were traveling through fine landscape having a hell of a riotous time, "As it should be. May it always be so."

Chapter One

Tongue River

I've been in love with Tongue River country since the first time I drove into the vast openness of miles upon miles of native grasslands, sage flats, dusty roads where wakes of salmon-colored dust trailed in my wake like a ghostly wall marking my passage. Rough-cut coulees sliced through plateau and bench land, scouring through hundreds of millions of years of history – long dead oceans revealed in layers of sandstone studded with fossils, primordial jungles holding dinosaurs now turned into thick seams of coal stretching north into Alberta and Saskatchewan, layers of muddy red clinker remaining from ancient coal bed fires that in some places still smolder, sending faint wisps of smoke above ground to be swept eastward by the winds blowing down from the Big Horn Mountains in Wyoming. Antelope graze along the narrow dirt roads. Elk hold in shadowed valleys as do Merriam's turkeys, mule deer, and black bear. Sage grouse drum out in those waves of sage that perfume the air along with the scent of ponderosa that grows in tall stands down through depressions in the land, along gentle slopes, and along eroding ridges.

Running through all this like an unexpected miracle is the Tongue River that heads far to the southwest in the Big Horns and empties a couple of hundred miles later into the Yellowstone River at Miles City. Along the way, the Tongue provides life for ranchers, wildlife, and of course fish, including rainbow and brown trout, smallmouth bass, white crappie (state record of 3.68 pounds) and carp. In the Tongue River Reservoir, northern pike (state record of 37.5 pounds), yellow perch, black crappie (state record of 3.13 pounds), channel cat, yellow bullhead (state record of 0.93 pounds) walleye and other species donated by residents of nearby Sheridan, Wyoming, including goldfish (mutated into koi), great whites, and piranha. Remember also that pretty much anything that swims in the pond above the dam has no doubt washed down into the river.

To drive alongside the river on the road from scenic downtown Birney (population 105 as of 2007) to the reservoir's dam on a 100-plus-degree July day is a revelation. Everything is dry, near death, desiccated, dusty, except for the river corridor which slices through the heart of this desert like an emerald scythe. Hay fields glow and wave in shades of green beneath a pitiless sun. The river shimmers blue, silver, and green while the colors of wild flowers grow along its banks – white, yellow, red, orange, lavender, light blue. Cattle and horse graze peacefully. Red-tailed hawks soar overhead. Golden eagles perch from old fence posts. Looking down on the river, large carp, maybe up to 15 pounds, feed in the shallows on nymphs and organic matter in the silt. Up by the dam and its campground, rainbows sip mayflies from abundant hatches. Ducks patrol eddies. Last season's brown trout redds are still visible in side channels.

The place attracts few people other than the motorized crazies up above in the reservoir and, as I mentioned, a few rainbows really do swim around in this gorgeous river flowing through the middle of bone-dry, lonesome southeast Montana. There really are a few browns, smallmouth and plenty of carp, but that's not really the point here. Tongue River country flows to its own rhythm, a lot like Coltrane did in *A Love Supreme.* Seems like anything cool in this land is under some kind of threat and the same holds true with this liquid tune. Open-pit coal mining a little bit to the southwest of here is tearing up the land, and oil pumpjacks bob up and down across the prairie. Now a new partner in crime is making its presence felt. Coal bed methane is riding roughshod over the coulees and bluffs for an energy-voracious country and using lots of water in the process. The oil and gas industry barons will leave the land bone dry and with a lot less life than they first found it if they continue with their rampaging ways. Even having lots of money can't always help.

A Montana state judge ruled that an energy company has the right to explore and drill for natural gas on an 82,000-acre Diamond Cross cattle ranch owned by the billionaire Forrest E. Mars, Jr. of candy bar fame. Mars' attorneys fought the proposed drilling but the company, Pinnacle Gas Resources – who owns mineral rights on some of this property – began drilling 90 minutes after the judge issued his ruling in January, 2008. The speedy response on the part of the company was because its leases were set to expire within a week if it did not act. At the time, Lonnie Wright, the son-in-law of Forrest Mars and the manager of the 82,000-acre Diamond Cross ranch, said that there was no choice but to let the company on the ranch property. "I got lots I could add but nothing that would help the situation," he said.

In mid-September, 2009, the river was still running good and blue. Diamond Cross Ranch's holdings seemed okay, but when a guy worth $14 billion can't get his way with the oil and gas boys you know some heavy darkness is going down.

The only people who ever believed me about brown trout swimming in the Tongue are no longer here. Gary LaFontaine had his own tales to tell about taking the fish in this remote watershed. He told me how he would cast a streamer far and wide then strip the thing back as fast as he could, often taking browns on nearly every cast. This sounded odd to me until I heard another angler, whose abilities I also respect,

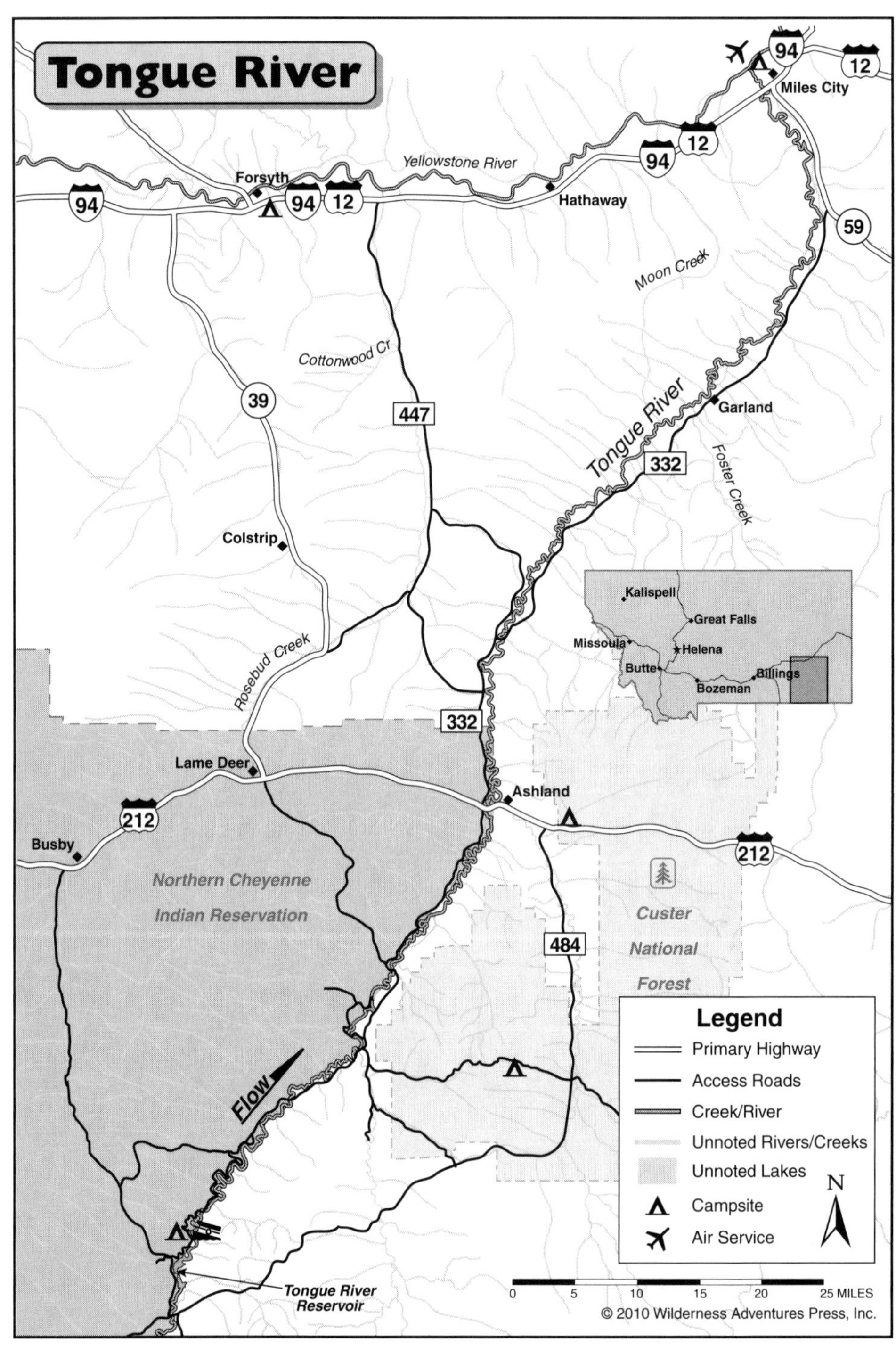
Tongue River
94
12
Miles City
Forsyth
94
12
Yellowstone River
94
12
Hathaway
Moon Creek
59
Cottonwood Cr
39
447
Tongue River
Garland
332
Foster Creek
Colstrip
Kalispell
Great Falls
Missoula
Helena
Butte
Billings
Bozeman
332
Rosebud Creek
Lame Deer
Ashland
212
Busby
Northern Cheyenne
Indian Reservation
Custer
484
National
Forest
212
Flow
Legend
Primary Highway
Access Roads
Creek/River
Unnoted Rivers/Creeks
Unnoted Lakes
Campsite
Air Service
N
Tongue River
Reservoir
0   5   10   15   20   25 MILES
© 2010 Wilderness Adventures Press, Inc.

say the same thing. My attorney Steve Potenberg and his father-in-law, writer Jim Harrison, float the Yellowstone often and on occasion they employ the technique.

"It sounds and looks crazy, but the browns, and some rainbows, come out of the deep channels in the middle of the river and smash the thing," said Potenberg. "It works."

I've yet to try it, but I will next fall.

The other person who knew about the browns in the Tongue was Bob Jones. On one of our trips there, we took a half-dozen between us in early May, using Cree Woolly Buggers cast as far as we could (upwards of 21 feet), allowed to sink and nearly dead drifted with the slightest of twitchings. The browns took slowly and we missed a number but got so we could sense the slightest pull on the line. The largest was Bob's of 21 inches and they averaged around 19 and two to three pounds.

One October, Ginny and I stopped at the campground on our way back from Biddle. You had to be there to partially understand. I noticed that some new redds were being constructed in some shallow water along the banks. Too tired to fish that evening, I walked along the river near dark with a flashlight and spotted browns working on their redds. They slid on their sides and pushed silt and gravel out of the way with their tails. Some of the trout were in the 20-inch range. These appeared to be females, as the smaller browns of 12 to 15 inches had well-defined kypes marking them as males. The next morning, I waded down below these spots and cast into undercut, grassy banks. Browns raced out and attacked my Bugger. They clearly weren't feeding but rather defended their territory. The third fish I took first smacked the pattern with his jaw, then pushed it violently with his snout before engulfing it. I could have taken countless trout. They were near peak aggression, but I exercised some restraint and climbed out of the water.

While packing up the Suburban, the sky clouded over, the air turned cold, and sleet began driving down from the northeast. Ugly weather was on the way. I couldn't resist one last look at the redds. In the gloom, I could make out the browns deepening and expanding their spawning sites. I was transfixed, then realized that we'd better make tracks to paved roads in a hurry or be trapped in the gumbo for who knew how long. As I said earlier, there are not a lot of trout in the Tongue, but that doesn't matter to me. The ones I've seen and caught are more than enough.

I know a number of my friends will not believe any of this, but I'm nearing 60 and no longer care whether or not people believe any or all that I say or write. Check out the river and the above technique on your own and prove me wrong. My conscience is clear and my heart pure.

I've heard a number of stories about excellent smallmouth bass fishing, but have yet to canoe the stretches of the river where the fish hold. I have caught a few in some runs above Birney, using Marabou Muddlers that were heavily weighted and even dosed with a split shot or two. Making quartering casts upstream I've taken enough two-plus-pound fish to realize that canoeing the river will be a near-future priority.

What I can state with dead certainty is that the Tongue has lots of carp, some over ten pounds. In late spring and early summer before the water warms and fills with weed growth and if the flow levels are near normal, the carp are suckers (a lame pun rises sluggishly here) for any nymph that looks like a Hare's Ear. Not gold-ribbed though, because the sparkle seems to spook them. You can sneak up on the fish as they hold in slower current or behind boulders, grazing on passing caddis pupae and mayfly nymphs. I've dropped a weighted fly just ahead of them; the term "dapping" (most commonly known as a method of fishing used in Great Britain by letting a fly pattern baited hook fall gently onto the water, and meaning to dip lightly or quickly into water, as a bird does) comes to mind. The carp are not selective and it's a blast watching them move slightly, open their big, rubbery lips and suck in the nymph. As soon as the hooks set they become quite offended at the alien intrusion and surge to the deeper and fast current seams out in the middle of the river. I have an old red glass Fenwick that I use for this because I'm afraid of snapping my other rods on the initial short-line set. This is excellent sport during heat of the day doldrums and, pound for pound, the noble carp is at least the equal of a trout.

I've never considered myself a sane individual. A life's history filled with far too much excess and an abundance of lunatic decisions obviates the need for that delusion. But there is more fishing than meets the casual eye in Tongue River country. Admittedly casting away to smallmouth bass in a spring-fed pond out on the alkali flats of southeastern Montana with the sun slashing down from a cloudless, burned-out blue sky in 110-degree heat is at least slight confirmation of this assessment of my somewhat addled mental state.

Though, even in this July furnace, there is some vague logic to the seeming lunacy. There is the incredible solitude amid the sage, prickly pear, and yucca dominated land that burns silently beneath the ancient, weathered face of the eroded foothills of the mountains. Indigo, ochre, and rust bluffs and cliffs yield to off-white mounds of rock and sand that grip this basin like toes from some enormous beast. Vultures circle overhead. The fish strike my streamer as soon as it touches the mirrored surface of the aquamarine gem. Two, three, four of them race to the Bugger and attack. Hell, the bass aren't big, maybe two pounds max, but I feel like I'm fishing someplace from a thousand years ago. Grasshoppers sporadically leap from the hot ground and bounce off my arms and legs as I cast and cast and take smallmouth after smallmouth. The only sign of civilization is a dusty, ragged two-track that leads to this place.

No it's not the glorious tourism-brochure Montana fishing of the Madison or Missouri or even the Yellowstone River that flows through my hometown of Livingston, now so many miles south and west of here. No snow-capped mountains, pine forests, elk, or large trout. But there are three mule deer grinding away on some desiccated native bunch grass in the shade of a rogue copse of ponderosa pines. I can hear their teeth crunching the wiry stuff. The animals look as mean as inner city thugs – lean, muscular, hides of bleached tan, eyes that look about the parched landscape with an expression of "tough is tough, deal with it".

This is what I love. What I live for. Good, hard, serious country with no people, a few places to camp, a little water and even a few fish. High plains Montana east of the Rockies in all its primitive glory. And there are fish far out this way – everywhere I look, if I do so with purpose and intensity. These smallmouths. Rainbows. Browns. Northern pike. Nothing trophy size but plenty of them at times and the pike swimming several hours northeast of here are natives of a thousand or more generations.

Damn fine land. Isolation. Stark beauty. And fish to catch. Home for a recluse such as myself.

Once while wandering the ragged roads of the Wolf Mountains southeast of the Little Bighorn Battlefield looking for the wild turkeys of those dried up mountains that are covered here and there with stands of tall and stately ponderosa pine, I stumbled upon a small trickle of clean water. I marked it for later and continued my fruitless quest for *Meleagris gallopavo merriami* (I find gratuitous use of Latin quite impressive). Later that evening at a camp along a clear, cold and very narrow creek that wound through dense tangles of alder, willow, and thorns or through chest-high thickets of grass I worked a small, grey Elk Hair Caddis through tiny riffles and runs or allowed the pattern to spin lazily on the surface of miniature pools that were camouflaged by shifting shadows and overhanging limbs. Wild smallmouth raced to the surface and took the fly. All of the fish, despite being only six to twelve inches, thrashed and leaped above the stream, often tangling the leader in the brush and, in the process, finding themselves quivering in a soft breeze riding down the valley. A quick pull on my short 2-weight popped the light tippet and the fish plopped back into the water, scurrying to dark cover. Others took its place, dark yet brightly colored fish with rich greens, coppers, whites, blacks, and golds. I fished for these beautiful fish for hours. Like with the bass of the spring-fed ponds, I couldn't help myself. Stars and planets made their appearance. Night hawks boomed and swooped above me as they fed on evening bugs including caddis and mayflies. Coyotes howled out on the flats in the west as a huge thunderstorm exploded into the sky miles away. Lightning illuminated its dark purple interior with an eerie golden-orange glow. The sound of thunder reached me as muted rumblings. And the fish kept feeding on into darkness. As the moon rose above a distant crease in the valley, I returned to camp, built a drink and sat beside the now nearly invisible creek. Rings of rippling water made by the eager trout spread across the pools in concentric circles of glowing silver. The hawks boomed and the coyotes continued chattering away, now clearly excited that the moon was up and the evening's activities would begin in earnest. I just sat there looking at the stream, the well-defined white band of the Milky Way and at the meteors fizzling in from the northeast. A very good place to be.

And down south a bit in the Big Horn Mountains of Wyoming, the North and South Forks of the Tongue hold populations of Snake River cutthroat, browns, rainbows, and brook trout. I was wandering a densely-wooded brook that bounced and burbled through a grass valley and then down a timbered canyon. Using the six-foot 2-weight, a small tippet and a #20 green Wulff, I sometimes successfully executed casts of maybe 20 feet, or merely dapped the fly in crystal pools while crouched behind deadfalls or brush. Enthusiastic and perhaps marginally crazed cutthroats pounced on the bug. Fish from eight inches to, again, fifteen inches. I learned later from a state fisheries biologist that the cutthroat here are planted and a twelve-inch fish was likely five to six years old. Striking trout with those parr marks, flaming orange slashes along their lower jaws, brilliant hues representing the entire colorful spectrum manifested by this species. I wandered for miles up this stream and often diverted to follow smaller tributaries that were sometimes only a couple of feet wide. They were all filled with the cutts. In muddy banks here and there were deep and fresh imprints of bear, coyote, cat, and marten. Canaries flashed bright yellow through the green leaves. I heard eagles and hawks screeching high above me as the raptors rode the thermals searching for prey. The rich, sweet smell of this fecund riparian corridor was everywhere. These Wyoming waters are popular among flyfishers, but the alpine settings make this inconvenience worth the occasional effort.

I've been fortunate as a writer to have the time and opportunity to fish pretty much whenever and wherever I pleased. I've caught large fish all over the place, but no fishing now gives me more pleasure than the waters of the southeastern portion of Montana. This wide-open country does not normally yield large fish, but the entire place is relatively undeveloped, virtually devoid of commercial guiding and touring operations. True, the roads are often impassable when wet. There are biting bugs and snakes. The weather can be tough. And help is often a long trudge away, but all of the obstacles are more than worth the effort. Those who live here are for the most part open and friendly, though many ranchers look at me when I ask permission to explore some small, brush-choked drainage slipping through some possibly snaked-infested draw way behind their home as misguided and a touch crazy. Permission is nearly always granted and all of them are curious about what I find, about my successes and failures. Several of these ranchers have become friends, regular correspondents. I send them my books and cards of thanks. Three of them have offered me places to stay when I'm in their country and have even interceded to the extent that they tell neighbors I'm harmless and to allow me access to other, even more esoteric creeks and ponds.

The money isn't overwhelming as a writer, but it's a good life. So many times when fishing these unspoiled waters in places that have not changed in centuries, the realization of my awesome aloneness in this world and this universe hits home with tremendous force. Stalking, casting, or just standing in one of these flows eliminates everything that connects me to the perceived security of life in Livingston. No computers, TVs, telephones, or sounds of traffic. This is what I'm after in life, but all of the natural nothingness pushes me headlong into confronting the reality that time is short and I'll soon be gone. In such cases I guess bourbon has its place.

So, it's back to the beginning and this small pond and its smallmouth bass. The heat is blistering. The air is dead dry, lifeless, and thick with the pungent, herbal scent of sage, but I keep casting to these fish, never tiring of the display of life in country most people think of as unpleasant, featureless, and lifeless.

Tongue River country is none of these.

TRIP INFORMATION

Timing: The river is something of a tailwater fishery, but from late-April through June the release from the dam makes fishing almost impossible for flyfishers. In late summer, strings of algae make retrieval of streamers an often tedious process.

Where: From the interstate at Miles City, take Highway 59 for about 13 miles south, then Hwy 332 along the river another 57 miles to Ashland, then a dusty affair called 556 the rest of the way along the Tongue.

Hub: Miles City is the best place to shop, stay, and eat. Up until about five years ago when Sheridan, Wyoming sold its soul to developers and the tourist buck, the town used to be real West. Now its four lanes of gridlock on the main drag and the place's residents are surly and they don't know why or for that matter, what hit them. The strip off the interstate in Miles City has all of the usual commercial jive like MacDonald's, Wal-Mart, Pizza Hut, all the major motel chains, and so on. Farther into town are some good old bars like the Montana Bar, 612 Main Street; Texas Club, good music, 716 Main Street; Cattle-AC, 420 Pacific Avenue; and the 600 Café, Inc for great food, 600 Main Street. Fishing gear and related items can be found at Red Rock Sports. Not a fly shop, but a good all-around store.

Appropriate Gear: rods from 4- to 7-weight rods. I prefer a 6-weight of nine feet, since it can be windy and the best water always seems to be on the far bank. Hip waders when it's not warm.

Favorite Patterns: The ubiquitous Gold-ribbed Hare's Ear Nymph, Montana Nymph, Bitch Creek, Elk Hair Caddis, favorite mayfly patterns, Buggers.

Special Regulations: Open all year

Black Nosed Dace

Why not? It works sometimes and it looks neat in the water.

Hook: Mustad #3665A, #9575 or #38941, sizes 4 through 12

Thread: Black-silk, monocord or nylon

Wing: Lower - Polar bear or white deer; Third - Black skunk or black bear; Third - Brown bucktail

Tag: Red yarn, very short

Head: Black silk

Body: Flat silver tinsel

CHAPTER TWO

Sage Creek – Pryor Mountains

"What is not brought to consciousness comes to us as fate."

Carl Jung

If there's any truth to the above observation by Jung, I'm reasonably certain that I'm a futuristic dead man with only slight hopes for resurrection, never mind redemption. Long, cold, dark Montana winters spent grinding through stultifying days filled with television sports reruns (I thought the Ball State-Central Michigan game was particularly exciting even the fourth time I watched the thing), partially written novels, and dysfunctional relationships, all of it without the mollifying influence of whiskey and, now, cigarettes, certainly obliterates much of what passes for consciousness in my life. So when the first genuine warm days of spring showed up during the middle of May several years back, the ones that threaten to pop the leaf buds and have all the little birds twittering well before sunrise, I hit the road looking for clear, running water, green grass, and an isolated place to camp.

I'm heading down to the Pryor Mountains and a little stream I've got going for a couple of nights. High time to flee the dirty, melting snow, wind, and grit of Livingston, and harass the down-sized brookies and rainbows swimming in the brushy creek that flows behind a treeless campground at the base of the mountains down where nobody ever seems to stay. I bring along some rib-eye steaks, club soda, and Honduran cigars. It ain't whiskey and Camel straights, but I'm older and much wiser now. I'll make do. And if things turn ugly and far-gone lonesome, I'll run along some back roads that slice through wide open, desiccated sage flats holding some antelope and turkey vultures, down into small-town-liquor-store Wyoming and score a bottle or two of Beam and a few packs of smokes, and then run oh so swiftly back above the border into Montana where I've learned with exactitude how to diminish myself in complete privacy. No one will know but me and I've been kidding myself for decades.

So the Suburban was loaded, and now I find myself rolling and lurching up a rough, gravel and dirt road that cuts between some old exposed rock on the planet, something like 48 trillion years old – a geology book tells me with pedantic certitude – Triassic and Jurassic sandstone and shale atop the Pryor Uplift of Madison limestone.

(A brief aside – the Crow Indians have closed the reservation portion of this road to non-tribal residents. On current state maps, the gravel byway is shown merely ending on the reservation in the middle of nowhere, a section of the road seems to have vanished much like those Russian villages and towns that are no longer on the maps of that country for some reason, any reason but a nuclear disaster. One hopes that the Crow did not suffer such a severe calamity and that this now non- or never-existent road succumbed to some inexplicable time vortex phenomenon. Whether this is a prudent move on the part of the tribe is a matter of perspective. The small town of Pryor and the adjacent and excellent Plenty Coups State Park are that much more isolated so the ability to generate money is diminished. Closing the road protects the sacred lands of the Crow from the marauding desecrations of those mindless souls who find fun in roaring madly about on ATVs. Perhaps the tribe should reconsider opening this thoroughfare and instituting a tribal-member-only season on the noisome machines. Only thinking aloud here. There's still another way into this marvelous little place as will be revealed at the end of this chapter.)

The air smells of new wild grasses mixed with wildflowers. Joe Jackson wails away on the system from an '85 Aussie concert about not getting what I want, 'til I know what I want. Cumulous clouds cruise by on a warm southwest breeze, and I know damn well what I want, but it's either illegal or has nearly killed me a bunch of times along the turbulent path that got me to this afternoon where I'll find what I want in the form of derricking four- to six-inch brook trout and rainbows into the tall bank side grass round sunset. Maybe I'd make it to the steak dinner or even all the way back home, but that's a touch of some of that unrecognized fate that the good doctor is talking about.

I artfully make the turn to the east that leads to the campground. The creek is full of early-season water and everything is very green. The grass already waist high. A few miles down the road, the campground is deserted and I pull into a place that has a weathered picnic table protected from the sun by a rusting metal roof supported by rusting metal poles. The fire pit is enclosed by a rusting circle of barrel-like metal. The grate is rusting, too. Outhouses are slowly leaning and sinking into the ground less than 100 yards away. I'm home.

I drag all of the gear out and arrange on and around the table. I put the sleeping bag and foam cushion in the back of the rig since it looks like rain. I've brought a delightful little fly rod for this water. A 6.5-foot, one-ounce, 2-weight. The thing comes in a case about the size of a double corona cigar tube. Uncle Orvis gave me this one way back when he thought that connecting my name to his equipment was sound marketing. He finally came to his senses and disinherited me, and I miss him so.

The creek drifts, glides, and bends through clumps of willow and alder mixed with dense grasses. The banks are covered with clumps of the grass along with prickly pear cactus and sage. A few small grasshoppers are bouncing around. One lands in

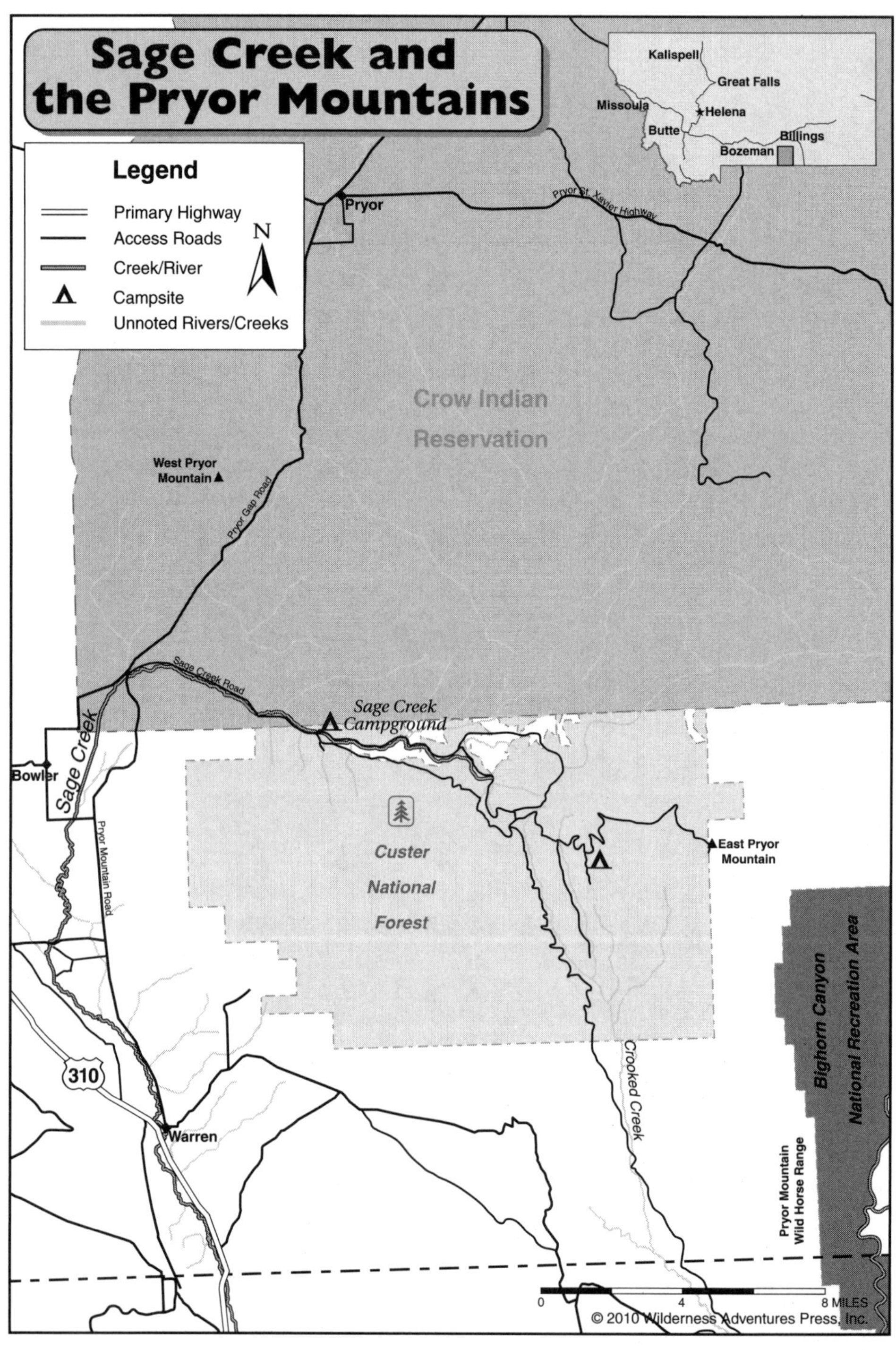
Sage Creek and
the Pryor Mountains
Legend
Primary Highway
Access Roads
Creek/River
Campsite
Unnoted Rivers/Creeks
N
Kalispell
Great Falls
Missoula
Helena
Butte
Billings
Bozeman
Pryor
Pryor St. Xavier Highway
Crow Indian
Reservation
West Pryor
Mountain
Pryor Gap Road
Sage Creek Road
Sage Creek
Campground
Bowler
Sage Creek
Pryor Mountain Road
Custer
National
Forest
East Pryor
Mountain
Bighorn Canyon
National Recreation Area
Crooked Creek
Pryor Mountain
Wild Horse Range
310
Warren
0
4
8 MILES
© 2010 Wilderness Adventures Press, Inc.

the stream and a trophy brookie of perhaps ten inches pounces on it before retreating to the shade of an undercut bank. Trout are rising everywhere, taking very small mayflies whose name, Latin or otherwise, I don't know. I tie on a small bug, about a #20 to a fine 6X tippet and work out about 20 feet of line. My initial cast lands at the base of a spiraling pool and my line begins to curl back downstream to me. As I take in slack, several fish – both rainbows and brook trout – rush the fly. A splashy take and the pattern is gone as I raise the rod and set the hook. A rainbow races back and forth arcing the slight rod, then leaps across the seven feet of open water into a bunch of overhanging branches. The tippet tangles. The trout wriggles from the line as it dangles inches above the stream. I snap the tippet. The rainbow thrashes then drops into the water and is gone. Vanished. Other fish start feeding again. I tie on fresh tippet and a new fly, cast again and, after a serious struggle of more than four seconds, ever so carefully work a husky five-inch brook trout to my feet. Cupping the tiny trout in my hand, I marvel at the intense coloration. The crimsons, indigos, sapphires, emeralds. The glimmering hard metal golds, silvers, and bronzes and especially the pure whites and blacks. The belly is flanked by a sophisticated shading of the deepest orange. The trout works its mouth open and closed in the water as it glides coolly through my fingers. Its gills flutter back and forth. Absolute perfection. As spectacular a fish as I've taken anywhere. Dropping my hand inches below the surface allows the trout to scoot free and race to the bottom where it becomes one with the shadows and gravels.

(Several years ago there were plans to restore native Yellowstone cutthroat in some spring-fed ponds on a ranch upstream and create a barrier so the various species wouldn't mingle. I've discovered nothing further on this and perhaps leaving well enough alone on Sage will be best.)

I continue fishing this way for hours until I notice that the sun is down behind the western hills and the sky is going pastel orange, red, and pink. Back at camp I build a charcoal fire, cook one of my huge steaks, devour it, then light a cigar, sip some club soda and watch as an early-season thunderstorm flashes and rattles in the distance. The weather moves off towards Billings and the stars and darkest night come out and drop down over me like the gentlest quilt of dead-black fabric. Coyotes begin to riff and howl up the valley. I enjoy the peace, the cigar, and the solitude. Maybe this is my unrealized fate. Then I climb into my sleeping bag and drift off.

On another visit, the gravel road that led through a gap in the northern beginnings of the Pryor Mountains bent and twisted like a rattlesnake with a badly broken back. The way grew steadily narrower and rockier and climbed gradually upward between immense, cracked walls and sheets of Madison limestone that are 650 million years old and rest upon partially exposed thrusts of basement rock of at least 1.5 billion years. Castle Rock towered above and behind us now and as we drove across a wide open grassy plain, the prominent geological feature eventually faded in the heat haze and the distance. Ginny and I are now headed some years later to Sage Creek Campground.

The Pryors are actually an extension of Wyoming's Big Horn Mountains that climb to more than 13,000 feet. The Bighorn (one word for the river, two for the mountains) flows between a ten-mile-wide rift that now separates the two ranges. This is harsh, surprisingly rough country. From I-90 to the east the Pryors look like long, gentle mounds, more like foothills than mountains, but as we drive farther in and eventually turn east on a dirt road that is baked dry but filled with deep ruts that indicate impassability during wet times, I realize that the seemingly innocuous and enticing side roads and two-tracks that wander off into the hills and through narrow canyons are more than likely potential death traps for us in our Suburban. West Pryor towers above us. Ponderosa pines give way to fir and, through my binoculars, I can see wind-beat clumps of sub-alpine fir thousands of feet above. The meadows are rich green that far up and patches of bright yellows, blues, whites, and reds catch my eye. Wildflowers still blooming up that way. Large patches of melting snow cling to feminine creases and dips in the steep upper slopes. The creek bubbles and sparkles as it pours through a steep-sided streamcourse choked with alder, willow, dense brush, cactus, and sage. This will be a tough little bugger to fish, but the water looks too good, even out here in all this dryness, to pass up. Maybe some rainbows of four or five inches. All my addictions are hopeless.

By the time we reach the Sage Creek turnoff, it must be 200 degrees out. The sun has baked the landscape to a seared yellow-white. The sky is a washed-out blue. We pull over by a large culvert where the creek flows clear and cool. I take off everything but my cutoffs and go for a dip among the tiny trout that dart up and nip at the hairs on my legs. I just sit down in the water and melt.

"Do you think anyone will come by, John?" asks Ginny.

"Hell, there's no one around for miles." We drop into the cool water of this magic little stream flowing all by itself in the middle of some of the hottest, driest country I've ever been in.

Well someone does come by. A truck load of cowboys who are stunned by the site of Ginny, but polite in that they immediately turn their gazes away from her and proceed up the road in quiet laughter and bright smiles.

"I'm mortified," she said "And I'll never listen to you again."

I've heard all this before. Life goes on.

We spend most of an hour swimming, soaking, sunning in the creek, watching the trout leap for small bugs or just appreciate the water as it races over shallow copper-colored shallows or swirls perfectly clear as it rushes out of the culvert. There are only the two of us enjoying the cool water on a scorching day out in a desert. Ignore the road and the culvert and it could be 200 years ago. A moist, cool time trip. Reluctantly we dress and head for the top of East Pryor.

After seven or eight miles that seem like 50, we turn off on a smaller road yet and lurch into camp. About a dozen picnic tables with wooden shade shelters, a couple of outhouses, plenty of wood around and no other people. All of these structures have been replaced with newer, better ones that blend into the land. There is now running water at a tap that smells and tastes of the oil and gas running beneath this country. We choose a site that scans the heights of West Pryor, provides a serious view up the creek's valley, and overlooks a couple of bends in the creek. While setting up camp, my attention is drawn by lots of silvery trout – rainbows and brookies – that are leaping and splashing as they madly chase emerging caddisflies and breeze-borne grasshoppers. A few of the trout look immense. Seven, possibly eight inches. I rig a one-ounce 2-weight and a #16 grey Elk Hair. Camp's done. Dinner can wait until the late afternoon heat dissipates. I smile at Ginny and wander off. She prepares for a dip in an emerald pool that has a large plank across it.

The grass is more than six feet high along the creek. Bunches of sweetgrass tower eight feet. The moist spring and early summer have turned this place into a scene from *Green Hills of Africa*. Even if there were no trout I would be in paradise. Wildflowers, more than a dozen species, light up the hills in splashes of intense reds, yellows, white, orange, blue. Western tanagers, meadowlarks, nighthawks, and swallows dive, chirp, and soar right over the tops of us. Looking down into a deep green water, I can see trout holding throughout the water column, keeping their various feeding positions with gentle flickerings of their fins. The fish cast dark, wavering shadows on the sandy bottom or upon the chocolate-colored mud deposited on the inside bends of the creek. The casting is tight with straight-up-above-me back casts and

swift 20- to 30-foot shoots between the brush. I mend and curve the line just before it hits the water. The first cast is greeted by a show-off rainbow that clears the surface of the water with the fly stuck in a corner of its jaw. The trout continues leaping until it crashes into some overhanging brush where it winds up dangling suspended from the branch-entangled tippet. The rainbow quivers and shakes until the line breaks and then it plops back into the water. I am crestfallen. This is an enormous fish. Perhaps nine inches. I cast again and hook a fish that sails over my head and lands on the grassy bank behind. I quickly retrieve it. A three-inch brook trout. Intensely colored with blues, oranges, golds, reds, emeralds, blacks, whites, purples. It dashes off when I release it. I take another dozen trout from this run and then another dozen at the next pool and on and on it goes. One rainbow reached ten inches. One brookie seven. The sun is setting. The light growing dim, but I could have fished this delightful brook all night. The land glows orange as the day nears its end. Purple shadows edging darker drift across the top of West Pryor. Nighthawks, always nighthawks out west, swoop and dive like fighter pilots along the stream. A coyote or two barks for a while. An eagle soars 1,000 feet or more above. The day is cooling. Down to 80 and a slightly warmer breeze brings the aroma of steaks grilling on a fire. I return to camp. Relaxed. Hug Ginny and accept a plate of the grilled t-bone and salad, and devour it.

A half moon rises just to the north of the Pryors and it casts black shadows across the dry grass. As usual, countless stars eventually come out.

We rose early one morning to make the drive up to the crest of East Pryor Mountain with hopes of spotting some of the area's wild horses. Hopefully the hot weather had driven them up into the high forest and cool meadows. Rounding a bend near the top we saw perhaps 150 of them roaming free in several bands way out here on the sage and cactus flats, or out on the south end of the range in the desolate desert of southern Montana and northern Wyoming. Or they could be hunkered down in one of the rugged canyons that tear through the mountains that reach almost 9,000 feet or they could be even grazing on the alpine grasses that far above sea level. The altitude we're aiming for, yet my mind is pulled back to that horrible Crooked Creek road that slowly narrowed to nothing more than a slim cut hard against a rock wall that fell hundreds of feet to the stream far below. We'd stopped out of instinct and experience well before things turned ugly and walked ahead to see what fate awaited us. Looked like death or worse to me, but the water down below, far below, looked like it could hold some nice trout. Pools, runs, and riffles that drifted in and out of shadows cast by willows and more tall grass. Too far away to see rises or shapes of holding fish, but I sensed the trout in that water. Some year I'd scramble down and check this one out, but for now it was a bunch of back-and-forths on the narrowing slice of rock and dirt to turn around and head up to the horses.

Then as we climb up on a broad grassy plateau that is contoured with soft eroded creases filled with ponderosa, the drainages breaking open into rugged canyons, we see the heads and flicking tails of the horses. As we top a rise the land falls away abruptly to the north and east and the horses are everywhere. Groups of four, five, or more lazily grazing on the rich native grains, colts rolling in patches of dirt, the stallions slightly distant from them and the mares. The males are alert, ears twitching, and they keep a sharp eye on us. I stop the Suburban and turn off the engine. Ginny grabs her camera gear and stalks off carefully down the two-track and works her way gradually to within 30 feet of one group – a black stallion, a roan mare, a buckskin mare and colt and, off to one side, a younger stallion with a dorsal stripe down his charcoal back and the vestiges of zebra stripes on his legs. The wild horses of the Pryor Mountains. These are the distant genetic relations to the Spanish horses brought over on galleons centuries before. Horses pirated away by Plains Indians. Horses that changed these Indians' way of hunting and living. Horses that eventually escaped from their Crow, Blackfeet, and Cheyenne masters and now, in a long-distance way, carry on the heritage. Blood typing by the Genetics Department of the University of Kentucky has confirmed that these animals are closely related to their Spanish ancestors. There may be as many as 25 family groups along with "bachelor" stallions. Most families or "harems" average five to six animals with a dominate stallion, a lead mare, a variety of other mares, and young animals.

The group Ginny is photographing allows her to approach even closer, though the lead stallion snorts and occasionally pounds his hooves to let her know who is in charge. I walk about a mile to another group grazing in a miniature valley below me. I stand next to a lone fir tree and watch. The horses notice me and move to within 20 feet of my vantage point, again snorting and giving us a strong once over. Then they resume their grazing. One of the stallions in this group has the striped markings along its flanks. I watch this family unit for over an hour as it slowly moves off out of sight down the beginnings of a canyon, then return to the car and Ginny. Several other groups of horses are feeding nearby and one bunch walks past us on the road. From what the woman at Britton Springs had told us, the wild horses are skittish and will usually move off at the sight of humans, often at a gallop. None of the horses we observed seemed concerned in the least. Cautious to be sure, but not frightened.

By now, the sun is only an hour above the horizon so we rattle our way to the rolling crest of the mountain and set up camp in the lee of an island of sub-alpine fir. The air is cool up here. Sixties. And the wind is kicking up to a gale. Large clouds approach from the south only to be torn into shreds by the wind and vanish into nothingness. We look out over the Bighorn Valley in Montana, beyond the rugged salmon and orange walls of Bighorn Canyon far to the north and east past the winking lights of Hardin and Crow Agency on off to the subtle rises of the plateau of Tongue River country. To the northwest our own Crazy Mountains glow blood red in the setting sun. Far to the south we can see the lights of Lovell and Cowley. We grill some game hens, sweet corn, and potatoes, boil tea and eat chocolate chip cookies. We sit around a small fire until well after dark as the moon rises over the Tongue River plateau and the stars come out. A few nighthawks and bats swoop past as they feed on insects. Then we turn in. As I look up at the sky and all of its mystery, I wonder at the Jungian subconscious/fate number before falling asleep reading James Ellroy's *L.A. Noir*.

TRIP INFORMATION

Timing: Mid-August into early October for clear water, and good bug action of caddis, mayflies, hoppers, and damsels.

Where: From I-90 at Laurel, take Hwy 310 about 45 miles to a gravel manufacturing complex at Warren. Turn left on the first gravel road you see, almost right of the highway (called BIA 5 on the *Delorme Montana Atlas Gazetteer*), then bounce and grind about a dozen miles, heading north, to Sage Creek and a right-east on BIA 211 for a half-dozen miles of gravel and dirt road to the campground that is marked by USFS brown sign. The nightly fee is $5.

Hub: Lovell, Wyoming back down south on 310 about 24 miles from Warren has groceries, motels, and gas, but no fly shop. The Western Motel at 180 West Main Street has nightly rates beginning at $53. The nearby Bighorn River and Canyon are worth a side trip.

Appropriate Gear: There are flies and some mosquitoes so bug spray helps. Wade wet which normally means creeping along the banks through the tall grasses. Good walking shoes with defined tread to avoid slipping help. Fly rods from 1- to 3-weight, 6 to 7.5 feet, leaders of 7.5 to 9 feet to 5X or 6X tippet. As mentioned, I like the Orvis 1-weight and I've also used Damon's five-foot, 2-weight – a rod that seems designed for this creek.

Favorite Patterns: Anything small from #16 to #20 including Elk Hair Caddis, Trico, BWO, Goddard Caddis, Yellow or Green Humpies, Adams.

Special Regulations: Open third Saturday in May through November 30

Adams

Hook: Tiemco 100 size #10-#20

Thread: Grey or black 8/0

Tail: Hackle fibers grizzly/brown/grizzly

Abdomen: Muskrat underfur

Hackle: Grizzly and Brown

Wing: Grizzly hackle tips

CHAPTER THREE

Clarks Fork
of the Yellowstone River

When I drive along Highways 310 and 72, I spend a dangerous amount of time looking at the Clarks Fork of the Yellowstone. If ever there was a brown trout stream with little or no access, this is it. Long, sweeping runs beneath grassy banks and towering cottonwoods give way to deep sapphire pools swirling against undercut banks. There are long stretches of gravel riffles that would be ideal to nymph for rainbows, too. But as I said, access was difficult at best until the FWP stepped in to provide access for anglers.

The good news regarding improved river access as reported by the AP in the summer of 2009: The state of Montana is going ahead with a plan to buy 172 acres along the Clarks Fork of the Yellowstone River for fishing and hunting access (called the Clarks Fork of the Yellowstone Fishing Access Site and scheduled to open by 2013). Homeowners neighboring the site blasted the decision, saying it will offer poor fishing and few game animals. The State Land Board, made up of the five statewide elected officials from the governor on down, endorsed the plan. It had previously been authorized by the Montana Department of Fish, Wildlife and Parks. Supporters say it is needed access in an area that offers little. FWP plans to pay $517,500 for the parcel, and spend perhaps another $100,000 for full development of fishing access to include a boat ramp.

So being a good Montana citizen, I scouted out this new find in late August and floated the river from near Bridger down to a bridge by Edgar, perhaps a dozen miles. The day was hot and clear, the river at somewhat low summertime levels. I cast hoppers to all the good-looking spots but moved only a few sluggish browns in the 15-inch range. I was not discouraged. The stretch of the river was filled with wildlife – kingfishers, blue herons, mallards, Canada geese, red-tails, golden eagles, western tanagers, chickadees, sharp-tailed grouse, fox, beaver, otter, white-tail and mule deer. A few fish and Ginny's companionship. All of this combined in a pleasurable mixture. We pulled up to a gravel and sand shoreline for a lunch of sausage, brie, grapes, sourdough bread and iced tea. While munching on some sausage I noticed a riffle bubbling over clean gravel downstream a little bit. And there were tails of trout breaking the surface as rainbows nosed among the rocks for nymphs. I extended the leader to nine feet and 5X, tied on a #14 Gold-ribbed Hare's Ear and worked down to the bottom of the run. Casting 30 feet up and quartering, I stripped line to maintain a dead drift. Within ten feet, a rainbow snapped up the pattern and leaped across the stream on its tail before submerging and dropping down into a dark pool below me. The fish jumped again when I pressured it with my 4-weight and then tired. Silvery and heavy at over two pounds. I released the trout and cast upstream again with the same result. I managed to take five rainbows, all two pounds or so, in this gravel stretch of 50 to 75 yards. The fish acted like they'd never been cast to before.

The rest of the float was spent fishing and marking similar structure with similar success and a couple of browns that took at the end of the runs along the shelves that marked a return to deeper water.

I could easily do this day after day, and my chances for larger browns would only increase as the days shortened, cooled, and moved into autumn. Rainbows and browns and a quiet, uncrowded river – a nice combination.

Besides the browns and rainbows there are a number of other species holding in the Clarks Fork according to FWP: arctic grayling, brook trout, brown trout, burbot, channel catfish, common carp, emerald shiner, flathead chub, goldeye, grayling, lake chub, longnose dace, longnose sucker, minnow, mottled sculpin, mountain sucker, mountain whitefish, rainbow trout, rainbow-cutthroat hybrids, river carpsucker, shorthead redhorse, smallmouth bass, stonecat, western silvery/plains minnow, white sucker, and Yellowstone and Snake River cutthroat.

The grayling, brook trout and cutthroat subspecies are found in the headwaters high in the backcountry of the Absaroka Wilderness. This water is only reached by long, strenuous hikes that climb far into true alpine surroundings.

I consider the Clark's Fork a brown-trout river despite all of the other species present. Browns attract most of my attention because of their stealth, voracious predatory nature, and size. While not native to Montana, brown trout are more often than not my favorite trout to fish for or, better put, to hunt. The following culled from the Nova Scotia Fisheries and Aquaculture tells a little more about these guys.

> *"The brown trout is a salmonid and is also known as German brown trout, German trout, Lochleven trout, or European brown trout. Brown trout naturally occur throughout Europe and western Asia. They range from Finland south to North Africa, west to Iceland and as far east as Afghanistan. Introduced throughout the world, they were first placed in Canadian waters in 1890. Today they are found*

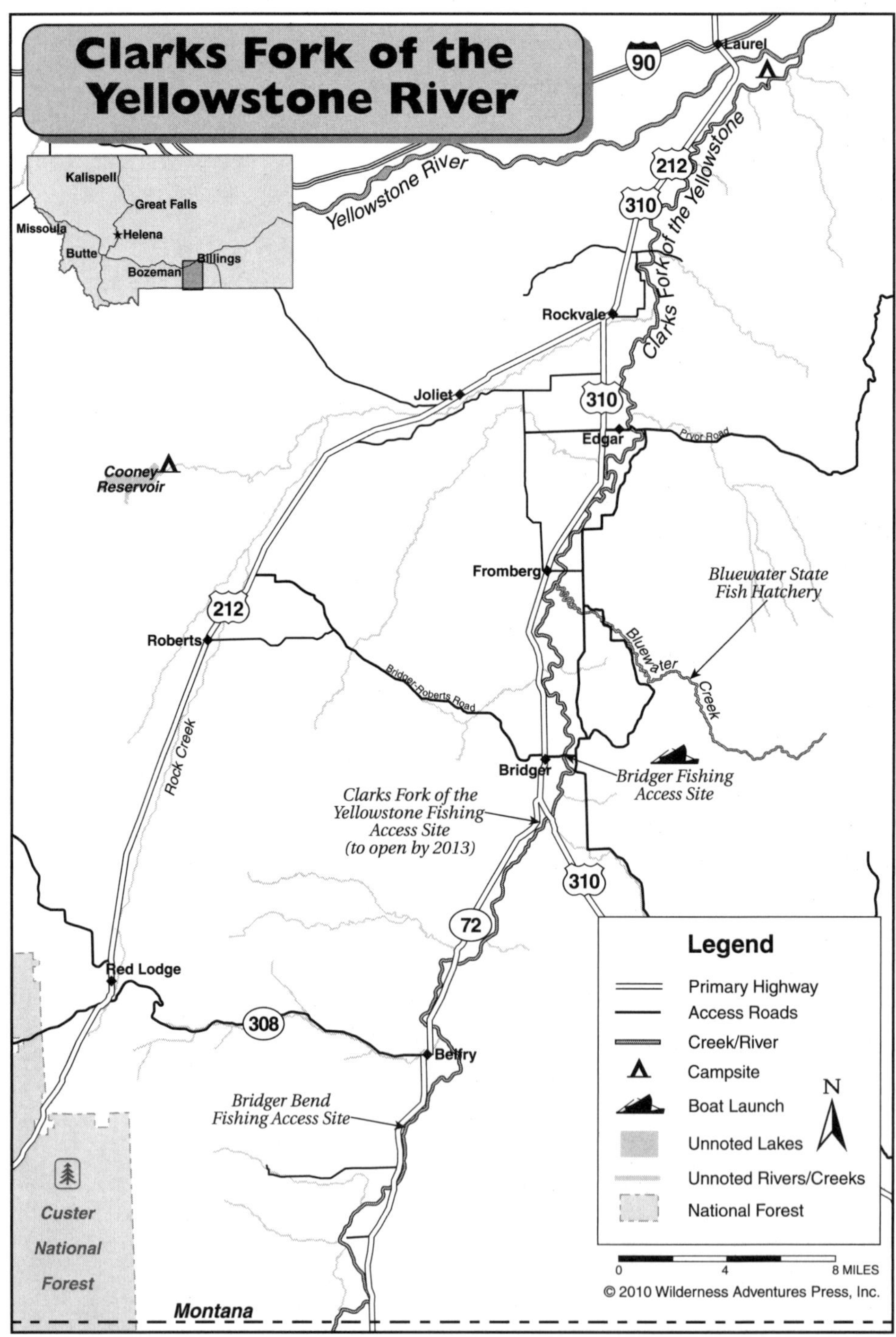

Clarks Fork of the Yellowstone River
90
Laurel
212
310
Kalispell
Great Falls
Missoula
Helena
Butte
Bozeman
Billings
Yellowstone River
Clarks Fork of the Yellowstone
Rockvale
Joliet
310
Edgar
Pryor Road
Cooney Reservoir
Fromberg
Bluewater State Fish Hatchery
212
Bluewater Creek
Roberts
Bridger-Roberts Road
Rock Creek
Bridger
Bridger Fishing Access Site
Clarks Fork of the Yellowstone Fishing Access Site (to open by 2013)
310
72
Red Lodge
308
Belfry
Bridger Bend Fishing Access Site
Custer National Forest
Montana
Legend
Primary Highway
Access Roads
Creek/River
Campsite
Boat Launch
Unnoted Lakes
Unnoted Rivers/Creeks
National Forest
N
0   4   8 MILES
© 2010 Wilderness Adventures Press, Inc.

in rivers, lakes and coastal areas in much of North America, all but a few states in the lower 48, and all provinces except Manitoba, Prince Edward Island, and the Northwest Territories...

...Brown trout get their name from the brown or golden brown hue on their bodies. Here are some other characteristics:

- *their sides are silvery or yellow and bellies are white or yellowish*
- *dark spots, sometimes encircled by a pale halo, are plentiful on the back and sides*
- *spotting also can be found on the head and the fins along the back*
- *rusty-red spots also occur on the sides*
- *the small adipose (or fatty) fin in front of the tail has a reddish hue*
- *sea-run brown trout have a more silvery coloration and the spotting is less visible*

They closely resemble Atlantic salmon and rainbow trout, but salmon have no red coloration on the adipose fin and rainbow trout have lines of black spots on the tail. Young brown trout (parr) have nine to fourteen dark narrow parr marks along the sides and some red spotting along the lateral line.

Brown trout can grow to be quite large, especially sea-run fish. Fish weighing up to 68 pounds have been recorded in Europe." *(Montana's state record is 29 pounds)*

The largest I've caught was well over ten pounds on the Bull River in far western Montana, though I've caught plenty in the five- to seven-pound range within a 100-mile radius of Livingston.

Apart from moving upstream to spawn, adults tend to stay at the same place in a river with very little movement to other stream areas. They can be found at these stations day after day, even year after year! Others move to or from estuaries in the spring or fall. The closest relative of the brown trout is the Atlantic salmon (Salmo salar). The brown trout's name (Salmo trutta) means salmon trout. The largest brown trout ever taken was hooked recently in Michigan weighing 41 pounds, 7 ounces. Brown trout prefer very similar habitats to our native speckled trout, except that they can tolerate slightly higher water temperatures. They often use lower reaches of rivers and streams that are unsuitable for other salmonid species.

Brown trout prefer cool clear rivers and lakes with temperatures of 54 to 66 degrees Fahrenheit. They are wary and elusive fish that look for cover more than any other salmonid. In running waters they hide in undercut banks, mid-stream debris, surface turbulence, rocks, and deep pools. They also take shelter under overhanging vegetation. Brown trout are meat-eaters (carnivorous). They eat insects from water and land, and take larger prey such as worms, crustaceans, mollusks, fish, salamanders, and frogs as their size increases. Browns spawn in the fall and early winter. In Montana this activity kicks off in late September and runs into December.

In addition to water temperature, I'm convinced that the angle of incidence and decrease in duration of sunlight are key triggering factors for spawning activity. They return to the stream where they were born, choosing spawning sites that are spring-fed headwaters, the head of a riffle, or the tail of a pool. Selected sites have good water flows through the gravel bottom. The female uses her body to excavate a nest (redd) in the gravel. She and the male may spawn there several times. A five-pound female produces about 3,400 golden-colored eggs that are four to five millimeters in diameter. Females cover their eggs with gravel after spawning and the adults return downstream. The eggs develop slowly over the winter, hatching in the spring. A good flow of clean, well-oxygenated water is necessary for successful egg development. After hatching, the young fish (alevins) remain buried in the gravel and take nourishment from their large yolk sacs. By the time the yolk sacs are absorbed, water temperatures have warmed to 45 to 54 degrees Fahrenheit. The fish (now known as fry) emerge from the gravel and begin taking natural food. Brown trout fry are aggressive and establish territories soon after they emerge. They are found in quiet pools or shallow, slow flowing waters where older trout are absent. They grow rapidly and can reach a size of five or six inches in their first year.

Yearling brown trout move into cobble and riffle areas. Adults are found in still deeper waters and are most active at night. They are difficult to catch and are best fished at dawn or dusk. Brown trout living in streams grow to about four pounds, but lake dwellers and sea-run fish grow larger. They mature in their third to fifth year and many become repeat spawners.

The river deposits its flow into the Yellowstone River near Laurel and unless you are a fan of oil refineries and petrochemical fumes, I'd give the place a pass, though as the following snippet of Lewis and Clark history suggests, this location was once an area of beauty and power – Clark's Fork and the 'Lodge Where All Danced'.

> *After leaving the site south of Park City (near Buffalo Mirage Access) on July 24, 1806, the Clark party stopped at the mouth of the Clark's Fork to dry out the contents of the two dug-out canoes which had taken water over the sides during the rapids run near Laurel. It is easy to see why Clark's journals talk of the strong currents and dangers of the Yellowstone River. Though calm on the surface, undercurrents and channels are hazardous. Clark's group floated past where the Clark Fork River flows into the Yellowstone River. It was during this time that Captain Clark drew his map showing the junction of the two rivers and making an 'X' to illustrate what he considered to be the best trading location near present day Laurel. This was also the place the Indians called the 'Lodge Where All Danced,' as a large council lodge 60 feet in diameter had been built on an island there.*
>
> *~ www.visitmt.com*

Here's one last angling item concerning the Clark's Fork – it's called Bluewater Creek. It flows from Bluewater Springs for 13 miles to the river, twisting through arid sage flats and even drier bluffs that hold some surly rattlesnakes. At the springs there's a state fish hatchery. A good gravel road leads from Fromberg to the hatchery, climbing through true northern high plains country. The narrow and very brushy creek holds fat one- to two-pound browns that jump all over hoppers, crickets, and ants. The first trick is to be able to dap a fly onto the water for a few feet of float needed to get the trout's attentions and also move to the take. The second trick is playing the feisty fish in the narrow confines. Break-offs are common. Much of the stream flows through private land, though there are stretches of state and BLM, and staying below the high-water marks can be sporting with the snakes and tangles of grass, alder, willow, wild rose, and so forth. Occasionally some of the areas hipster residents take to these healing waters in a naked way and they tend to let others know that their presence is unwelcome. Well, to this I say "To each his own, but I'm playing through in search of brown trout." A Joe's Hopper works well here and this is something of an exercise in esoteric angling for those needing a variety fix.

TRIP INFORMATION

Timing: Before runoff in April through June and by mid- to late July into early October. The snow lingers well into summer in the high country of the 12,000-foot plus Beartooths. The autumn colors are magnificent.

Where: Take Highway 310-212 south from I-90 at Laurel to 310 to Hwy 72 just south of Bridger to the Wyoming border. The river cuts back north again into Montana's Beartooth Wilderness, and this stretch is reached by steep mountain trails. Also, Bluewater Fish Hatchery Fishing Access does permit camping. There is a seven-day limit. Toilets and access for camp trailers is available. Open all season. Located adjacent to the Bluewater Fish Hatchery complex on the Bluewater Creek.

Hub: Columbus, which is also the hub for the Stillwater and West Rosebud, is a nice Montana town along the Yellowstone River. The main drag is called Pike Street and is off the highway about one-half mile. The New Atlas Bar is a great place for a drink or two, 528 E. Pike Avenue, 406-322-9818. The 307 Bar, Grill, & Casino features a full bar, restaurant, and a casino. Varied menu. Open daily from 10:00am to 2:00am. Breakfast served from 8:00am to 1:00pm on weekends. 842 E. Pike Ave., 406-322-4511. Git's Big Sky Motel located at 740 E. Pike Avenue is okay for a few nights. For current information on grayling in the area, call the Montana Department of Fish Wildlife and Parks at 406-247-2940 (Billings) or 406-994-4042 (Bozeman).

Appropriate Gear: Four- to 6-weight rods from eight to nine feet for the middle and lower stretches. In the upper water, since you'll be hiking in, a 4- or 5-weight pack rod, floating and sink tip lines, lightweight hip waders and boots work well. The water is ice cold even in July so the extra weight is worth the effort. Bear spray and noise maker or lots of talking. Backpacking gear if you're young, fit and masochistic.

Favorite Patterns: On the lower stretches Stimulators and Sofa Pillows work in late spring and early summer matching large stoneflies, including the salmonfly. Rainbows and browns in the middle and lower stretches love these, as they do large Hare's Ear nymphs and Elk Hair Caddis later in the summer near dusk. Hoppers play well, too. I'm a big fan of Charlie Brooks' Assam Dragon (and all his other designs). We're dealing with wild, native cutthroat here so the pattern is not all that important. Wulffs of all colors, Hare's Ear nymphs work really well,

Buggers for curiosity's sake, Elk Hair Caddis, Rat-FacedMcDougal (if only for its name). I'm a believer in wet flies and need to fish them far more than I do. A pair that come to mind (see patterns below) are the Skunk Hair Caddis Wet Fly and the Ringneck Soft Hackle Fly. There are dozens of other patterns and they all work even (or especially) on big browns. Cast quartering up stream allow the fly to drift down below you and then swing it out with the current.

Special Regulations: Open entire year.

Skunk Hair Caddis Wet Fly

Hook: #6-10 wet fly
Weight: (optional) 12 wraps .015 lead-free wire

Thread: Black 6/0 pre-waxed thread
Body: black skunk tail hair

Rib: copper wire
Hackle: black hen hackle
Head: black thread

Ringneck Soft Hackle Fly

Hook: Daiichi 1140, 1550, Mustad 3906 or similar: sizes 12-18

Thread: 6/0 Danville's, black
Body: Thin body of natural peacock herl

Hackle: Black ringneck pheasant neck feather

CHAPTER FOUR

West Rosebud Creek

The West Rosebud races downhill like it just knocked off a Mini Mart, shooting the attendant while doing so, and is now running like mad with $19.47 in paper and coin to make a connection with the corner meth dealer. Hell, it's the first glorious week of September, and the flows are supposed to be sedate, summer casual and here I am clinging to bank-side limbs more to remain upright than to wade farther upstream to cast to likely-looking holding water. I was using a Joe's Hopper because of its high floatability quotient and visibility. Even so, I was having a hard time seeing the thing as numerous Yellowstone cutthroat slashed at the bug as it flew by them in the frantic current. I managed to catch a number of fish from 10 to 14 inches but playing them was most likely a delightful visual from the Spastic Ballet as I teetered and yawed on the rocky streambed with the icy water pulsing through my legs. This stretch was just below Emerald Lake. The distant ice of Grasshopper Glacier and the towering peaks of the Beartooths were visible in brief snatches as I staggered from foothold to foothold.

Later that afternoon, I worked a section of river near one of the two national forest campgrounds along the creek. There were a few pools running tight to log jams every 50 yards or so and, in each of these and any other patch of slightly deeper-than-normal water, I cast the hopper and before the thing had floated 10 feet a cutthroat rose in a splashy rise and tagged it. The fish were all 14 to 17 inches, running and sometimes leaping in the warm, sunny air. Fine fishing in beautiful surroundings. We'd planned to camp but both places were gated, closed. A printout with a picture of a stocky man was tacked to each campground bulletin board. The guy had been missing for two weeks and anyone with information concerning his whereabouts was told to contact the Stillwater sheriff. Even with a .357 magnum and a 20-gauge for random grouse shootings, we decided to head somewhere else to camp. We hadn't drawn for a serial killer permit this season and had no wish to risk our future hunting privileges.

The West Rosebud is the prettiest of three streams that are all similar in nature to the fact that their origins and the canyons they cut through are similar. They all headwater in the wind-swept-snow-and-ice-covered high country of the Beartooth Mountains and they all eventually merge with the Yellowstone River at Columbus. Actually, the two Rosebuds join the Stillwater above the small town of Absarokee. There are fishing accesses and boat put-ins on the Stillwater from Fishtail down to Heh-Kep-Pe on the Yellowstone. This stretch drifts through private ranch land and is wonderful floating water for browns, cutthroat, and rainbows. There are also brook trout in these waters. The upper Stillwater has a good campground and the fishing is pocket-water action for cutthroat to maybe 15 inches. Hiking the trail into wilderness country leads to better action, including some large fish in mountain lakes that are accessed oftentimes by faint mountain-goat-like trails. The East Rosebud heads, surprisingly, at East Rosebud Lake, elevation 6,740 feet. There's a campground and a number of summer places on the water. Fishing is spotty to slow for larger trout, but a boat or float tube is needed for brown, brook, and rainbow trout. The view of the mountains is mind-blowing, but the drainage itself was ravaged by recent fires. This may have resulted in a burned-out landscape but the addition of nutrients during runoff despite increased siltation has led to some large insects and insect numbers here and there leading to a few fat cutthroat. Search and destroy, mile-an-hour wading is the plan here. Trails here and at the heads of the other two waters lead far back into wilderness high country where a few lakes even hold grayling...

...I've been captivated by grayling since the evening I watched very old films of my grandparents fishing for these fish in Alaska. We watched these in the den of their home in Lake Forest, Illinois more than 40 years ago. The flickering black-and-white images of them unloading their gear from what looked like a Fokker single-engine, overhead-wing plane; the wild mountains behind the streams they were fishing with bamboo rods; the blurry scenes of the fish thrashing along the surface when they were hooked; and the brief close-ups of the grayling before they were released or whacked on the head with a rock and shoved into wicker creels - all of it. My grandmother fished all over the world in places anglers had never heard of way back in the 1930s and 40s, but she always said, and her eyes sparkled when she did, that catching grayling in the far north was her favorite.

The fish are unique to freshwater because of their large dorsal fins that are marked with carefree bands of turquoise spots. They eagerly take dry flies, fight fairly well, are beautiful and are excellent table fair, especially when smoked over cherry wood then stuffed in morel mushrooms that are sautéed in butter, dry sherry, and minced garlic, then seasoned with sea salt and freshly-ground white pepper. Quite good - especially with sourdough French bread, unsalted butter and a decent bottle of white wine (not Chardonnay, please). I've had many fine and interesting times fishing for grayling. Like when I was working along a high mountain lake shore and I started hearing Moon River being played on an organ. I thought that I was having one of my periodic episodes, but rounding a rock bluff I saw a camper with Minnesota plates pulled over on the side of the logging road that hugged this lake. A white-haired woman was playing a Farfisa organ powered by the rig's generator. Her husband was

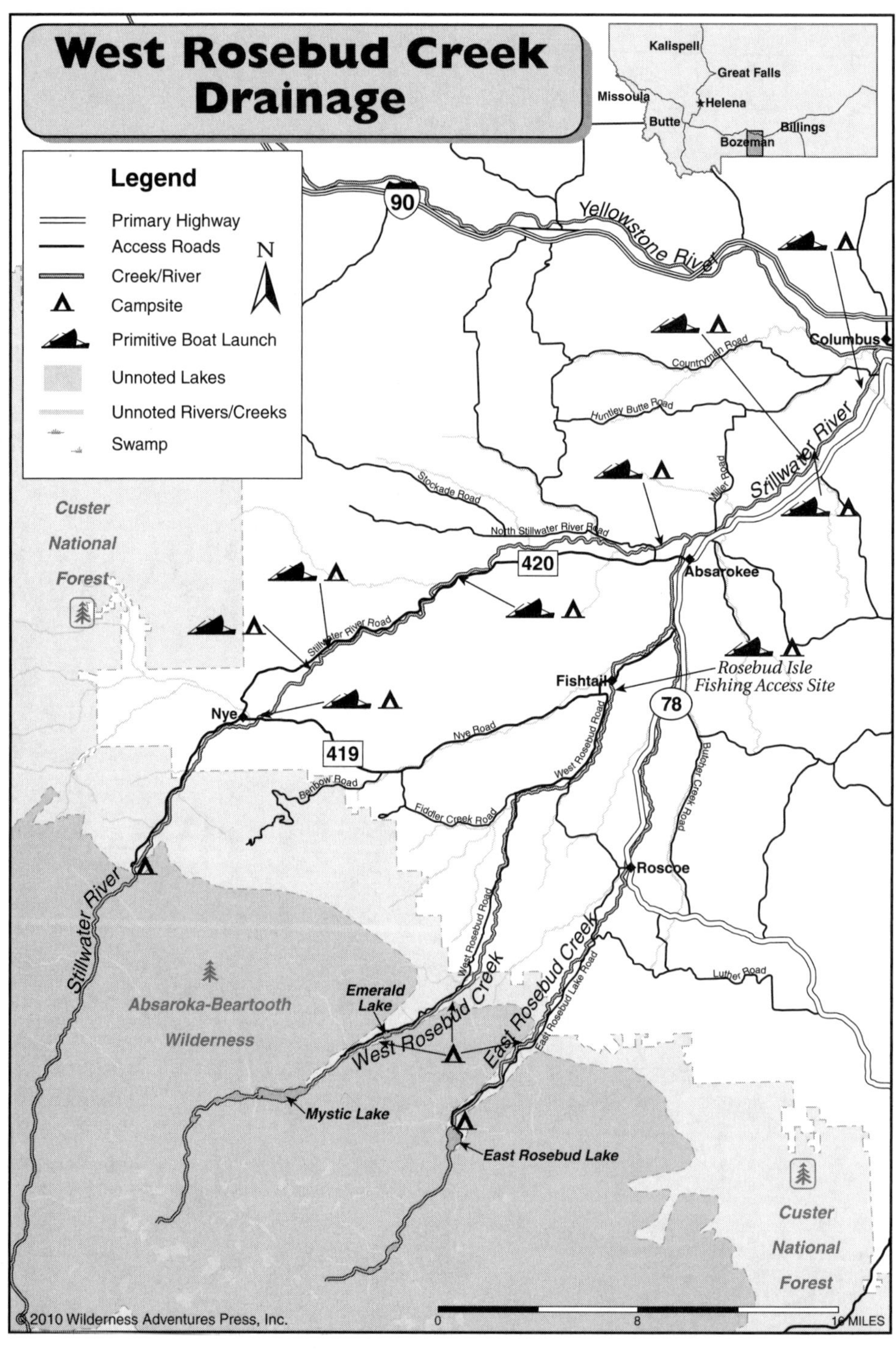
West Rosebud Creek Drainage
Kalispell
Great Falls
Missoula
Helena
Butte
Billings
Bozeman
Legend
Primary Highway
Access Roads
Creek/River
Campsite
Primitive Boat Launch
Unnoted Lakes
Unnoted Rivers/Creeks
Swamp
N
90
Yellowstone River
Columbus
Countryman Road
Huntley Butte Road
Stillwater River
Miller Road
Stockade Road
North Stillwater River Road
420
Absarokee
Custer
National
Forest
Stillwater River Road
Nye
419
Fishtail
78
Rosebud Isle
Fishing Access Site
Nye Road
Benbow Road
West Rosebud Road
Fiddler Creek Road
Butcher Creek Road
Roscoe
Luther Road
Stillwater River
Absaroka-Beartooth
Wilderness
Emerald
Lake
West Rosebud Creek
East Rosebud Creek
East Rosebud Lake Road
Mystic Lake
East Rosebud Lake
Custer
National
Forest
© 2010 Wilderness Adventures Press, Inc.
0   8   16 MILES

parked in a lawn chair working on a toddy and puffing a cigar. Ah, the good life. And a lake near Kalispell that always has nice, sizeable fish in it, though one time a few days after I'd fished it, a ranger discovered a body in a parked car near shore. The guy had apparently committed suicide. Perhaps his last sight of this world was the grayling dimpling the smooth, sapphire surface of the lake as they fed on midges. Perhaps.

The best fishing for grayling is way back in the mountains – far up, sometimes above timberline, up there with the eagles and the clouds. In the Beartooth Mountains, where West and East Rosebud Creeks and the Stillwater River originate, there are a few lakes with viable populations of grayling. Before chasing them it is necessary to check with the Montana Department of Fish, Wildlife and Parks to acquire current information (contact numbers in Trip Information below). Sure, there is excellent fishing at lower elevations in Alaska and Canada, but I prefer the high country of Montana. Tucked away beneath glacial cirques where avalanche chutes funnel tons of snow and rock down into clear, cold lakes – those are the places.

There is not much time to fish for grayling here. Snow, many feet of it, blocks most trails until mid-July. By late September, the peaks have vanished from sight, hidden by dark, boiling clouds that hold the first storms of winter. When the lakes are open, swarms of mosquitoes and horseflies make tying on a #20 pattern a nightmare. Millions of minute insects flying just above the water or trapped in its surface film tempt the grayling. A perfect cast is often rewarded with the sight of a maddeningly discriminating grayling sucking in a midge right next to the angler's cautious offering. A person has to be persistent, lucky and, most of all, driven to seek fish under these conditions.

So what is it about grayling that draws ardent admirers back over and over to these outposts of solitude? The scenery, to be sure, but there is something more. There is a magic spell that swirls around grayling.

The first time the power of the fish is felt at the end of a quivering, slender leader, the sight of the dorsal fin slicing through the surface of turquoise water, the shimmering purples and silvers – this, too, is part of the attraction, but only a part. Grayling addiction has many facets. Its grip on the angler, like all addictions, is tenacious.

Montana or arctic grayling (*Thymallus arcticus* for the fish's supposed thyme-like scent) are found primarily in streams, but adapts readily to lakes. The fast-flowing, frigid waters of Alaska, Alberta, British Columbia, Manitoba, the Yukon and Northwest Territories, and Saskatchewan have large numbers of grayling, but if you want to find the fish in the lower 48 you'll have to come to the Rockies of Montana, Wyoming, and Utah.

The ice ages of North America wiped out most species of fish. The massive sheets of ice ground up everything in their paths. The knife-like ridges and near-vertical cirques of Glacier National Park offer striking evidence of this tremendous gouging action. When the icecaps begin to recede, perpetual winter abated and fish gradually returned. Warmwater species carved out larger and larger territories as the climate warmed. But the grayling were here all along, surviving in near-freezing waters at the edge of the towering fields of ice.

The range of the species was extensive, from Michigan and Minnesota, cutting a wide swath through the Rockies into Utah then well into eastern Siberia.

Over the millennia, they evolved into an elongated, muscular shape that was ideal for the fast currents and riffles of the headwaters they prefer. A large, sweeping dorsal fin provides stability and maneuverability, which is helpful during the constant search for aquatic insects and crustaceans, especially freshwater shrimp. The dorsal fin is the grayling's most distinctive feature with irregular, but clear rows of turquoise spots. Occasionally, the fin's upper edge is tinged with white or pale pink. The tail, pectoral and anal fins are usually a yellowish color, but the pelvic fins more often than not have lengthwise stripes of black and pink.

As settlers spread westward, the grayling began to rapidly disappear. Outside of Montana and a few portions of Wyoming, the grayling are gone from the Rockies. Grayling used to inhabit most of the Missouri River headwaters, and were recorded by the 1803 Lewis and Clark Expedition as a "new kind of white or silvery trout". The last remaining native population in Montana is holding out in the Big Hole River drainage in the southwestern corner of the state. West of the Continental Divide, the Montana Department of Fish, Wildlife and Parks has pursued a policy of stocking the fish in several lakes. Grayling can be raised in hatcheries, but they do better when reared in special lakes set aside for that purpose, then netted for transplant elsewhere.

Grayling naturally inhabit oligotrophic ("scant nourishment" or "few foods") waters. These are deep, clear lakes that do not have much plant or animal life. Where trout struggle to survive or may even die out, grayling can exist, frequently producing populations that are far too large for their surroundings and resulting in stunted fish. Fisheries biologists have recognized this ability to survive in near-barren waters. This, in turn, has provided a fishery in pristine, backcountry waters that were formerly barren.

"We've given them substitute habitat, and that means lakes instead of streams," said George Holton of the Montana Department of Fish, Wildlife and Parks. "Grayling can withstand low oxygen levels, and thus survive in lakes that would winterkill trout."

Many of these lakes have small, almost indistinguishable, outlets and inlets. This can be a problem because grayling spawn almost exclusively in small, fast-flowing streams. A number of the lakes are stocked annually; the fish sometimes packed on foot or, at other times, dropped from the air (a curious sight as thousands of silvery creatures are disgorged from the belly of a low-flying aircraft).

Most of these lakes require at least an overnight hike, usually up steep terrain. Because mountain weather can turn nasty in a matter of minutes, rain gear and a lightweight tent with a rain fly are necessities. Wood is often scarce or nonexistent, so a dependable (if there is such a thing) gas stove should be brought along. A number of quality pack rods are available that can be strapped to the backpack with only a slight increase in weight.

Most grayling mature by three years (often as early as two). At this age in Montana they are about a foot long. The female lays from 1,000 to 13,000 eggs in a territory defined by the male. No redds are built, but the males vigorously defend the breeding areas, repelling invaders with dorsal fins extended. The fin is also erect when the fish are hooked, perhaps as a display of anger or aggressiveness. Most grayling live less than six years and a fish over two pounds is considered a trophy in the lower 48. The largest grayling recorded in North America is five pounds, 15 ounces from the Katseyedie River in the Northwest Territories.

The fact that they survive at all is remarkable. Many waters in Montana are ice-covered in August. Consider a lake buried under 50 feet of snow and another four or five feet of ice, the water black and nearly lifeless underneath.

The grayling more than make up for winter's inactivity with summer feeding binges. The vision of hundreds of swirls, fish leaping out of the water and crashing back, slurps, plops, and gurgles amid clouds of insects, the air literally humming

with life, is fantastic. At these times extremely small patterns – #18 to #22 – tied to 7X tippet are needed. Larger flies and tippets are blithely ignored by the fish. On other occasions, a medium-sized Woolly Worm cast in the middle of a pod of fish will provoke a determined strike, while minute patterns are proving ineffective. It is prudent to carry patterns like the Adams, BWO, Black Gnat, Elk Hair Caddis and Hare's Ear in #14 to #22 and Woolly Worms in #10 to #14 in olive and also black.

The fish are gregarious by nature and will feed in groups of three, four, or more. Schools frequently work the shore, the rise rings marching towards the angler like some carefree, slightly lunatic infantry battalion.

On this day, a frenzy is upon the grayling. No time to be that discriminating connoisseur who delicately sips emerging caddis from a perfectly smooth lake surface reflecting the hot yellows and golds of aspen and larch in autumn, a time when matching the hatch is important. Any cast, and nearly any pattern works right now.

The attraction of grayling is not only in the fishing, nor is it exclusively the wilderness experience, that chance to escape the madness of cities and rush-hour traffic. It is also the sound of the fish feeding in the night, the sky blasting starlight on snowfields high above camp. The grayling moving to their own rhythms as they have done for thousands of years.

One aspect of Montana I used to take for granted was public access to all of the rivers, creeks, streams, and sloughs, but not anymore. Events of recent years have made me much more active and aware of my fishing rights as the following shows.

Aside from the fact that Montana has some of the finest trout waters anywhere in the world – the Madison, Yellowstone, Bitterroot, Bighorn, Beaverhead and on and on – what sets the state apart from the rest of the country and also the world is its stream access law that gives anglers the right to fish on nearly every river, stream, and creek that flows.

Montana is unique among other western states and most states in general. In 1984, the Montana Supreme Court held that any river or stream that has the capability to be used for recreation, such as fishing and floating, can be used by the public regardless of whether or not the river is navigable and who the owner of the streambed property is. The result is that anglers and floaters have full use of most of the rivers in Montana for fishing and floating, along with swimming and other river-related activities. This is known as the Montana stream access law, a law that has been under attack by out-of-state interests since its inception.

On Mitchell Slough in the Bitterroot Valley, a stream that local residents have fished for decades, wealthy out-of-staters attempted to close access but were overruled when the Montana Supreme Court ruled in 2008 that the 16-mile-long stream is open to the public and that the landowners are not entitled to fence it off as part of their private sanctuaries. The court said the slough roughly follows the historical course of a waterway mapped 130 years ago, and therefore is subject to public access and required permitting, as are other natural waterways. The 54-page decision overturned two earlier rulings by state district courts that found the slough was not a natural, perennial-flowing stream.

Opponents to the law as it applied to the slough include former pop star Huey Lewis, Charles Schwab, Private Wealth Partners managing director Kenneth Siebel and a home belonging to Anthony Marnell II, the head of a casino construction company, is built over a tributary to Mitchell Slough.

In 2006, Lewis said in the Times that those in favor of public access on Mitchell Slough had "done a masterful job of casting this as a class-warfare issue... 'Rich out-of-staters' is an expletive, and they try to make it a battle against them and rich out-of-staters. There are 25 people, and 20 are not rich and not out of state." Lewis also said of Montana that there is "more cheese, fewer rats" than in California.

Along the North Fork of the Blackfoot River, a large fly-fishing outfitter/guiding operation has run a fence directly up to a bridge crossing the stream in violation of the law. This practice is common throughout the state. On a recent trip, I noticed this exclusionary practice on bridges spanning streams that included the Dearborn, the Musselshell drainage, Swift Creek, the Yaak drainage, and the Teton.

No big deal you say. There's plenty of public access through state holdings, national forests, BLM land, and national parks. Perhaps, but should the state's access law ever be overturned, and its under threat every second of its life, kiss fishing goodbye to a lot of rivers like those mentioned above along with others that include the Ruby, Boulder, Big Spring Creek, Blackfoot, and on down the line. Large portions of these rivers wander through private holdings.

In April of 2009, Montana's governor Brian Schweitzer signed HB190 – the stream access bill that allows landowners to build fences that keep cattle in, but not those that keep fly fishermen out. This is an important victory against out-of-state landowners and developers who have spent loads of cash from a large war chest in a greedy attempt to overturn the access law.

Anglers in the state may fish between the ordinary high water marks of a stream. The Montana legislature in 1985 defined the ordinary high water mark as:

> ***"Ordinary high-water mark"*** *means the line that water impresses on land by covering it for sufficient periods to cause physical characteristics that distinguish the area below the line from the area above it. Characteristics of the area below the line include, when appropriate, but are not limited to deprivation of the soil of substantially all terrestrial vegetation and destruction of its agricultural vegetative value. A flood plain adjacent to surface waters is not considered to lie within the surface waters' high-water marks.*

This means that an angler or a floater has full recreational use of a river below the rivers ordinary high-water mark.

> ***"Recreational use"*** *means with respect to surface waters: fishing, hunting, swimming, floating in small craft or other flotation devices,*

> *boating in motorized craft unless otherwise prohibited or regulated by law, or craft propelled by oar or paddle, other water-related pleasure activities, and related unavoidable or incidental uses.*

A floater or angler who encounters any artificial obstructions may also climb above the high-water mark to get around these obstructions in the least intrusive way possible (however, "the law does not address portage around natural barriers, and does not make such a portage either legal or illegal"). The statute clearly states that this is legal; but the law does not give the public right to cross private property to reach the rivers.

Obviously wealthy landowners who thought that they were buying their own private Montana are angry. The conflict comes because the Montana stream access law says the public owns the rivers. For recreation, including hunting and fishing, everyone has a right to get access to virtually any waterway that flows through private land. But many landowners have put up fences to keep people away from the streams, an act that is now in violation of the stream access law.

For example, lack of access to the Ruby River has discouraged anglers. There have been a number of complaints from fishermen who have been yelled at and photographed and who have even heard warning shots fired as they fished prized trout streams flowing through private land, which is legal as long as they stay within the high-water marks.

The fight is contentious to say the least along the Ruby River, designer trout water with a good population of large brown trout that hold tight to brushy banks and along

the bottoms of sapphire runs and pools. The river drifts through a valley of landowners who have put up fences to keep people off most of the river's lower stretch.

Some landowners "erroneously are trying to lay claim to a public resource," said Dick Oswald during the height of the conflict a few years ago. Oswald is a fisheries biologist for the Montana Department of Fish, Wildlife and Parks in nearby Dillon. "I suspect they didn't do their homework before they bought land. This is America, not feudal Europe."

"Montana has the last of the wild trout fisheries; the rest are shot," said Reid Rosenthal in an article in the *New York Times* in 1997. Rosenthal is president of Country Roads, a company in Sheridan that manages many ranches that have been bought by wealthy fishermen and sells fishing vacations along the Ruby River. His view is typical of those opposed to the stream access law.

Rosenthal said he and his clients did not oppose public access to the Ruby but wanted a change in regulations that allow each angler to keep five trout a day. Mr. Rosenthal said allowing such catches would destroy the fishery. But proponents of public access point to a memorandum Rosenthal wrote to his ranch-owning clients in support of fund-raising for a campaign to overturn the stream access law by taking it to Federal District Court, and the Supreme Court, if necessary. In the memorandum, made public by the pro-access Montana Wildlife Federation, Mr. Rosenthal said, "Don't kid yourself, this situation is really one of social resentment, jealousy and envy, not fishing access."

Perhaps tired of all of the flack he received for his elitist position, Rosenthal later said that he no longer supported a campaign to repeal the access law. "I wish I'd never written that damned thing."

Montana governor Brian Schweitzer has said the state is committed to defending the river access law. "If you want to buy a big ranch and you want to have a river and you want privacy, don't buy in Montana. The rivers belong to the people of Montana."

For now, people can access Montana's trout streams even if they have to climb over, under, or go around obstructions like those presented by the outfitter on the North Fork Blackfoot. But everywhere I go I hear stories (hopefully just that, stories) of out-of-state Montana landowners building up a huge war chest to wage yet another attack on Montana's stream access law.

"The attempt to make heaven on earth invariably produces hell," said Austrian philosopher Karl Popper; and I believe Jefferson said "the price of freedom is eternal vigilance".

Whether you live here or visit from somewhere else, nothing could be more applicable than these two quotes for the state of trout fishing in Montana.

None of these streams are at the top of my list of fishing waters because they do not have all that many fish, there is not a great deal of holding water and a fair amount of people use the area. That being said, if I could only fish the West and East Rosebud Creeks and the Stillwater River, I would not have a lot of trouble staying happy.

TRIP INFORMATION

Timing: The streams in this region usually fish best after runoff because they are snowmelt-glacial melt waters and often too cold in the spring. Runoff can continue through July because of the 12,000-foot-plus elevation of the Beartooth Mountains. From summer through mid-October at the latest.

Where: Take the Columbus exit off I-90 about 35 minutes west of Billings, then Highway 78 through Absarokee (ab-zor-kee) and another seven miles to 419 and a mile to the West Rosebud Road.

Hub: Columbus is a nice Montana town along the Yellowstone River. The main drag is called Pike Street and is off the highway about one-half mile. The New Atlas Bar is a great place for a drink or two, 528 E Pike Ave, 406-322-9818. The 307 Bar, Grill, & Casino features a full bar, restaurant, and a casino. Varied menu. Open daily from 10:00am to 2:00am. Breakfast served from 8:00am to 1:00pm on weekends. 842 E. Pike Ave., 406-322-4511. Git's Big Sky Motel located at 740 E Pike Ave is okay for a few nights.

For current information of grayling in the area call the Montana Department of Fish, Wildlife and Parks at 406-247-2940 (Billings) or 406-994-4042 (Bozeman).

Appropriate Gear: Light, short rods work well in this country. I've even used my old Orvis one-ounce, 2-weight with fine results. Three-weight or less and around seven feet is premium. Leaders of nine feet tapering to no more than 4X because of the fast water. Hip waders with felt soles.

Favorite Patterns: A lot of the fishing is short-cast, hit-or-miss pocket water, so attractors, the brighter and more colorful the better. These types of patterns also float better than most others due to bushy hackles and the use of deer hair. All attractors including the usual suspects – Humpies, Wulffs, H&L Variant. Joe's Hopper, Parachute Hopper, Hare's Ear, and all similar nymph patterns.

Special Regulations: Open entire year.

H&L Variant

Hook: #10 to #18
Thread: 6/0 black
Tail: White calf hair

Body: Half peacock quill, half peacock herl

Wing: White calf hair
Hackle: Brown or ginger

CHAPTER FIVE

Stillwater River

For years, whenever I fished the Stillwater River I would drive past the various fishing access points along the lower stretches of the stream that flowed easily through a beautiful Montana agrarian valley. I was intent on fishing for wild trout in the freestone, tumultuous stretches of water that poured out of the Beartooth Mountains on the Custer National Forest. By no means was this a mistake, it was merely an oversight on my part that caused me to overlook some wonderful float fishing when the water is still high enough, often through the summer in wet years. Otherwise the various fishing access points mentioned in the trip information section are good places to begin wading for browns, Yellowstone cutthroat, rainbows, and the ubiquitous mountain whitefish.

Because a good deal of the river is steep gradient whitewater with rocks and boulders, I prefer to use my 16-foot Mad River Explorer or my 12-foot Old Town pack canoe. Working the chutes, glides, and riffles from either of these crafts is a delight. I've rigged a basic lead-weight anchor and rope setup for holding in prime areas when I'm alone. Using one of my favorite rods, a seven-foot six-inch bamboo South Bend 290 with an Ari Hart Gallatin reel I picked up for relatively (relatively meaning over $300) cheap lends a certain gentrified air to my otherwise back alley fishing. A seven-foot leader tapered to 4X works well with Woolly Buggers and one of my favorite big-fish nymphs, Charles Brooks' Assam. Many years ago I had the privilege to have a few drinks with Brooks at a bar in West Yellowstone. The weather was dark, wet, and cold but we were warm sitting by a fire talking about this and that. Brooks taught me a lot about big fish angling – his best point being, "It's straight forward. To get the attention of big trout you need to drift something large along the streambed, otherwise you're wasting your time." So later that year, I purchased his book, *Nymph Fishing for Larger Trout*. I studied the thing over the winter and as the seasons followed, I realized how right Brooks was. I've read all of his other books and would recommend them to anyone.

Coming around a sweeping bend below the Whitebird Access, I dropped anchor and began casting upstream dredging a deep run that dropped into a blue-water hole beneath some overarching cottonwoods. On the fourth drift, the line stopped dead. Then as I lifted up on the rod, the fish roared across and downstream. One hand on the rod and the other pulling up the anchor, I floated downstream, mostly bow first, in pursuit of the fish. After maybe a hundred yards, the canoe ground up on a sand and gravel ridge in midstream. I staggered out and held on as the trout thrummed along the river bottom then ran a couple of times upstream before leaping twice. This was a big brown of several pounds. He ran once more thrashing the surface and then the flex of the cane wore him out. He was easily four pounds and deep colored in the search-and-destroy browns, blacks, golds and honey shadings of big males. Released, he sulked away in slow defiance.

I noticed hoppers all around so I added to my tippet, tied on a Joe's Hopper and fished my way down to the confluence with the Yellowstone, taking dozens of cutthroat, rainbows, and browns along grassy and brushy banks. Emerald fields flashing gem-like under irrigation spray rolled off to the bluffs that sheltered the river valley. Angus cattle grazed with brain-dead nonchalance here and there. Hawks, herons, some golden eagles, and a few hungover ravens watched as I slid downstream. This was another of those easy going days that made me feel like I knew what I was doing.

I have no love for the mining industry, but on rare occasions it sometimes does something right as detailed in this May, 2000 editorial (I've yet to see anything of any scope of a positive nature since this time) in the *New York Times* titled *A Promising Accord in Montana:*

> *In the past, the mining industry in Montana has made few environmental concessions to anyone. But in a surprising and salutary development, the Stillwater Mining Company, which operates two platinum mines in the Beartooth Mountains at the edge of the Absaroka-Beartooth Wilderness, has signed a good-neighbor agreement with a coalition of local environmental and citizens' groups operating under the umbrella of the Northern Plains Resource Council.*
>
> *This striking agreement holds the East Boulder and Stillwater mines to a higher set of environmental standards than those required by state and federal authorities. It institutes oversight committees with members drawn from mine management and citizens' groups. The company will place thousands of acres under conservation easements, and it will finance audits of its own environmental performance. Most important, it has agreed to an open exchange of information with the council and will invest in what the council calls "groundbreaking new water treatment and waste reduction technologies."*

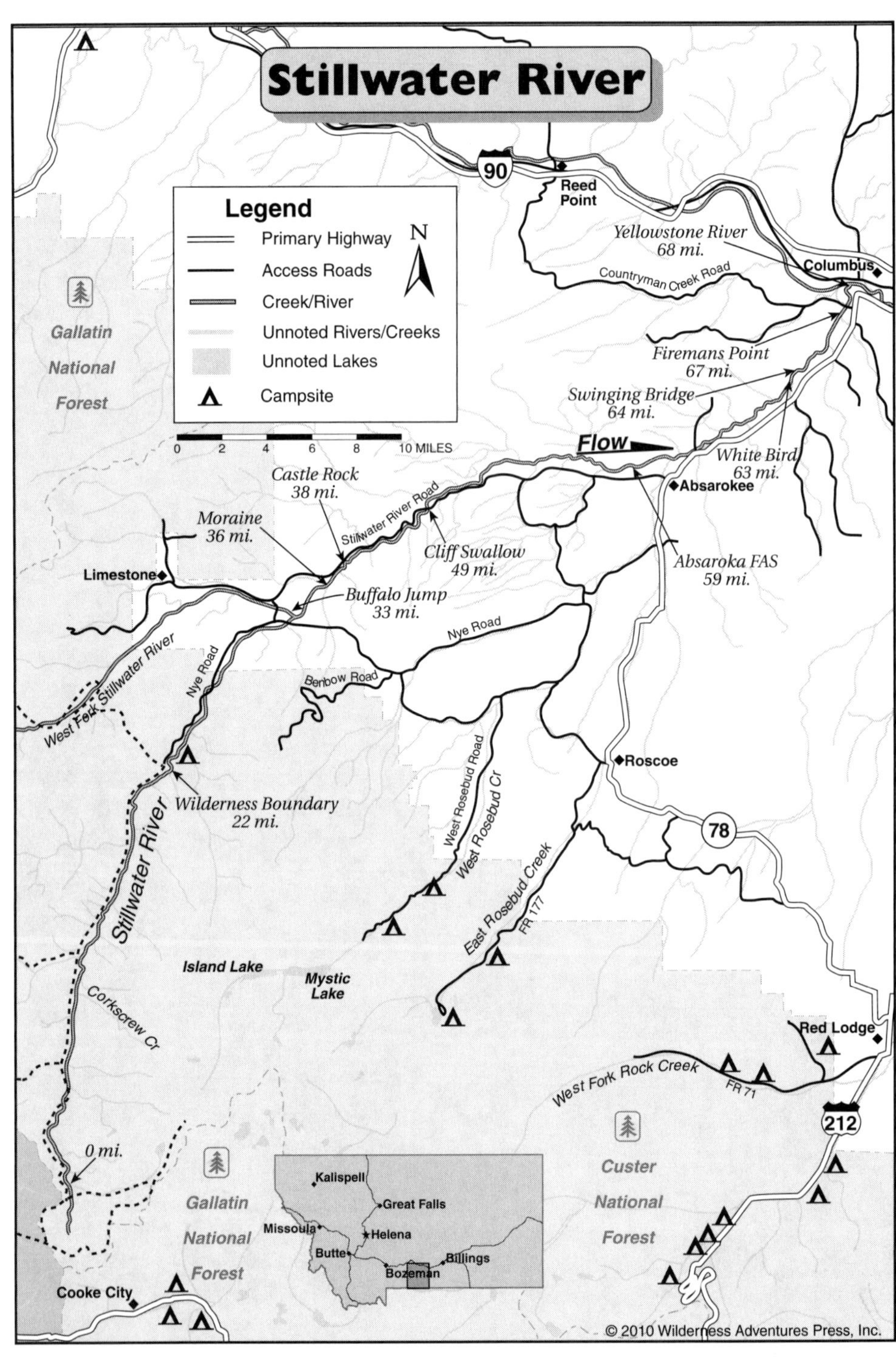
Stillwater River
90
Reed Point
Yellowstone River 68 mi.
Countryman Creek Road
Columbus
Legend
Primary Highway
Access Roads
Creek/River
Unnoted Rivers/Creeks
Unnoted Lakes
Campsite
N
Firemans Point 67 mi.
Swinging Bridge 64 mi.
Flow
White Bird 63 mi.
Gallatin National Forest
0 2 4 6 8 10 MILES
Castle Rock 38 mi.
Moraine 36 mi.
Stillwater River Road
Cliff Swallow 49 mi.
Absarokee
Absaroka FAS 59 mi.
Limestone
Buffalo Jump 33 mi.
Nye Road
West Fork Stillwater River
Nye Road
Benbow Road
Roscoe
78
West Rosebud Road
West Rosebud Cr
Wilderness Boundary 22 mi.
Stillwater River
East Rosebud Creek
FR 177
Island Lake
Mystic Lake
Corkscrew Cr
Red Lodge
West Fork Rock Creek
FR 71
212
0 mi.
Custer National Forest
Gallatin National Forest
Kalispell
Great Falls
Missoula
Helena
Butte
Billings
Bozeman
Cooke City
© 2010 Wilderness Adventures Press, Inc.

It is possible to attribute the fact of this agreement to the profitability of these mines, which has given Stillwater Mining greater latitude to negotiate. But this agreement could not have come about without enlightened leadership at the company or the dedication of negotiators for local citizens and environmentalists. The result makes genuine environmental protection consistent with continued productivity. With luck, this may become a model for similar agreements elsewhere.

In more recent developments in the summer of 2009, Montana's U.S. delegation was quick to criticize a bankruptcy judge's decision to allow General Motors Co. to drop its precious metals contract with the mine. GM will instead get its palladium and rhodium, used to make catalytic converters, from suppliers in Russia and South Africa.

From Democratic Sens. Max Baucus and Jon Tester: "We are deeply disappointed with the completely unacceptable actions taken by General Motors over the past few weeks," Baucus and Tester wrote to G.M. CEO Fritz Henderson. "We urge you to reconsider this decision and instead re-engage with domestic palladium producers as you move forward in the coming months and years."

So the mine along the Stillwater hangs on by a thread and its future is decidedly uncertain. The operation appears to be interested in maintaining both the environment and the support of conservationists, but none of this is carved in stone. Situations like the one above give me at least some hope concerning the fate of trout streams in Montana, but then there's the other, tarnished side of the precious metal coin as delineated below.

Trying to stop the mining of a gold deposit potentially worth billions of dollars is like trying to slow down a steamroller by placing cartons of eggs in front of it. The eggs get scrambled along with anything else that gets in the way of the outfit as it lumbers inexorably down its inevitable road of huge profits and altered landscapes.

Such was (and may be again with the soaring price of gold) the case with the Seven-Up Pete Joint Venture, located a few miles outside of the small community of Lincoln about 80 miles east-northeast of Missoula. Phelps Dodge (the majority owner in the project at 75.25 percent) and Canyon Resources are currently engaged in preliminary exploration of the reserves located in the headwaters of the Blackfoot River just above its confluence with the Landers Fork in the McDonald Mountain area. Both the main Blackfoot River and the Landers Fork are home to native populations of cutthroat trout and dwindling numbers of bull trout, a species that often exceeds 10 pounds. Other portions of the drainage contain brown, rainbow, and brook trout along with sizeable numbers of indigenous mountain whitefish and forage fish.

To get a general idea of the scope of this project, these initial activities cost the two companies more than $30 million. Presently, the mine is on hold.

And according to information found on Montana River Action's website: "In 1998, the environmental community sponsored Voter Initiative 137, banning the use of cyanide to separate gold from ore in all new mines and the initiative was passed by Montana voters. In 2004, the mining community sponsored Initiative 147 with the intent to return cyanide heap leaching, open pit gold mining to Montana, but this initiative was soundly defeated by a vote of 256,658 against and 185,695 in favor."

Still from the MRA website:

> *"We all thought we had heard the last of Seven-Up Pete Joint Venture and the failed mining company Canyon Resources, but like a recurring nightmare, Richard De Voto, the president of Canyon Resources, is now suing in federal and state courts for the $70,000,000 they had expected to make on their venture before I-137 was passed, saying I-137 'deprived them of lucrative profits.' The lawsuit names the State of Montana as defendant and asks the court to strike down I-137 because it interferes with existing contracts, and demands "takings" compensation for temporary and permanent losses. When his demands for compensation by Montanans were struck down by the courts, Mr. De Voto resorted to some spiteful remarks, saying the mining industry 'would not touch Montana with a 10-foot pole.' It must be said that Canyon Resources is in the very risky business of gold mining and should not be able to bill Montanans when this project fails...the low-grade gold is still there and someone will want to mine it. Jewelry accounts for 84 percent of all gold mined, while only 6 percent is used for electronics. The remaining 10 percent goes to coinage and gold hoarding by people in insecure times. We must not jeopardize Montana rivers and compromise our lands for such luxurious, non-essential consumption."*

According to the companies' initial Conceptual Plan of Operations drawn up years ago, during the 15-year or so life of the open-pit, cyanide-heap, leach-process mine, more than 600 million tons of rock would be dug up and moved to a nearby location. This is the equivalent of 10,000 freight trains hauling 100 fully-loaded cars. On the average, only 0.03 ounces (less than $12 worth at current prices) of gold per ton are expected to be recovered. Modern technology and gold prices of at least $1,000 per ounce makes this miniscule amount of ore profitable, despite tremendous costs in equipment, engineering and labor. This included moving portions of Highway 200 about 1,000 feet closer to the Blackfoot River. Piles of tailings from the leaching process would tower more than 600 feet above the road.

"Frankly, we will be altering the landscape," said project manager John Marsden. "Essentially, we will be moving the hill from one spot to another.

"This is a world-class gold deposit. The question is can it be mined and processed profitably, and can it be permitted. We believe the answer is yes."

Those who enjoy the beauty of the valley, including the Ponderosa-pine-covered butte about to be mined, may disagree with Marsden concerning his "win-win" assessment. But it's hard not to like the guy or senior project geologist Jim Volderberg. As employees of the mining company, they are quite obviously excited about the project. They both even like to flyfish, play pool, and drink beer. Regular guys. Spend enough time with these two, and a person, even a stone-cold flyfisher, could begin to believe in the mammoth project........ Almost.

While the mine is huge in scope, the process is relatively simple. The rock is drilled and blasted. Then the ore is hauled either directly to a lined leach pad engineered for crushed ore, or to a crushing facility and then to a pad designed for crushed ore. Dilute cyanide solution is then applied to the ore to dissolve precious minerals, in this case mostly gold.

While at the site, Volberding showed me a chunk of gold-bearing rock. It looked like a piece of concrete speckled with smaller pieces of stone. The gold is not visible to the eye: it is measured in dimensions of microns. Until recently it was not technically possible to extract such deposits profitably. The geologist said that the gold perked up into the rock millions of years ago as a result of a now-extinct geologic feature similar to Yellowstone National Park's Mammoth Hot Springs.

"To a geologist this is an exciting find, and this is the only place that is exposed," said Volberding. We were standing on a pine-covered, grassy slope several hundred feet above the valley. The Blackfoot River twisted and curved along the edge of timbered mountains rolling to the south. Off that way is the site of the Seven-Up Pete gold deposit that, according to the manager, is a "tar baby" that sucks up man-hours and money. A much more difficult and costly area to mine.

Putting aside the fact that the open-pit mine will dramatically alter the landscape and damage the aesthetics of the place, the greatest concern to fisheries biologists, environmentalists, local residents, and flyfishers is the possibility of a cyanide leak from one of the leach pads. Cyanide, even in dilute levels, kills fish and other life forms by inhibiting their ability to absorb oxygen. Trout have been identified as the most sensitive fish to chronic or acute cyanide poisoning. Concentrations as low as ten parts per billion free cyanide can rapidly and permanently affect the swimming ability of salmonids. Invertebrates are even more sensitive. A leak could decimate the Blackfoot River, which has been on the rebound largely through the efforts of groups like Trout Unlimited and the state Department of Fish, Wildlife and Parks.

Cyanide solutions used in the mining process can also leak into groundwater resources. Once in the groundwater, there is no known method of cleaning up the aquifer short of pumping the water to the surface for treatment, which is an extremely costly process. The cyanide ponds attract wildlife, and at least 10,000 deaths of animals at these sites around the country have been documented, according to the National Wildlife Federation. Spills of cyanide are not rare occurrences. According to the Department of State Lands, three out of five active heap leach operations registered in Montana in 1989 received water-quality violations due to illegal discharges of cyanide solution.

The leach pads at this operation will have composite pad liner systems of compacted soil and a geomembrane liner consisting of two compressed six-inch layers of clay. All of this will be overlaid with a PVC liner of sufficient thickness to withstand the pressure from 600 feet of rock.

Other problems could be changes in the flow of the groundwater, and Marsden said they are drilling extensively to map this underground system with the intentions of designing the mine so that no damage is done in this area. He expects to exceed the standards of the Beale Mountain mine near Anaconda, an operation touted as state-of-the-art when it comes to the environment.

Hundreds would have to work the site, creating a potential overload disaster for the small town of Lincoln. Marsden said that some workers may live in Helena, an hour away, to help mitigate some of the impacts on services and facilities like law enforcement, water, and schools.

The project sounds pretty good, but Phelps Dodge has a track record of neglect, abuse, and environmental violations. Its operations in the Southwest have been cited and fined frequently for discharges into nearby water systems, and some of its smelters are considered among the dirtiest in the country. According to a Mining Report Card prepared by the Mineral Policy Center, the company's greatest problem concerning management practices "is not expertise, but commitment...Phelps Dodge's defensive approach to seeking permits pays financial dividends in the short run, but its basic assumption – that regulators' expectations are merely a nuisance for the lawyers to handle – has led to serious long-term problems."

Concerning reclamation, the Center states, "The Phelps Dodge Corporation receives its lowest grade in this category. The company's Southwestern operations fail even the most minimal standards of reclamation...Reclamation activities have taken place at some Arizona properties, but the record here is relatively unimpressive. Each time, initiative came from a regulatory agency, not the company itself."

Another problem is the fact that federal land is not involved. Private and state land is, meaning that the primary regulatory agency will be the Montana Department of State Lands. Based on past mining abuses overseen by the department, this is a lot like having the fox guard the hen coop.

Years ago, the Big Blackfoot Chapter of Trout Unlimited passed a resolution that stated in part, "...the Big Blackfoot Chapter publicly states its grave concern about the potential impacts that the Seven-Up Pete Joint Venture may have on the Blackfoot River...to assure that the company can conclusively prove that the technology it will employ during and after the proposed mining operation will result in complete containment of cyanide and all other pollutants...and be it further resolved, that, through the regulatory process and all means available, the chapter will call for the total reclamation of all sites disturbed during the mining operation including the requirement that Phelps Dodge provide sufficient bond prior to the commencement of further exploration of mining to support all reclamation costs."

From the windy ridge at the proposed mine site, the view up and down the valley is beautiful. Timbered mountains running in all directions. It is hard to comprehend that the ground I'm standing on might, in the future, be a huge hole more than 1,000 feet deep and that this butte will be a pile of rock lying next to the highway just a short distance from here.

I ask myself: Twenty years from now will there still be trout swimming in the river running so peacefully below me?

There is nothing as devastating as a hard-rock mine or that of an open-pit coal mine where the land is concerned. These enormous scars on the planet's surface never heal. In Montana, they are all over the place. The coal mines near Decker in the southeastern part of Montana use equipment that is built on a scale that dwarfs conventional earth-moving equipment. Some of my favorite country is out on the

coulee and bluff lands that roll off to the horizon not far from the Decker mines. I wrote another novel about mining in Montana and actually got the sucker published. It's called *Hunted* and is an attempt to make others aware of what this form of mineral extraction does to the landscape. The book concerns the 1872 Mining Law, and despite outrage and concerted efforts by people across the country, this abomination remains unchanged to date. I'd like to say that I'm sorry for dragging the ugliness of the mining issue into this book, but I'm not. What is truly overwhelming and depressing is driving around the West and on north through Alberta and seeing mine after mine, clearcuts everywhere resembling some massive, earthly skin disease, and all of the related destruction. If relentlessly banging on people's heads is what it takes to get even one soul truly outraged, then that's what I'll do. Good country is my sanity and salvation. Those that destroy it are my enemies. And they don't call Montana the Treasure State for nothing. Millions of tons of precious metals have been dug, blasted, and filtered from the ground and nearby streams. Enough gold has been mined to sink a large freighter. Much more of the same holds true for silver and copper. And rarer metals of equal or greater value are now coming into their own in the eyes of mining company executives and investors on world markets.

So what does all this have to do with trout and flyfishing? In Montana, and other parts of the mineral-rich West, nearly everything in some river drainages. Sloppy disposal of tailings, settling pond failure, leaching of cyanide into the aquifer, soil erosion – any one of these can spell disaster for trout populations not just for a year

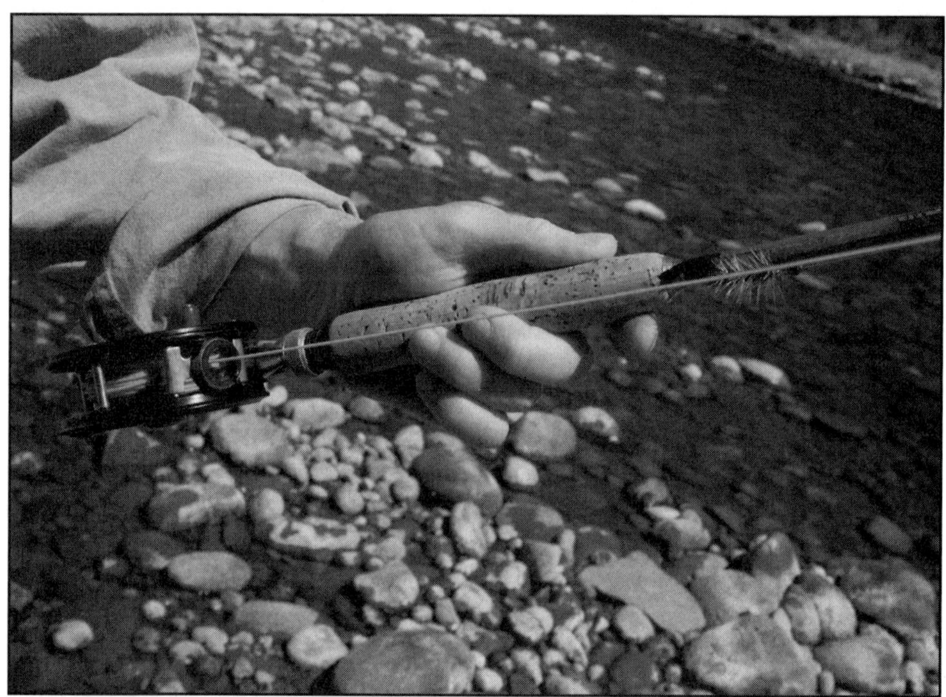

or two but for decades. Look what has happened around Butte, once the nation's largest copper-mining location. Nearby streams are so full of heavy metals that trout find survival there difficult or impossible. This area and on west to Anaconda is the nation's largest Environmental Protection Agency Super Fund site.

According to EPA findings, the hard-rock mining industry creates between one and four billion tons of solid waste each year. Almost no hard-rock mining sites are currently required to be restored to pre-mining condition, except where state laws require it. Groundwater impacts are frequently ignored by the BLM. The Mineral Policy Center estimates that the cost of cleaning up historical hard-rock mining sites is somewhere between $20 billion and $50 billion.

"There are lots of degrading things to the environment – logging, grazing, etc. – that will heal themselves over time, but mining scars will be with us long after the earth is a cinderball and there is no sun," said the late Gary LaFontaine to me one time while we fished the Little Blackfoot.

Gary's words pretty well some up a lot of our feelings.

But enough of this ecological jive. There's plenty of good water tearing down out of the mountains. From the campground at the end of the road that follows the river, I headed up the trail. Mind-blowing canyons, mountains, ice and snowfields and thick pine forest draping steep slopes stretched far down into the southern horizon. I almost forgot to drop down to the pocket water and fish. Almost. Lately I've turned more and more to bamboo rods. This time I was using a five-foot nine-inch treat, manufacturer unknown, beautifully restored by an artisan in Skowhegan, Maine. Short leader of seven feet tapered to 4X with a #12 Yellow Humpy was all the angling sophistication required here. Short casts of 20 to 25 feet or usually less along the quiet edges of foaming water turned Yellowstone cutthroat on nearly every cast. None huge, a couple to maybe 14 inches, but this was more of the joyous fishing of my youth that I can never get enough. Fantastic country that's so far gone beautiful, it feels like I'm alone working the icy snowmelt stream somewhere on a more sensible planet. Each fish was wild native perfection full of rose, red, crimson, emerald, cerulean, aquamarine, yellow, and deep-orange cutts along the lower jaw. And they were strong from living in this rapid, chill environment. Even the smaller ones of six inches felt like tough guys on the little rod. I saw no one, though I knew others were hiking far into the Absaroka Beartooth Wilderness high country. Eagles worked thermals thousands of feet above, circling in enormous gyres defining vast chunks of three-dimensional territory. I could not imagine what these sharp-eyed predators were seeing.

I focused on the pockets and miniature pools ahead of me and managed to work a mile of raucous water before calling a halt to the proceedings, climbing back up a steep slope to the trail and walking downhill to my Suburban at the parking area.

Classic lower river drift fishing or delightful free-form mountain stream action. I used to come to the Stillwater for day trips. Now I come for several days to do both fully. Fine water winding through true Montana terrain.

TRIP INFORMATION

Timing: Before runoff in April through June and by mid- to late July into early October. The snow lingers well into summer in the high country of the 12,000-foot plus Beartooths and the autumn colors are outrageous.

Where: Take the Columbus exit off I-90 about 35 minutes west of Billings, then Hwy 78 through Absarokee (ab-zor-kee) then 78 for several miles to 420 and all the way, about 16 miles, to the campground. Put-ins for floating are located on 78 heading upstream from Fireman's Point to Swinging Bridge to White Bird then along 420 are Absaroka, Cliff Swallow, Castle Rock, Moraine, and Buffalo Jump.

Hub: Columbus is a nice Montana town along the Yellowstone River. The main drag is called Pike Street and is off the highway about one-half mile. The New Atlas Bar is a great place for a drink or two, 528 East Pike Avenue, 406-322-9818. The 307 Bar, Grill, & Casino features a full bar, restaurant, and a casino. Varied menu. Open daily 10:00am to 2:00am.

Breakfast served from 8:00am to 1:00pm on weekends. 842 East Pike Avenue, 406-322-4511. Git's Big Sky Motel located at 740 East Pike Avenue is okay for a few nights.

For current information, call the Montana Dept. of Fish Wildlife and Parks at 406-247-2940 (Billings) or 406-994-4042 (Bozeman).

Appropriate Gear: Four- to 6-weight rods from eight to nine feet for the middle and lower stretches. In the upper water, you'll be hiking in a 4- or 5-weight pack rod, floating and sink-tip lines, lightweight hip waders and boots. The water is ice cold even in July, so the extra weight is worth the effort. Bear spray and noise maker or lots of talking. Backpacking gear if you're young, fit, and masochistic.

Favorite Patterns: On the lower stretches, Stimulators and Sofa Pillows work in late spring and early summer matching large stoneflies including the salmonfly. Rainbows and browns in the middle and lower stretches love these, as they do large Hare's Ear nymphs and Elk Hair Caddis later in the summer near dusk. Hoppers play well, too. I'm a big fan of Charlie Brooks' Assam Dragon (and all his other designs). We're dealing with wild, native cutthroat here so the pattern is not all that important. Wulffs of all colors, Hare's Ear nymphs work really well, Buggers for curiosity's sake, Elk Hair Caddis, and Rat Faced-McDougal, if only for its name.

Special Regulations: Open entire year.

Assam Dragon

Hook: #4 to #10, 2X-3X long
Weight: 0.03 wire, 12 wraps

Body: Natural brown seal fur 0.125 inch wide to 0.0625 wide, 3 to 4 inches long

Hackle: Brown dyed grizzly
Thread: 3/0 brown

CHAPTER SIX

Musselshell River

They traveled the wilder parts of the world as their parents and grandparents had done the Grand Tour – it was expected. They went into the world with open minds, wide-eyed, sufficiently healed. They sought sophistication and charm, not in the Louvre and the Uffizi, but in the tapestried halls of nature."

From The Diamond Bogo by Robert F. Jones

All sorts of words in several forms come to mind whenever I fish the Musselshell. Thoughts, phrases, passages from revered writers, but none more revered than my friend, the late Robert F. Jones. Bob and I shared a love for good country and all that goes with it – big game, birds, whiskey around late night fires, stories that were mostly true, and the brown trout of this river. Each time we walked alongside this river or worked upstream casting Woolly Buggers, grasshopper imitations, Elk Hair Caddis, or perhaps some weird mouse pattern we'd thought up in the flickering light of one of our blazes; we fished with the intensity and love of men who knew what they held dear in life, what mattered most, the wild natural world – all of this that had kept us from going crazy over the years was vanishing at an astonishing pace; and we knew that we were blessed to have rivers like this one in this modern, insane age, a stream with large, secretive brown trout that were always here even when we failed to move even a single one of them despite hours of determined casting. The Musselshell was how we thought flyfishing should always be – the land magnificent, unspoiled, the trout never easy, the isolation felt within the riparian corridor so complete that the sound of a passing car on the distant highway went unnoticed, walking up to a blue heron seemed normal and the strong tug of a brown at the end of the line was right. We shared other rivers like this: the Mettawee in Bob's home state of Vermont, the Bitterroot of years ago (not the drift-boat-rubber-raft gridlock of today), the Ogilvie in the Yukon, and the Tongue are some of them.

But whenever we wanted to recall and create between us images of what flyfishing means for some, conversation always drifted inevitably to our time on the Musselshell. The river is not large. Not floatable. Tough to walk and wade. The browns are really fickle to the point that a person begins to wonder if there are any fish in the damn thing, and the mosquitoes can be difficult, as in North Woods ravenous. All of these apparent negatives are why we loved the river while, thankfully, so few others do. Even skilled flyfishers shun the water for their own reasons – muddy in places, too small, tough casting. All we ever encountered were one or two bait fishers from Billings, a couple of hours east of us. They'd take a couple of browns and we'd wish they didn't, but we'd learned that all but a very few men who fish are usually worth knowing and who the hell are we to question these others, anyway?

One afternoon during the downtime of the heat of an early September's day, we were discussing some of the large trout we'd seen and heard about in the river and what exactly it would take to entice one of these into striking. We decided that the fishing should be at dusk or cocktail hour because that was when the true predators started to prowl (check any bar) and that the fly had to be large. As this conversation was unfolding, we heard a slight rustle and some delicate gnawing in our food box. A quick glance through the eye of a flashlight revealed a mouse not much larger than my thumb with its head burrowed into the sacred bag of Fritos.

Bingo! We looked at each other with an awareness that transcended anything Kesey and his band of Merry Pranksters brought forth in his Acid Tests. I'd brought a basic tying kit and we set about constructing our mouse on a large hook with spun-then-shaped grey deer hair, some chamois for a tail and all held together with grey thread on a large streamer hook. Something was missing.

"Whiskers," said Bob. Nothing in the kit would do, but just then as with all great moments in our chaotic angling adventures a horse whinnied across the Musselshell. A black mare. Bob splashed across a shallow riffle, pulled a handful of rich, green grass and gently approached the horse.

"Here you go, girl. Easy. Easy," he murmured in a seductive voice. The mare came to the rusting barbed wire and leaned over nickering just as seductively. A love story unfolding on the high plains of central Montana. Bob fed the horse handfuls of the grass while stroking the rich black mane. Eventually, as with all relationships, this one ended, though happily. The mare resumed her grazing. Bob returned with several strands of jet black hair. Trimmed and tied in at the head and our mouse imitation began to breath, but was still lacking something.

"Eyes," Bob said. He was on a roll. "Mustache die would work. Have any?" and he gave me a wise-ass look full well knowing that I'd never had a mustache let alone any coloring. "Oh, hell. Let's drive into Harlowton and ask at the Stockman's."

"How'd you know there was a Stockman's in Harlowton?"

"What Montana town doesn't have one?"

Forty-six miles (round trip), three mugs of the Stockman's ice cold beer later, a quick dash to the local Midtown Market for some Just For Men mustache coloring, two more rounds – vodka-and-cranberry this time – at The Two Dot Bar and we were

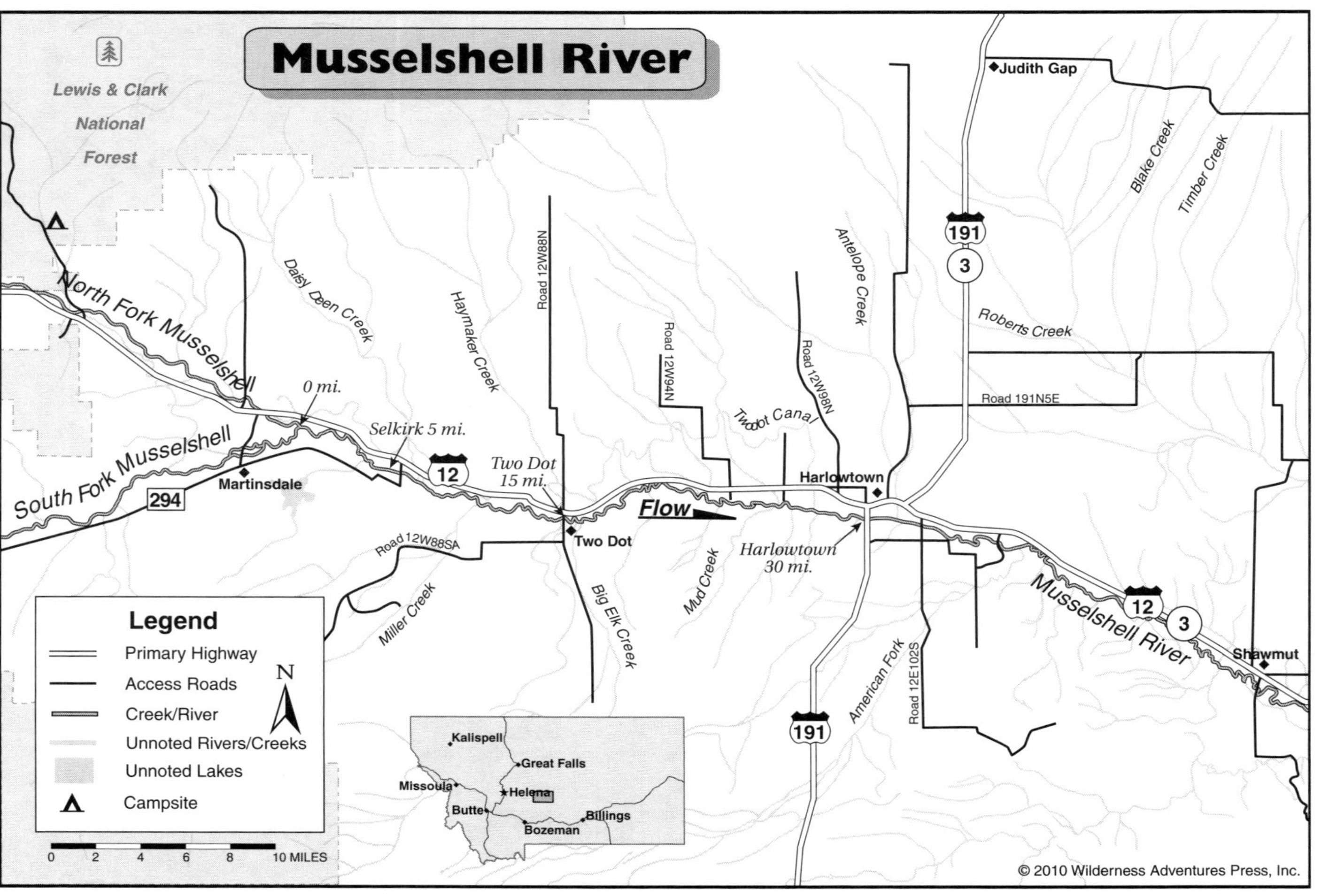
Musselshell River
Lewis & Clark National Forest
Judith Gap
Blake Creek
Timber Creek
North Fork Musselshell
South Fork Musselshell
294
Martinsdale
0 mi.
Selkirk 5 mi.
12
Daisy Dean Creek
Haymaker Creek
Road 12W88N
Road 12W94N
Twodot Canal
Road 12W98N
Antelope Creek
Roberts Creek
191
3
Road 191N5E
Two Dot 15 mi.
Two Dot
Flow
Harlowtown
Harlowtown 30 mi.
Road 12W88SA
Miller Creek
Big Elk Creek
Mud Creek
American Fork
191
Road 12E102S
Musselshell River
12
3
Shawmut
Legend
Primary Highway
Access Roads
Creek/River
Unnoted Rivers/Creeks
Unnoted Lakes
Campsite
N
Kalispell
Great Falls
Missoula
Helena
Butte
Billings
Bozeman
0   2   4   6   8   10 MILES
© 2010 Wilderness Adventures Press, Inc.

back in camp. Nothing had changed and the mouse would be sightless no longer. I delicately and thoroughly applied the coloring and we had a mouse.

"Needs a name," Bob said.

"Jolt for Jones and Holt," I said.

"Works for me. Time for a drink and you might think about grilling some steaks for us before we go fishing."

Following dinner that also included baked potatoes, corn, sour cream and fresh butter purchased from the Hutterite madness up the road, we rigged the mouse to a seven-foot section of 20-pound leader attached to the butt section of Bob's line. His Orvis 5-weight was armed. We each took a beverage with us and puffed away on cigarettes (ah the cold, old days when I smoked and drank in gay defiance of death) and headed downstream to a deep pole protected by a large willow and grassy bank. The light was going as we headed to a gravel bank below this spot where the autumn before I'd watched the current wash away the swirl of a truly big fish. Handing me his drink, Bob pulled line off the reel and false cast against the bank well below the pool.

"Going to bounce the fucker off the grass for realism," he said with Merit Light clenched between his teeth, smoke rising straight up above him in the warm, still air of dusk.

The mouse made a "whooshing" sound as Bob rocketed the hairy thing back and forth above our heads. A bat dive-bombed the thing and rushed off with a faint, high-pitched squeak. Then Bob launched the mouse that "thwacked" against a bare spot in the grass and "plopped" into the water, some dirt falling with it. He made one strip and the largest damn brown trout either of us had ever scene – bigger than the 27-plus-incher that towed us down the Bighorn one spring and bigger than the eight-pounder I'd landed on the upper Clark Fork years ago – came from out of nowhere and smashed down on the little mouse. The creature's mouth was as large as a pair of shovel blades – all white inside with rows of enormous teeth. As Bob reared back to set the hook the brown crushed down in a splash that sent water in all directions and reaching nearly to where we stood. Stone and sand just ahead of us was soaked. The rod pumped twice and bowed more, then doubled, then the leader snapped with a "pop" that sounded like a thick firecracker. The sound echoed off a nearby hill and died in the gathering gloom.

Bob had chomped through his smoke. He spit out the butt and lit another then reached a hand out to me. I handed him his drink. We looked at each other and drained our mugs.

"Big fish," I said.

"No shit," he said. Then we both laughed a long time for no other reason than this was what we always lived for, always chased. We went back to camp, built up the fire and talked into the night beneath a thick, bright Milky Way as nighthawks boomed overhead and great grey owls hooted in a nearby stand of trees. One large meteor seemed to fizzle out directly above the pool of the large brown. A coyote howled. Life was good.

And all three of the glasses…were full of sand. That was how they had their tea in the Sahara.

From The Sheltering Sky by Paul Bowles

The Musselshell Breaks is a lonesome, disheveled section of landscape. Eroding gouges in mostly barren soil lead down to dry washes at every desiccated twist and turn of this dusty yellow road. The Missouri Breaks, an even larger example of this arid chaos, encroach upon our tawdry little expedition from three corners of the horizon. To the south lies flat, empty distance sometimes called the Big Empty. Indeed, it seems that only by an unspoken natural generosity of this awe-inspiring place coupled with a ragged collection of Montana maps, are we making any headway into this country in search of purportedly large smallmouth bass, a gamefish not often associated with Montana, but present none the less.

As the miles bounce and jolt by, the outing was beginning to take on the sere overtones of Bertram Thomas's 1931 expedition to the Rub' al Khali or Empty Quarter of the Arabian Peninsula, except that our road was indeed somewhat traveled where Thomas had not even the benefit of a sand-blown two-track to guide him. Advantage this day going to contemporary children on the run in a 1983 GMC Suburban.

It had been well over an hour since we'd turned north off the velvety pavement of Highway 200 at the small outpost of Winnett, a hardy enclave of humanity tucked precariously beneath a towering ochre wall of Eocene sandstone. Our destination was the mouth of the Musselshell River where it contributed its meager flow to the dark blue immensity of Fort Peck Lake, an impoundment dating from the 1930s. Years ago while trespassing on the sacred private holdings of a large ranch perched on the other side of the Musselshell, we'd tried to reach the bass of whispered rumor, fish that were purported to exceed five pounds and willingly smash any streamer cast their way. The attempt failed due to numerous barbed-wire fences, busted cattle guards, and finally nothing but jumbles of clinker, sandstone, and cactus.

But today was fine – mid-70s, puffy clouds, a gentle wind pushing through the long needles of Ponderosa pine that wound around the hills and gentle buttes in stately symmetry. The air smelled of pine, sage, and water-hungry earth. Every ten miles or so an established, weathered ranch complex flickered in and out of view, metal roofs coruscating in the August sunlight before vanishing like mirages as we whipped around another bend, dust billowing behind us.

By "us" I mean my wife, Ginny, and myself. We roam thousands of miles each year across Montana and often get carried away in our amblings to the extent that we find ourselves in places north of the Arctic Circle on some barely navigable travesty like the Yukon's Dempster Highway, where we spin in all directions overwhelmed by the mountain ranges rolling off in all directions in the perpetual daylight of summer. Enormous rivers filled with grayling and arctic char power beneath thick stands of boreal forest. Or we wind up in Wichita when we were headed for Casper. So, searching for smallmouth bass in the arid northern high plains is little more than a walk around the block in our addled minds.

Ginny exclaims, "How beautiful!" and points through the bug-splattered windshield to the northeast. "That water is gorgeous. Can't wait to go swimming."

I see no water, only blue sky, dry bluffs, clumps of juniper, more Ponderosa, sage, some antelope, and a couple of mule deer flicking enormous ears against the pesterings of biting flies, but allow Ginny her delusions or illusions. Pulling over on the grassy spine connecting two knolls, we pause for some bread, summer sausage, and cheese. Orange pop for her. Iced tea for me. Still no water in view. The afternoon is warm now, in the upper 80s. The horizon dances through waves of heated air giving the sky an unfocused look, as though water is washing over the Breaks. Things turned upside down. Water on top, land below. No big deal. We'll be near lots of normal water soon enough when we reach an ephemeral flow called Crooked Creek. Snack finished, we climb back in the Suburban, now host to a number of flies who've decided to go along for the ride. Again, no big deal.

Mildly intoxicating images drift through my mind. Visions of casting a 7-weight with a large, weighted Marabou Muddler far out into gentle whorls of Musselshell current dissipating in the waters of Fort Peck, the streamer sinking down into cool, dark water and then swiftly though erratically retrieved before an iron-strong smallmouth hammers the fake, flees to the depths as the old Battenkill sings away, fly line slicing the still surface of the lake as the fish then sprints away from me. I'm eager now. Ready for the chase.

After several more miles of beatific isolation, we crest a mound and take in the view, a vista that encompasses many miles. A broad valley reminding me of Africa's Great Rift Valley stretches north, south, and east. Behind in the west lies where we've

just been. The mouth of the river and the deep waters of the lake are supposed to be a couple of hundred feet below us.

Except that there is nothing. Nothing at all but a vast prairie of scrub willow, native grass, cactus, lots of grey-green sage, more antelope and mule deer grazing desultorily in the simmering heat. But there's no rolling river. No deep-water lake. No water at all.

Looking through binoculars I see a thread of blue that twists quickly round a reddish-brown hill and out of sight. The Musselshell. We've found it and perhaps Fort Peck, and only 20 or 30 miles distant. It's the extreme low water of late summer that is playing with our heads. But we're not fooled. We know where the wet stuff and the smallmouth are now. A mere sprint. We could be there by 4 a.m., but what the hell? We're older, a touch wiser and take things easier these days, so we decide to pass on the brief stroll and the waiting bass. Next spring after runoff when water levels are 30, 40 feet higher will be a good time. Soon enough. Getting out and seeing the country today is reward enough. It's okay to let the venture end this way. Mentioning this to Ginny draws an agreeable nod. We drink some cold water from a jug stored on ice in the cooler, climb back in our rig and head back home.

Just one more 525-mile day trip in a series of many. Ah yes, even when it's a bit twisted along the Musselshell, life is still good.

The brown current ran swiftly out of the heart of darkness, bearing us down towards the sea with twice the speed of our upward progress; … I saw the time approaching when I would be left alone of the party of 'unsound method'.

From Heart of Darkness by Joseph Conrad

Those words from Joseph Conrad's novel come to mind every time I walk through the eight- to ten-foot-tall grasses that grow luxuriantly along the Musselshell in the summer. I feel like I've wandered through some temporal doorway into the edge of vast boreal landscape that runs alongside one of many unnamed rivers in the Northwest Territories. Illusion often equates to artifice, that in turn becomes reality in a fervent mindscape. But the fecundity of this river valley, its healthiness, lushness is like no other in the state. After talking with a Dehcho Dene tribal member one July in the Territories about those anonymous streams, I learned that the waters are filled with "pike" – a local term for walleye – especially in late June. Back home in Montana, I tied a number of bright yellow, heavily-weighted Woolly Buggers to mimic the lead-head jigs I'd used in northwest Ontario's Wabigoon River in the early 60s.

Back then the Wabigoon, now destroyed by mercury poisoning from a pulp plant operated by the Dryden Chemical Company – bastards – beginning in 1962, was full of walleye to eight pounds that would suck in the jigs often to be sucked in themselves by large northern pike. One greedy fellow ate a two-pound fish I was reeling in. The northern predator was eventually landed when my father pulled off his pants, knotted the legs and slid the northern's head into them. The fish weighed 44 pounds (my father carried a scale to weigh the various crates we portaged on the three-week venture – he was a little nuts like the rest of us and liked to chart the weight decrease as we consumed the various food and beverage items). The fish, as well as First Nation people living along the Wabigoon drainage, are now loaded with the pulp plant mercury – bastards – and are paying a horrific price for this industrial greed – neurological damage, birth defects, destruction of a commercial fishery, but, as is my wont, I digress.

Staggering vaguely back on track, the Buggers I concocted were #4 and #6. On the next visit to the far north stream, to the best of my knowledge unnamed, I hacked my way upstream through thick undergrowth while being devoured by mosquitoes, moose flies (size #2) and black flies. Woodland bison chomped leafy vegetation in the dense forest on a slight rise, taking note of my struggles with slight head turns and sporadic grunts. Death by a marauding bison would have been a mercy killing. Standing thigh-deep in mucky stream bottom – now a stationary target for my buzzing companions – I cast the pattern along the banks and stripped it back slowly. Walleye or "pike" after walleye or "pike" hit the thing and I soon had a nice group of two- to four-pound walleye or 'pike" to fillet and fry up for dinner amidst the swarms of indigenous insects later that sunlit night, perhaps around midnight. The same fishing conditions and action, only for brown trout, can be found on the Musselshell using Buggers when the stars are aligned properly.

Strange recollection, perhaps awkward incidence…so that's the drift of my Heart of Darkness episode…and life was good up there, too…

…several years ago, I took my wife up to the river one full-blown gorgeous October day. We weren't married then, but I'd decided to change all of that. We walked the river, Ginny photographing whatever caught her eye while I worked upstream casting a Woolly Bugger along undercut, grassy banks, into log jams and through deep runs. The browns weren't active, but I managed to turn a few. Each a jumper as is the style of Musselshell trout. They were healthy, brightly-marked with their distinctive blood-copper spotting and dark honey bellies. All of them in the 15- to 18-inch range. The day was in the 70s. The sky cloudless and Montana blue. The cottonwoods were a blazing shade of yellow that only memories in the mind can describe. Back at camp I said to Ginny that I had something we needed to talk about. She looked worried, probably thinking "I hope he's not planning to start robbing MiniMarts again".

I reached into my pocket and pulled out my grandmother's engagement ring and asked if she would marry me.

Her eyes sparkled with the colors of the day and she said yes. I placed the ring on her finger. We hugged and kissed and she spent the next hour turning the ring in the sunlight watching it sparkle. Life was good.

The Musselshell is special. I've had some of the best days of my life with this river. I hope it always remains what it is now, even well after I'm dead and gone. I'll do anything to protect this country.

TRIP INFORMATION

Timing: From mid-April until runoff muddies things in mid- to late May. Then from late June through early November.

Where: Highway 212 follows the trout water from near Martinsdale down to Shawmut in the central part of the state. Very little of this river flows through public lands, but there is a fishing access at Selkirk a few miles east of Two Dot on Hwy 212. Access can also be gained from the numerous bridges that cross the stream all the way to Roundup. The quality trout fishing fades away within a half-dozen miles downstream of Harlowton and is replaced with a smallmouth fishery that would be excellent if irrigation drawdown didn't hammer it. Below Roundup think catfish until you reach the CM Russell Wildlife Refuge in the Missouri Breaks, where large smallmouth roam the waters of the Musselshell where it drains into Fort Peck Reservoir.

Hub: Harlowton is a small place of less than 1,000, but has most necessary services including: Country Side Inn, 309 3rd Street NE, 406-632-4119; and Stockman's Bar, 406-632-4621, with pizzas, angus beef burgers, pork chop sandwiches as well as other assorted sandwiches, and homemade chili. Ray's Sports and Western Wear has most of what an angler needs. Located on the east end of town by Highway 191, 406-632-4320. Martinsdale, a small town about seven miles from the river has a fine restaurant and also offers good rooms for $40 to $60 per night. The restaurant is open from Thursday through Sunday – 11:30am to 7:30pm, except for September through December when it's necessary to call to find out the open hours. The place is called the Crazy Mountain Inn, 406-572-3307, stay@ crazymountaininn.com. The Mint Bar is just a stroll across the wide street.

Appropriate Gear: Three- thru 5-weight rods, eight feet or shorter. Seven and a half- to nine-foot leaders from 5X down to 2X for streamers. Wet wade in warm weather or bring chest waders. Insect repellant.

Favorite Patterns: Woolly Bugger, Marabou Muddler, Joe's Hopper, Dave's Hopper, Elk Hair Ccaddis, Hare's Ear nymph, BWO, Adams, Stimulator.

Special Regulations: Downstream from where the north and south forks meet – open all year.

Jolt Mouse

Hook: Mustad 9672, or any 2X long streamer hook. Size 2
Thread: Grey 6/0 monocord

Body: Coarse deer hair, natural
Tail: Strip of chamois
Ears: Chamois or any other thin, tan leather

Whiskers: black horse mane hair
Eyes: Just For Men dark brown mustache dye

CHAPTER SEVEN

West Boulder River

The way these Yellowstone cutthroat trout reacted to the unsettling appearance of my Cree Woolly Bugger as it settled lazily through the clear water column of a large pool in the meadows section of the West Boulder River was reminiscent of the way a distant memoried girlfriend from college days in Missoula responded when I poured a pitcher of beer over her head at the employee Christmas party at The Shack while she was playing a juvenile kissing game with some hapless hippy in the back corner of the greasy spoon. Like the then-soaked blonde, the trout went nuts swimming in mad circles (she ran) and diving for cover (she zipped into the restroom) before false-charging (she reappeared yelling obscenities in my direction) the streamer. Perhaps there is a behavioral connection that needs to be explored here. The only one that comes to mind is that anomalous actions – e.g. abrupt appearance of arcane fly pattern and sudden beer dousing – forced upon any sentient (and with the girlfriend I'm possibly being generous in this regard) species produces a measure of chaos. By the fourth cast, the fish were lined up shuddering (known as agonistic behavior) in ranks, the braver among them rushing the Bugger then breaking off the charge at point-blank range. The motions of their finnings causing the Bugger to spin and jiggle in the water. When I stripped the pattern a foot or two, the biggest of the cutthroat slashed at it, one hooking itself and circling madly before jumping a few times and then coming to my feet. The trout was a brilliantly-colored specimen of 17, maybe 18 inches. Rich shades of red along the cheeks, the cuts of the jaw; orange, indigo, emerald, orange, white and blackest of black spots lit up the firm, stocky cutthroat. I released the fish and watched it streak to cover along the stream's bottom. The other trout were all atwitter rushing pell-mell about the pool. After several minutes the situation righted itself and order was restored with the phalanxes of fish stacked in military order in the water a few feet out from the far bank. They appeared to be waiting for the alien to return to their midst, which it did as I launched another Woolly Bugger. Once again, the bravest of the brave attacked and I landed another fine cutthroat. Two more casts. Two more fish.

Reaching these meadows was an upward hike on a fair trail for a little over three miles through thick pine forest into the Absaroka-Beartooth Wilderness. As the meadows near, thousands of acres of burned-over land appear. Scars from the red-hot fires of a parched summer several years ago. New pines and succulent undergrowth is making a strong return. The land is rejuvenating itself. What's unsightly to humans is the natural way of wild lands, and rewarding to see. Fire-created soot and silt has nourished the land and been flushed from the streams. All seems well. I'd been worried when I came here the year after the fires, but I needn't have. The fish were fine. Grizzly tracks marked moist areas, deer were abundant as were hairy woodpeckers, Cooper's hawks, and golden eagles.

I decided to take my obtrusive act about a half mile across the tall, lush grass meadows in the direction of the magnificently shining distant mountains. In about 15 minutes I reached the creek again. The stream was now a forested flow with downfalls, deep pools, shallow riffles, and undercut banks protected in places by fir tree root balls. I removed the offensive Bugger, added about two feet of 5X tippet and tied in a #14 Royal Wulff. This is one of my favorite patterns and has been for many years. I enjoy watching the brightly-colored fly bob and twirl on the sparkling surface of the West Boulder. Yellowstone cutthroat rose from nearly every holding spot and took the Wulff with an audible slurp and a splash that sent out circles of crystalline spray shimmering prismatic in the sunlight. Walking along through the shallows, along gravel bars and banks, or briefly through the trees was pleasant. The fish were everywhere and cooperative. The air smelled of pine and the water tasted of ice melt from distant snowfields and tannin. The wind moaned through needled tree tops and mountain chickadees chattered among themselves. An hour's fishing and 20 trout from eight to fifteen inches. It was that kind of day. Later, towards dusk the fish would be larger, but we would be back down to the Suburban by then. Another time with lightweight camping gear and sunset fishing would prevail...

...The narrative now makes a slight divergence to the neighboring state of Wyoming. While this book is about Montana adventure the pursuit of happiness and excitement often follows up drainages and past man-made boundaries drawn on maps, especially in this case when chasing Yellowstone cutthroat. Once these arbitrary and quite unnatural lines of demarcation are violated anything can happen as we shall see...

...For some of us, not making the uncommon effort to define failure and success on our own terms can transform life into a largely disappointing experience. The fact that the Cubs have yet to win a World Series in my lifetime (or my father's or in nearly a century) is a personal object lesson in perseverance and loyalty. Losing my hair is perceived as a sign of high testosterone levels. And on it goes through convoluted time.

So when Ginny and I set out for the hinterlands of western Wyoming in search of what the Wyoming Game and Fish Department calls the Wyoming Cutt Slam I had already internally acknowledged that I would probably not catch (and release)

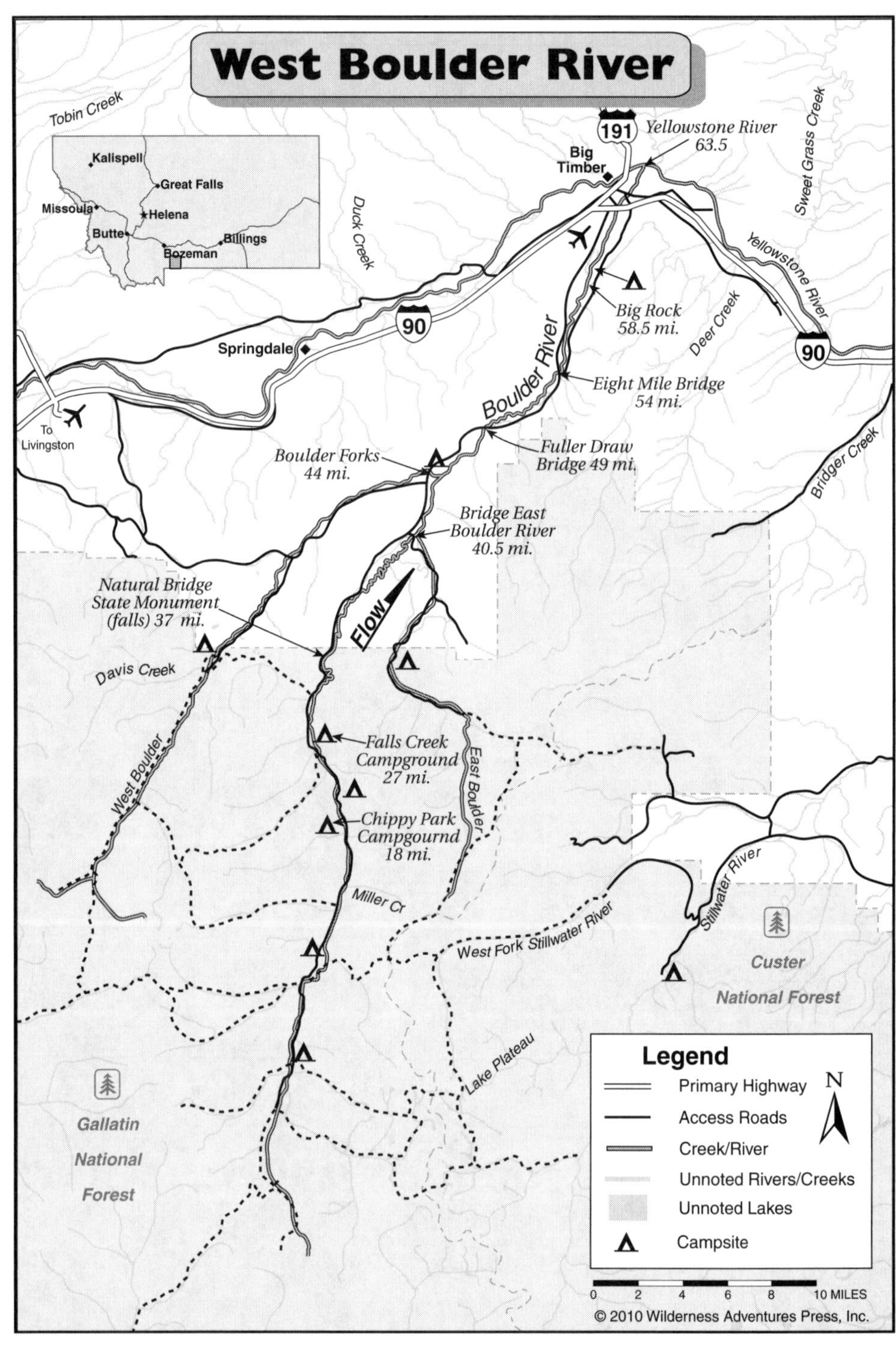

West Boulder River
Tobin Creek
Kalispell
Great Falls
Missoula
Helena
Butte
Billings
Bozeman
191
Yellowstone River
63.5
Big Timber
Duck Creek
Sweet Grass Creek
Yellowstone River
Big Rock
58.5 mi.
Deer Creek
90
90
Springdale
Boulder River
Eight Mile Bridge
54 mi.
To Livingston
Boulder Forks
44 mi.
Fuller Draw
Bridge 49 mi.
Bridger Creek
Bridge East
Boulder River
40.5 mi.
Natural Bridge
State Monument
(falls) 37 mi.
Flow
Davis Creek
West Boulder
Falls Creek
Campground
27 mi.
East Boulder
Chippy Park
Campgournd
18 mi.
Miller Cr
Stillwater River
West Fork Stillwater River
Custer
National Forest
Lake Plateau
Gallatin
National
Forest
Legend
N
Primary Highway
Access Roads
Creek/River
Unnoted Rivers/Creeks
Unnoted Lakes
Campsite
0 2 4 6 8 10 MILES
© 2010 Wilderness Adventures Press, Inc.

the four sub-species of cutthroat trout in question – Yellowstone (*Oncorhynchus clarki bouvieri*), Bonneville (*Oncorhynchus clarki utah*), Colorado (*Oncorhynchus clarki pleuriticus*) and Snake River (proposed classification of *Oncorhynchus clarki behnkei*). If I did succeed, I would need to submit a form stating where and when I caught the individual cutthroat along with digital photo documentation of each variety. Then I would receive a color certificate honoring my achievement. There are no expectations on my part concerning fulfilling the Slam, but should this eventuate, I definitely plan on having the full-color certificate framed and hung in a prominent location in our living room.

I'm not into competition or quest of any kind. I was initially reluctant to participate in the program, but reading the information on the department's website changed my mind. It stated that the Cutt-Slam is "a program designed to encourage anglers to learn more about Wyoming's cutthroat sub-species and develop more appreciation and support of the Wyoming Game and Fish Department's cutthroat management program". I much prefer native species to introduced gamefish as in casting to the westslope and Yellowstone cutthroat, mountain whitefish, Montana arctic grayling (*Thymallus arcticus montanus)* and bull trout as opposed to what most flyfishers prefer chasing – brook, brown, and rainbow trout.

Inured to what most psychologically healthy individuals consider abject failure, I figured two, possibly three, species landed would be a rousing success, but I had no idea how this peripatetic angling road trip would play out. The slowly-realized sinister nature of the adventure may haunt me for the remainder of my life, possibly even threatening the long-term stability of my rock-solid marriage.

As I was once again to experience, the angling gods are a capricious and cruel lot.

We set out for the South Fork of the Shoshone River outside of Cody near the southeastern corner of Yellowstone Park. The road was paved, degenerating into gravel winding through development after development then a long-running series of trophy and dude ranches. Once on the Shoshone National Forest, every trailhead and turnout was jammed with pickups and SUVs pulling horse trailers. The high country big game season was in full swing. Despite all of this human degradation, the sharp, jagged mountain peaks, escarpments, and sawtooth ridges are spectacular especially with a fresh dusting of pure white snow. At the end of the road, we stop and work our way up a trail to some passable pocket water. There are excellent pool and riffle stretches all along the way to the parking spot but all of this water is on private land and therefore off limits. This is unlike Montana, where an angler can access water from public roads and bridges and wade to his heart's content as long as he stays within the high water marks. In Wyoming, water that flows through private holdings is PRIVATE! No exceptions. We tend to take this freedom for granted in Montana, but it is truly a gift not to be squandered or given up to out-of-state wealthy who have accumulated a massive war chest in an attempt to overturn the state's stream access law. Not on my watch. Not while I'm still kicking.

On this trip, I packed a number of specialty rods that I don't use all that much but treasure all the same. For the South Fork, I rigged up an Orvis six-foot, one-ounce, 2-weight – a deceptively strong and accurate rod. Lightweight rods are a delight on small streams such as this one as long as the fish are played quickly so that they are not exhausted to the point of dying. Attached to the end of a 4X tippet is a Royal Wulff. The first four casts to likely-looking holes produced small Yellowstone cutts that ran in splashing circles briefly, then came splashing to my wet hands. Ginny photographed the little guys as I admired them before turning them free.

The South Fork is far too residential and locked up for our wild tastes, so we decided to cut the fishing short and move on down the road. Since we have a long distance to cover for our next cutthroat adventure somewhere in the southwestern part of the state, we decided to chew up some highway after a snack of sharp white cheddar, sausage, sour dough bread, and orange juice.

As can be seen from this truncated, comic-tragic narrative, eventually all angling may be viewed as being at least tangentially connected. Chasing the other three sub-species of cutthroats found in Wyoming is grist for another book, so I'll leave this subject where it stands.

I went back to the end of the meadows where Ginny was photographing damselflies, rising trout, and the valley back towards the mountains. We ate a sandwich, cheese and apples, drank some water and headed into the forest for the brief climb well above the stream that quickly began dropping down through the rocky gorge.

Within at most a minute's scramble, pools, runs, glides, pockets, riffles gliding over golden-copper streambed dominated the walk. I switched to a Yellow Humpy, waded in and worked my way upstream about a mile below the meadows. This looked like classic cutthroat water, but it isn't. I took a number of browns from the diminutive four-incher that pounced from next to a midstream boulder to a sleek fourteen-inch male that rose from the bottom of an elongated pool. The fish was colored in those golds and coppers of his stream and the spots were blood red. A remarkable fish. A half mile farther and about 200 yards through the pines, I repeated the process. A solid day in this water would yield dozens of fish. Nothing major, maybe 16 inches down near the trailhead, but truly joyous fishing. The kind that is easy and most importantly, fun.

A stream like this is intoxicating, hypnotic, drawing the angler from pool to riffle to run to pool and on and on. The fishing was steady with trout splashing after the fly on each cast. The air was rich with the scent of pine and the cold water and I realized that with a well-provisioned backpack I could spend the entire span of warm weather months in this country living off wild trout, morels in the spring and chanterelles in the fall, wild onions and perhaps a poached grouse or two. Good country like this is a treasure and Montana has many lifetimes of this wonderful, nearly surreally beautiful landscape. As fine as all this fishing is, I realized that I needed to turn around and head back. I wanted to be back to the Suburban in full daylight, even the fading, golden light of a sinking sun.

After another mountain mile walking through the forest, we left the tall trees and walked into the late afternoon sun to our rig. This had been a good day.

TRIP INFORMATION

Timing: Late July into early October. The snow lingers well into summer and the autumn colors in the high country are outrageous.

Where: A couple miles east of Livingston turn south on Swingley Road then bob and weave ever upward for about 15 miles before turning right on the West Boulder River Road (well marked). The trailhead is at the parking lot and the trail climbs for another four miles to the meadows.

Hub: Livingston is the hub. Fly Shops abound, including Dan Bailey Fly Shop on Park Street just west of Main Street – 800-356-4052, info@dan-bailey.com. There are a bunch of places to stay but along with Dan Bailey you might as well go for the whole Rancho Deluxe movie trip and stay at the Murray Hotel which has a good restaurant – The 2nd Street Bistro, 406-222-6433 – and the infamous Murray Bar, 406-222-6433, 201 West Park Street, 406-222-1350. Other restaurants and bars are located along Main, Park, and Callender. Grocery stores, hardware stores, and everything else are all within a few blocks of Main Street. That nitwit Anthony Bourdain did a *No Reservations* number on my home town and managed to create a nightmare dude travelogue. If you ever wander into this travesty on TV do so while heavily sedated. Smoke 'em if you got 'em.

Appropriate Gear: Since you'll be hiking in, a 4- or 5-weight pack rod, floating and sink-tip lines, lightweight hip waders, and boots. The water is ice cold even in July so the extra weight is worth the effort. Bear spray and noise maker or lots of talking. Backpacking gear if you're young, fit, and masochistic.

Favorite Patterns: We're dealing with wild, native cutthroat here, so the pattern is not all that important. Hopper imitations, Wulffs of all colors, Hare's Ear nymphs work really well, Buggers for curiosity's sake, Elk Hair Caddis, and Rat Faced-McDougal, if only for its name.

Special Regulations: Open entire year.

Rat-Faced McDougal

Hook: Standard dry fly #6-14
Thread: Tan

Tail: Light tan elk hair
Body: Natural grey deer, spun and clipped

Wings: Grizzly hackle tips
Hackle: Light ginger

Chapter Eight

Yellowstone River

Nobody wants me
They left me all alone
So I'm a singin' the blues, but thank you Lord
For giving me another day

Nobody Wants Me by Norton Buffalo

The words and the melody of that song run through my head more often than not when I fish the Yellowstone. The river reminds me of the song and the other way around. Norton died in October of 2009 and his words for this song and many of his others will carry added meaning for me now. I knew him in a way that was his hallmark – like a long-time friend sorely missed and joyfully visited with once again. I believe he was this way with everyone he encountered. I've talked with the guy when he played in Whitefish over the years, beginning with the filming of *Heaven's Gate* in the Flathead Valley. Always funny, full of life, mischievous, like the night at the Great Northern when he said to the crowd, "We're going to be playing late tonight, but I'll write excuse notes for those of you who'll need them tomorrow", and off he and his band went on an energetic run on *One Kiss To Say Goodbye* and a bunch more hours of bliss. I remember his playing around town back then and down through the years, my fishing in the surrounding mountains in those days and as always, the joy of living in Montana. Norton's music has fishing rhythms all through it for me and no more so than when I'm on the Yellowstone, a watery musician in its own way and, like Norton, plays melodies as sweet as any I've ever found...

...The fish sails through the air. I pull back hard on the oars to give my friend more room to work the brown trout as it crashes and flies down this deep run next to a sheer wall of dusty-yellow rock. When the huge fish took the fly, my friend (sometimes known as Johnny Surf the Space God, but that's a story of journalistic revisionism not for the faint of heart) and I had been discussing how much television had done to ruin pro football – complete discontinuity as in kickoff, timeout, three plays, coaches challenge, commercial break, and four minutes of analyst (as in brain dead jock and terminal sports hack) babbling about whether both of the receiver's feet were in bounds as 397 different replay angles loop over and – like the line on my friend's reel is doing right now – then a punt, more beer and truck commercials, a long pass but flag on the play for defensive pass interference and another coach's challenge with a little red flag and a brief commercial break while all of this is sorted out and on and on for three or more hours. And abruptly as in a godsend, the brown smashed the Cree Woolly Bugger putting an end to the inane conversation about a dead sport. My friend's Australian shepherd, Rupert, is up on the front seat, his large ears flying in the wind, barking instructions at us as he plays the fish or rather as it plays him. The brown is well over two feet long. This was revealed in its first leap as the trout arced above the water and then crashed back through the surface with that distinctive big fish "thwack". The crazed trout is well into the old reel's backing as it powers its way towards a wicked spate of cascades and mid-stream boulders. He tries to check the brown with no success. More line tears off the reel. I can tell by the pitch of Rupert's barking that things are getting desperate.

"I've got to pull out now or we'll get sucked into Lynda's Trap," I yell. Lynda's Trap, a hundred-yard stretch of standing waves and a vortex-like swirling hole along a stone cliff shoreline, is named for a woman both of us know, someone who had impressed us with her psychotic personality and drunken raging temper. A lunatic neither of us ever wanted to encounter again. We're the only ones that call this piece of water by that name. Being quite stealthy, at least in our own minds, this is one of our little angling secrets.

"Hang on, damn it. I've almost got him," shouts Johnny Surf as the trout reaches for the sky once again, taking still more line from his ancient and banged-up Ari Hart reel. "See what I mean?"

I don't, but this fish is closer to 30 inches, the biggest brown I've ever seen on the river, so I look ahead and plot a course through the roaring maze of whitewater that is now only 100 yards away. I can hear the pounding and crashing of the river even above the wind. I can smell the damp richness of water. What the hell. If we die, we die. I can hear it all now over drinks at the Stockman's Bar uptown:

"Hear 'bout the two idiots who drowned in the river near the golf course today?"

"What happened to them?"

"Guy hooked his fish of a lifetime and the other fool tried to row them through that hole above Mayor's Landing while the first one hung on to the fish," and the speaker takes a long pull from his drink while those gathered around him lean forward expectantly. "Got pretty much most of the way through, then they lost an oar and they crashed into a boulder. Smashed the boat to shit and they all drowned. Found the bodies tangled in a log jam down by Springdale," and the speaker drains his drink and asks for another. He's silent for awhile and then adds, "Had a dog with them. Damn shame to lose a good dog that way. Here's to the dog."

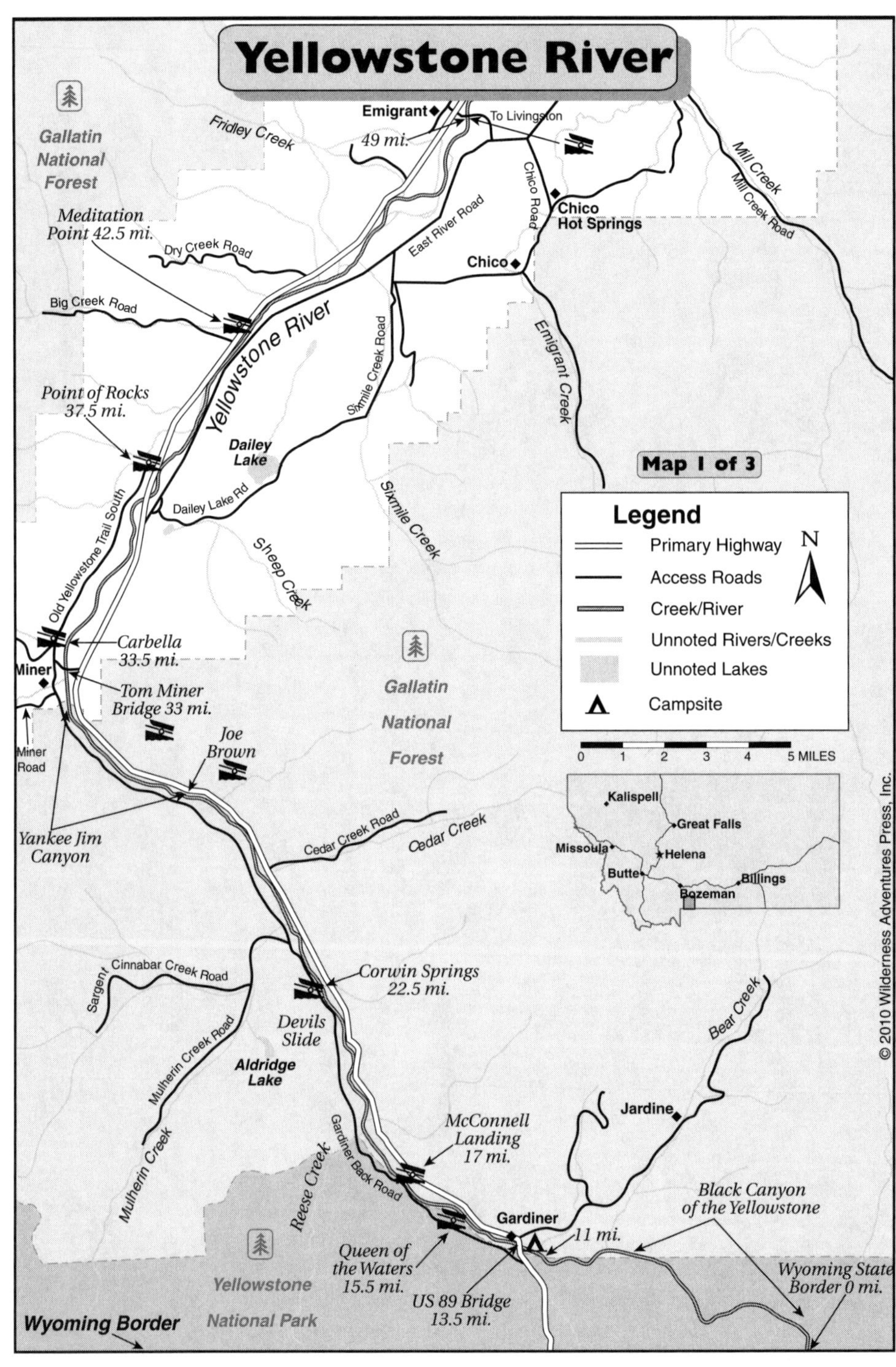
Yellowstone River
Map 1 of 3
Gallatin National Forest
Fridley Creek
Emigrant
49 mi.
To Livingston
Chico Road
Chico Hot Springs
Chico
East River Road
Meditation Point 42.5 mi.
Dry Creek Road
Big Creek Road
Yellowstone River
Sixmile Creek Road
Emigrant Creek
Mill Creek
Mill Creek Road
Point of Rocks 37.5 mi.
Dailey Lake
Old Yellowstone Trail South
Dailey Lake Rd
Sixmile Creek
Sheep Creek
Legend
Primary Highway
Access Roads
Creek/River
Unnoted Rivers/Creeks
Unnoted Lakes
Campsite
N
0 1 2 3 4 5 MILES
Miner
Carbella 33.5 mi.
Tom Miner Bridge 33 mi.
Joe Brown
Gallatin National Forest
Miner Road
Yankee Jim Canyon
Cedar Creek Road
Cedar Creek
Kalispell
Great Falls
Missoula
Helena
Butte
Billings
Bozeman
Sargent
Cinnabar Creek Road
Corwin Springs 22.5 mi.
Devils Slide
Bear Creek
Mulherin Creek Road
Aldridge Lake
Jardine
Mulherin Creek
McConnell Landing 17 mi.
Black Canyon of the Yellowstone
Gardiner Back Road
Reese Creek
Gardiner
11 mi.
Queen of the Waters 15.5 mi.
Wyoming State Border 0 mi.
Wyoming Border
Yellowstone National Park
US 89 Bridge 13.5 mi.
© 2010 Wilderness Adventures Press, Inc.

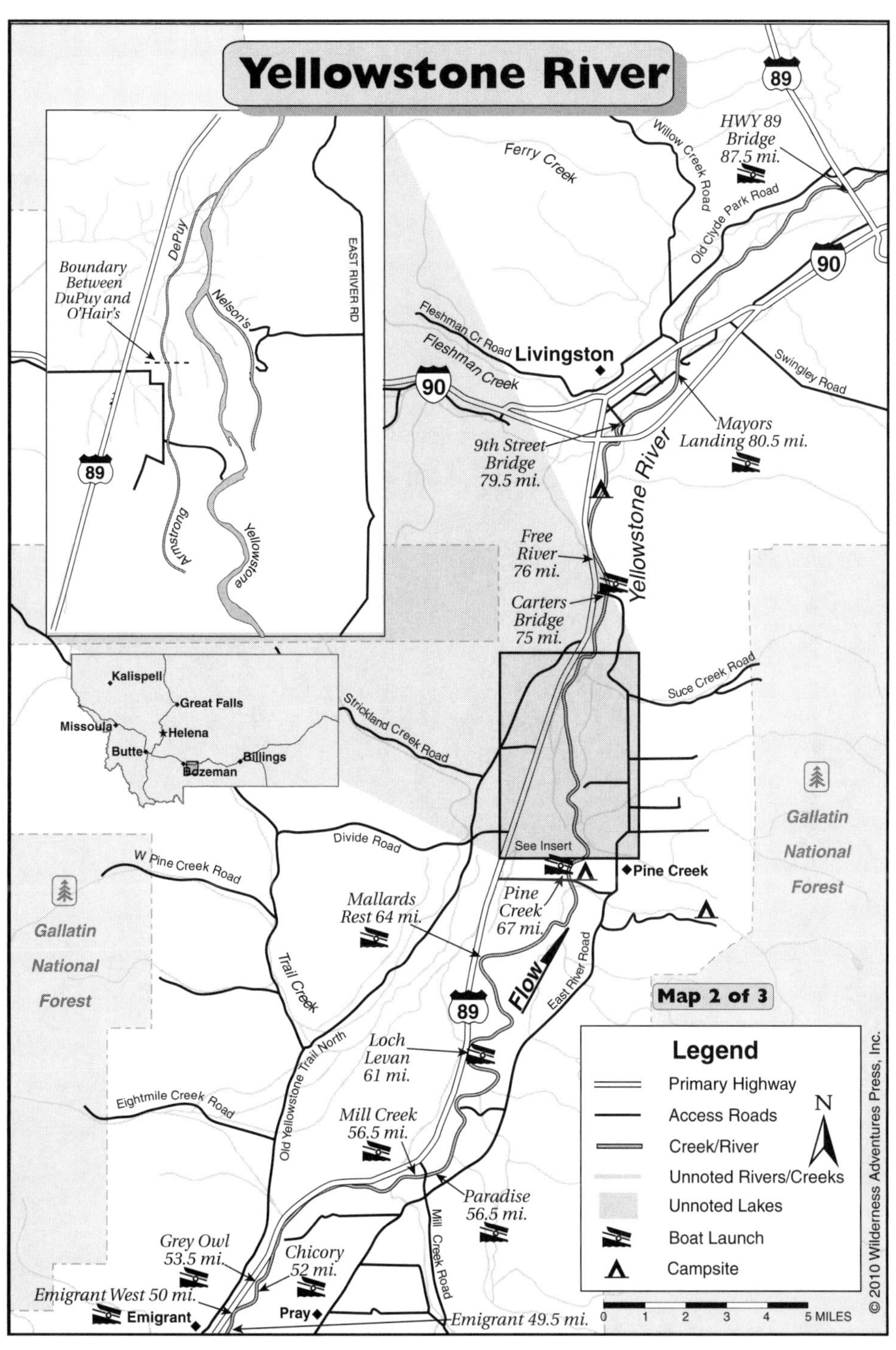
Yellowstone River
89
HWY 89 Bridge 87.5 mi.
Ferry Creek
Willow Creek Road
Old Clyde Park Road
90
Swingley Road
DePuy
Nelson's
EAST RIVER RD
Boundary Between DuPuy and O'Hair's
Fleshman Cr Road
Fleshman Creek
Livingston
90
9th Street Bridge 79.5 mi.
Mayors Landing 80.5 mi.
Yellowstone River
Armstrong
Yellowstone
89
Free River 76 mi.
Carters Bridge 75 mi.
Kalispell
Great Falls
Missoula
Helena
Butte
Bozeman
Billings
Strickland Creek Road
Suce Creek Road
Gallatin National Forest
Divide Road
See Insert
Pine Creek
Gallatin National Forest
W Pine Creek Road
Mallards Rest 64 mi.
Pine Creek 67 mi.
Trail Creek
Flow
East River Road
Map 2 of 3
Old Yellowstone Trail North
89
Loch Levan 61 mi.
Eightmile Creek Road
Mill Creek 56.5 mi.
Paradise 56.5 mi.
Mill Creek Road
Grey Owl 53.5 mi.
Chicory 52 mi.
Emigrant West 50 mi.
Emigrant
Pray
Emigrant 49.5 mi.
Legend
Primary Highway
Access Roads
Creek/River
Unnoted Rivers/Creeks
Unnoted Lakes
Boat Launch
Campsite
N
0 1 2 3 4 5 MILES
© 2010 Wilderness Adventures Press, Inc.

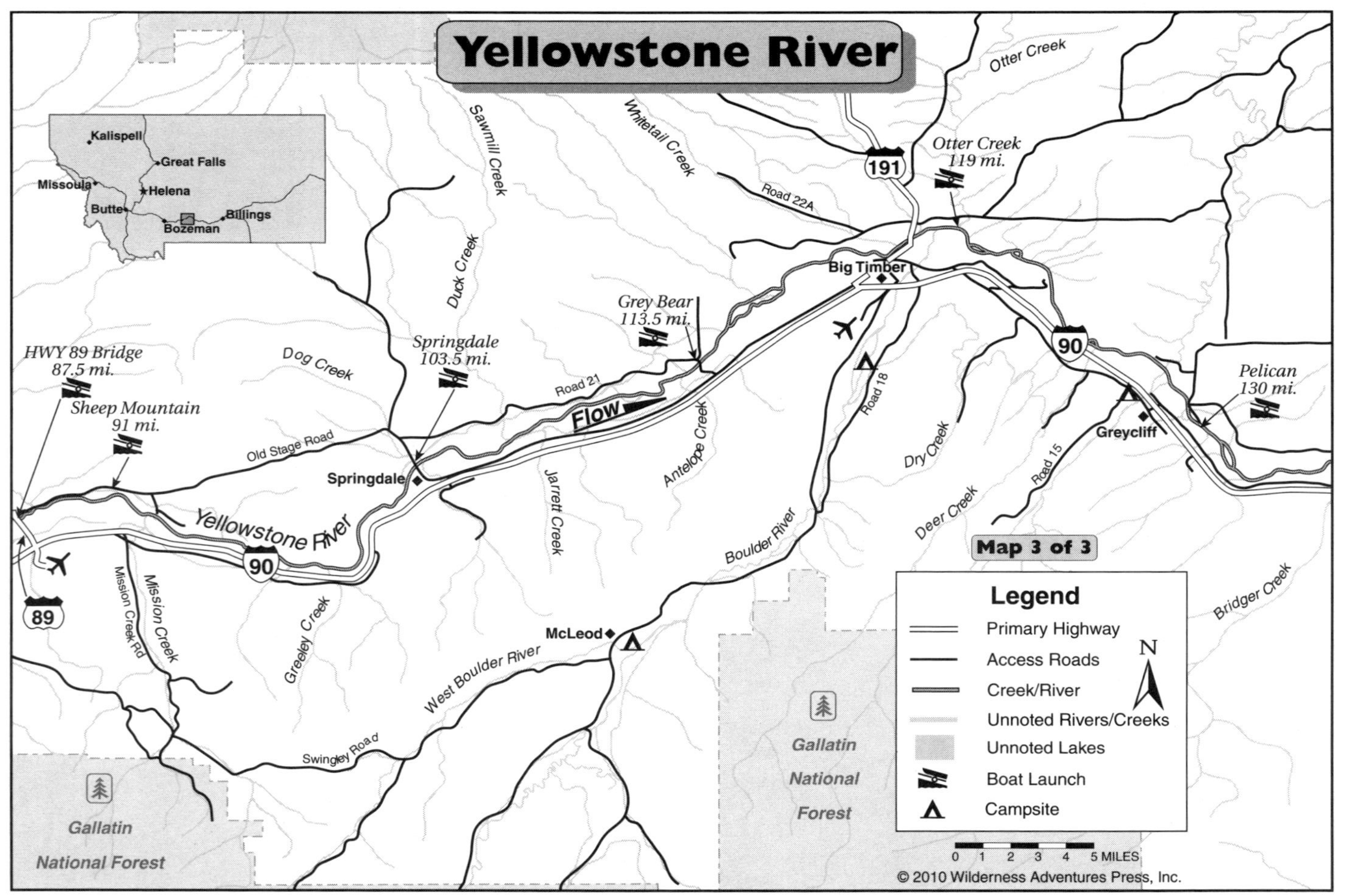
Yellowstone River
Kalispell
Great Falls
Missoula
Helena
Butte
Billings
Bozeman
Otter Creek
Sawmill Creek
Whitetail Creek
Otter Creek
119 mi.
191
Road 22A
Big Timber
Grey Bear
113.5 mi.
90
Dog Creek
Springdale
103.5 mi.
HWY 89 Bridge
87.5 mi.
Duck Creek
Road 21
Flow
Antelope Creek
Road 18
Dry Creek
Deer Creek
Road 15
Pelican
130 mi.
Greycliff
Sheep Mountain
91 mi.
Old Stage Road
Springdale
Yellowstone River
90
Jarrett Creek
Boulder River
Map 3 of 3
89
Mission Creek Rd
Mission Creek
Greeley Creek
McLeod
West Boulder River
Bridger Creek
Legend
Primary Highway
Access Roads
Creek/River
Unnoted Rivers/Creeks
Unnoted Lakes
Boat Launch
Campsite
N
Swingley Road
Gallatin
National Forest
Gallatin
National
Forest
0 1 2 3 4 5 MILES
© 2010 Wilderness Adventures Press, Inc.

My reverie is broken as we ride the crest of the first standing wave, this one about four feet high. The boat rocks and spins with the force of the twisting water, then we are in the air, briefly, before slamming into the side of a rock shaped like a bottle of Gallo wine. Probably skull-popper Burgundy. The current holds serve. Both oars snap and are torn from my hands. My friend is hanging on to the boat up front with one hand, his beautiful Hoagie Carmichael fly rod clutched in the other. The gem is worth thousands and belongs in a museum, but Johnny Surf said, "The guy built this to fish with and that's what I'm going to do with it." Rupert is not around. Nowhere to be seen. Next a huge whirlpool spinning out of control below, the big rock twirls us around at about 45 rpm before shooting us into a series of smaller obstructions. We batter our way through this gauntlet, the teak gunwales of the boat and then we blast over and into a submerged rock that tears a small hole in the bottom. The jolt knocks my friend overboard, and my last vision is of man and fly rod going head first into the river, feet high in the air. Then the boat capsizes and I am underwater. The sun is shining brightly. I clearly see the rock through the aquamarine current before I am slammed into it. Then I'm out.

The sun's heat and white light bring me around. The first thing I see is Johnny Surf and Rupert standing in the river near shore. He's holding the brown trout at arm's length. The dog is sniffing the fish's gill plates. I also notice pieces of the teak floating languidly in the calmer water and my friend's fly rod in several mangled pieces, the reel smashed, lying on the cobblestone beach. Rupert looks fine, but blood is streaming down Johnny Surf's legs.

"Hell of a fish, Holt," he said. "Between hauling your sorry ass out of the water and dragging this guy in, we had quite a time. Damn dog herded the thing to shore every time it tried to swim away. At least one of you is worth a damn."

"Right."

I slowly get to my feet. I ache and hurt all over. There is a fair-sized knot on my forehead, but other than that I'm fine. We've been lucky, especially when considering some of the other mayhem we've been involved in over the years, driving cars down sidewalks, being shot at by crazed murderers on the run from the cops, parking an old Datsun wagon in the middle of an Illinois cornfield to watch the sun come up (corn stalks were too high but the beer and Beam smoothed out the disappointment). Only a gash on my friend's leg and my bump, though we are out a few grand on the custom-made rod and some repairs to the borrowed drift boat. Fortunately the guy who loaned us the craft moved back to Beloit, Wisconsin for reasons he refused to list, let alone explain. We had time to set things right. Patching the puncture to make the boat sea worthy was no big deal for a couple of longtime Bondo putty artistes and we still had Johnny Surf's old beater fiberglass Fenwick and an imitation Pflueger reel made by Sears sometime in the last millennia and it probably had a fresh silkworm gut line. We'd be fine. Just another day on the river.

I walk over and look at the brown finning in the shallows. I mark it against a rod fragment (that later translates to 27 inches according to the Stanley tape). I then spend several minutes reviving the fish that is still lolling in the slight current near shore. The behemoth finally trundles off. An old, scarred male with subdued colors – browns, blacks, reds, aged bronzes, and whites. He'll live to wreck another drift boat.

"Shit," is all Johnny Surf can say. Then he takes off his shirt and starts walking towards the highway that leads to town. Rupert rushes to the river and retrieves a small piece of the boat's wreckage, then catches up with his buddy. I follow both of them.

"Well, that was a fine fish and it was one hell of a ride," he said. "We survived. Lived to fight another day and such bullshit." Just as we reach the road, we see a rusted '63 GMC cattle truck coming our way. We flag down the noisy rig, climb into the cab and are back to town in minutes. The driver looks at us. He is up from his place in the West Texas hill country where he bird hunts and lives alone most of the year; that is except for June through August when he heads north to spend some time on his small place at the base of some mountains north of town. He's about 70, lean, tanned and tough. We've met before. Talked a bit about not much of anything. Another good old boy. He knows who I am and succinctly says, "I don't want to hear about it", and returns to puffing on his Chesterfield and drinking from a can of Pabst.

He asks where we're parked and we say up at Pine Creek and down at the Hwy 89 Bridge. He says "don't start", turns around and runs us the few miles down I-90 and then up 89 and our rig. We say thanks and he says, "Owe me a drink when I see you next", and drives off in a cloudy mixture of dusty and oily exhaust.

Just another day on the river for a couple of Bozos on the bus.

A few years ago when I canoed the length of the river for the hell of it, something I'd thought of doing for a long time with the idea of writing a book about the journey, I fished many miles of the river. All of this reinforced my conviction that I can quite easily get by with six, maybe seven, patterns – Woolly Bugger, Elk Hair Caddis, Hare's Ear nymph, Royal Wulff, Bigg's Special, Joe's Hopper and a small dry like an Adam's or Blue Winged Olive. I could drop the hopper and use a large Elk Hair, but I like fishing a Joe's Hopper, the way it floats, the way big and little fish hammer the thing. Using other patterns is fun, but not necessary. If the fish are picky beyond these seven I guess I'm out of luck and I don't care. Nor do I use a dropper or a strike indicator. I learned to nymph without one so I stick with what I know. A number of guides have their clients (hate this term, sounds like a law office gig) use a Bugger on the point and a dry of some sort on top for a dead drift approach. The fun in Bugger fishing is working the pattern to suit the conditions and the mood of the day and the fish. Sometimes a dead drift works, but maintaining slight contact and the merest hint of motion works even better. Other times, a pronounced constant stripping action seems best, often in deeper water, and on clear days when I think subtlety and not brazen behavior would be preferred.

The choice is obviously the individual angler's. Simpler is better for me and I can tie the above seven patterns in my sleep. Varying size and color shades takes care of the rest. I make some exceptions for northerns where bigger and truly ostentatious is better, as in red-and-white Woolhead Bendbacks and chartreuse barracuda flies. Though to be honest (why start now, Holt?), anything of size moved with some semblance of life will work on the species.

I always took fish – browns, Yellowstone cutthroat, rainbows, brook trout, mountain whitefish – with these patterns. I never had any need of any others on the Yellowstone, though I could have used Stimulators, Madam X's and on and on.

To suggest the possibly arcane possibility of winter fishing in Montana will draw various derisive reactions from all but a few anglers. Most of us think of the state as being locked down under a deep blanket of snow and ice with temperatures hovering around zero as a mean wind howls down from Alberta. A good deal of the time in much of Montana this is the case.

Yet, just south of Livingston in the Yellowstone River's Paradise Valley the situation is sometimes quite different, especially on the area's three famous spring creeks – Nelson's, Armstrong, and Depuy. Even in the dead of winter, say in December or mid-February, there are days that are partly cloudy with temperatures in the upper 40s to lower 50s, even 60 on occasion. Last year I observed just two days below zero here in Livingston. The region is so well-known for its mild winters that more than a century before, the Crow and Blackfeet used to winter their horses in the Yellowstone Valley because of this relative mildness and availability of grass – that is, when the two tribes weren't fighting each other. Factor in the constant, well-above-freezing temperature of the spring creeks and the chance for adventurous souls to catch rainbows, Yellowstone cutthroat, and browns – sometimes on dry flies – becomes a very real proposition.

The advantages to this time of the year are: the lack of crowds and increased accessibility to the water; fish that, while not as aggressive, are also not as selective; and the fact that motels and restaurants are eager to serve visitors during the slow time of the year. Wait staff friendlier than ever, now recovered from summer's tourist onslaught. The nightlife at bars such as the Murray, Z Bar, and Stockman's is in full winter mode amidst a classic high-plains Montana town hunkered down somewhat quietly until mid-spring. And there are those glorious days when the air is calm, the sun is blasting away, temperatures are moderate – much like spring or early autumn – and the fish are eager to please.

The disadvantages are obvious – often wickedly cold weather and fierce winds that can approach 100 mph. But, if you're the adventurous type and like to gamble, this is the time to fish Montana when few others, other than cabin-fever-crazed locals, do. The fishing can be tough. Often the very skilled have a hard time here. One trick, though not all that popular on this small fly water, is to wing a #6 Woolly Bugger bank-tight and strip the thing back as fast as you can. Frequently the trout, especially the rainbows, will go nuts chasing the thing down.

All three creeks are marked by impeccably clear water loaded with nutrients. This leads to rich aquatic plant life that in turn generates abundant aquatic insects

– mainly mayflies and their nymphs, along with caddis and midges. The streams drift through rich ranch land with the Absaroka Mountains towering in the east and Yellowstone Park less than an hour to the south. Armstrong and DePuy's are located off Highway 89 less than 10 miles south of Livingston. Nelson's is reached by the East Side road, also less than 10 miles from town. Countless famous anglers, a number of former presidents, actors, derelict writers, and thousands of trout bums have worked these waters over the decades. Because the number of rods is limited to 16 per day or less, reservations for the prime months are often needed a year or more in advance. Winter doesn't have this problem. The low number of anglers allowed on these waters has helped maintain the high quality fishery and the spectacular setting.

In the summer, the trout are wary and quite selective, often taking dries and nymphs smaller than #20 – things like Pheasant Tails, BWOs, emergers and so on. Tippets tapered to 7X and smaller attached to the ends of 15-foot leaders or longer are the norm. What rod to use can be a tradeoff. Light outfits of 2- and 3-weight are great, but if the wind is blowing, a five or six is needed to turn over the leader and also to make a cast of any distance. This terminal tackle and small patterns are also in play during the cold months.

I like all three creeks. Choosing one over the other is tough. DePuy's probably is considered by many to be the best of the three. Armstrong is where I've had my best luck taking a number of fish in the 20-inch range. I guess Nelson's is my favorite because I knew the parents before they both passed away a few years back. Friendly, generous, and full of fun, they reminded me of the Montana I first stumbled on 40 years ago. Hell, take your pick. All three are filled with trout. Some of them very large but also very well-schooled. They've seen the offerings of some of the finest fly casters in the world. All three are gorgeous streams. And all three are a blast to fish as you wade cautiously to a feeding fish or work a nymph along weedy seams in often shallow water of only a few inches or through deeps runs of several or more feet. Cattle wander and bawl nearby. Coyotes howl. Eagles and hawks soar by. Deer and even elk graze the benches. Classic Montana here.

Bring plenty of warm clothes, warm chest waders, fingerless gloves, sun screen and sunglasses.

So, if spending time in Montana when the land is covered with snow, often dozens of feet of the stuff up in the mountains, and when the fish and area residents are laid back, appeals to you, I can think of no better place than Livingston and the spring creeks of the Paradise Valley.

October in the Yellowstone Valley is heaven on earth. Warm days, cottonwoods in full raging yellow-orange, browns lit up in spawning finery, fewer anglers and usually those of well-meaning determination. Down by Indian Fort off the Interstate near Reed Point, wading the braided channels often turns rainbows and browns. If the day is warm, hoppers are flitting about and even a large Elk Hair works. On cloudy afternoons, streamers draw browns from slight dips in the gravel streambed and from under brushy banks or even up from deep channels. But as always, I prefer the golden sunshine special days that are the condensed purity of all the fine days of the preceding months. A time when there is an urgency driven by the awareness of another approaching winter, yet still a period of relaxed reflection and learned patience.

More than a half-century ago, John D. MacDonald of Travis McGee fame wrote a novel titled *Wine of the Dreamers* about a dismal time "when Earthmen dreamed their dreams, laid plans to travel beyond their own planet, the Watchers stepped in – for escape from Earth was the dream that must be destroyed." Well, looking from my hiding place beneath my bed, .357 magnum firmly clutched in my right hand, TV remote in the other, I can often see the need to dream myself off the planet these days, too. But then comes one of those magnificent October days on the Yellowstone fishing a side channel all alone. A small Joe's Hopper cast above an overhanging cottonwood of stately dimensions, a gentle glide over a slight depression in the golden gravels and "zing", a nice rainbow flashes beneath the sun and for a brief time, all seems right with the world. That's the power of flyfishing, for the pursuit's ability to transport me far beyond my self-indulgent concerns with the mundane aspects of the day to day. To hell with the Watchers ...

... I'm a singin' the blues, but thank you Lord, for giving me another day.

TRIP INFORMATION

Timing: The river can be fished all times of the year, but I pass on the stretch from November through mid-March. Too cold for my taste and the fish need a break from angling attentions, a chance to rest and regroup, especially along the heavily-fished stretches from the Paradise Valley down to Big Timber. There is often an un-fishable mini-runoff in late-April or early-May. Rarely is the water in good shape for the famed Mother's Day caddis hatch. September and October are more often than not glorious and also prime fishing.

Where: In Yellowstone Park, roads follow the river the entire way from the outlet of Yellowstone Lake. From the north entrance of the park, Highway 89 traces the river's course to Livingston before giving way to I-90 all the way to Billings. Below here, the Yellowstone is largely a warmwater fishery.

Hub: I mentioned some places in Livingston in the West Boulder chapter. Here are some other ones. Hatch Finders is a neat little fly shop tucked away in downtown Livingston with good advice and fellowship – 113 West Park #3, 406-222-0989. Contact information for the three spring creeks is as follows: Armstrong Spring Creek – Judy O'Hair at 406-222-2979; DePuy Spring Creek – Daryl or Theresa Smith at 406-222-0221, daryl@depuyspringcreek.com; and Nelson's Spring Creek – Roger or Mary Nelson at 406-220-6560.

The Livingston Bar & Grill is no longer owned by artist Russell Chatham, but it is still a fine place to eat – 130 North Main Street, 406-222-1866. The Stockman's is a good bar with the best burgers in town – 118 North Main Street, 406-222-8455. For take-out lunches for fishing or any other time, Mustang Catering is as good as it gets – 215 West Lewis Street, 406-222-8884, carole@mustangcatering. com. A special place to stay along the river just south of town is Yellowstone River Cabins at $90 to $145 per night depending on the season – Dee Dee Van Zyl, Ursula Neese, 4950 Hwy 89 South, 406-222-2429, 888-669-6993, deedee@ yellowstoneriverinn.com.

Appropriate Gear: Bring plenty of warm clothes, warm chest waders, fingerless gloves, sun screen and sunglasses. Rods from 4- to 7-weight and up to nine feet are fine. Double taper, weight-forward, rocket taper, triangle taper – the choice is yours. Sink tips have some value in deep runs and holes. Chest waders. Be ready for wind. Wilderness Adventures Press' 11x17 map from Gardiner to downstream of Livingston is a good source of information for those unfamiliar with the river.

They're available at Dan Bailey's or from Wilderness Adventures Press at http://store.wildadvpress.com.

Favorite Patterns: Nearly every fly pattern ever invented has been tried with some success. The best bet is to check in at a local fly shop and ask what patterns are producing right now.

Special Regulations: Open entire year. Combined trout: four brown trout and/or rainbow trout daily and in possession, only one over 18 inches. Catch and release for cutthroat trout. All tributaries between YNP Boundary and Springdale – Catch-and-release for cutthroat trout. All tributaries downstream from Springdale – Open entire year. Combined Trout: includes cutthroat trout.

Cree Woolly Bugger

Hook: TMC 300 or Mustad 79580, sizes 6-10

Thread: Black 6/0
Body: Medium, brown chenille
Tail: Black marabou

Hackle: Cree (or badger) hackle palmered over the body

Chapter Nine

Gardner River

Cars were lined up back around the bend as gawkers rolled down windows aimed cameras and camcorders towards the scene of all the action. Others bravely left the perceived safety (sanctity?) of their vehicles to walk down to the river's edge for a better view. All of this was life threatening, in my eyes. The creature in question was known to be stubborn, aggressive, and hostile with a bad temperament. Still the throng continued to swell and move closer to the action.

I looked at Ginny and muttered "God! Haven't these idiots ever seen a guy playing a fish before?"

"Relax, John. You're a star," she said.

"My ass," I muttered.

"Hey, what'd you catch 'em on?" one guy yelled.

"Orange garlic marshmallow," I kindly offered knowing full well that the use of bait in Yellowstone Park was (mostly) illegal.

I brought the Yellowstone cutthroat to my feet. Beautiful fish full of deep oranges, reds, blues, greens, and whites with large jet black spotting. Sixteen inches on a Joe's Hopper.

"Hold him up so I can take a picture," some bozo yelled, a fat guy wearing a 'Save the Manatees' t-shirt, orange and blue argyle socks, baggy Bermuda shorts, and some sort of ball cap with what looked like antlers on it.

"Not this time around, sport," I said and released the trout. At least one of us could go invisible. I should have known better than to fish just below the bridge crossing the Gardner River a couple of miles and hundreds of feet below Mammoth Hot Springs. Anything that moves and looks slightly different from suburban docility found back East is photographed to hell and back in the park during the summer. When I'd hooked the fish, the traffic was moving thickly, but steadily north and south along the road between the north park entrance and Mammoth Hot Springs. As soon as my rod doubled over and the trout jumped, some sort of alien radar clicked on and vehicles begin pulling madly over to the roadside while simultaneously grabbing and pointing image-capturing paraphernalia in my direction. We're a very weird species.

I looked once again at Ginny, shrugged and laughed a little. We walked up a hill away from the river and back downstream as it moved thankfully far from the road and the herd of tourists.

I've always enjoyed fishing the Gardner. When most people think of Yellowstone, they don't realize how little of it is in Montana, just 3 percent with 96 percent in Wyoming and the remaining percent in Idaho. Only four or five miles of the river is in Montana with the rest flowing south towards Sheepeater Cliff and on through Gardner's Hole past striking streams that drift through lush meadow and pine forest with names like Fawn, Panther, Indian, and Obsidian. All of this water holds small brook and rainbow trout and is the only part of Yellowstone (along with Joffe Lake) that may be fished using worms by children 11 years and younger. Claiming to "have the mind of a child" is not a valid excuse, though. There's a nice campground in the area. The Gardner flows beneath the Norris-Mammoth Road bridge. The water and the fishing are quite good for a mile downstream – walk the mile downstream well away from the river and work up, but after this canyon cliffs crowd in and the wading turns rough before turning dangerous to deadly below Sheepeater Cliffs and Bunsen Peak before pouring over Osprey Falls. Continue if dying is something you've always wanted to do. The next fishable stretch lies far below the bridge that crosses the river on the Mammoth-Tower Junction Road. It's a scramble down and a trudge back up but the fast moving, boulder pocket water is worth the effort for trout that run a little bit larger than those in the Montana section. Lava Creek adds nutrients to the flow when it enters downstream of the bridge and also doubles the Gardner's volume.

The water in Montana is a pleasure to work. The stretch up from the entrance is large-boulder pocket water that holds fat cutthroat and, in the fall, large browns run up from the Yellowstone at its junction town by Gardiner (note the difference in spellings for the town and the river, a minor curiosity). Dropping a weighted stonefly nymph or any other large pattern into these plunge pools requires accuracy with often short casts and solid line control. Any slack and a trout will take, then slip the hook. Above this water all the way to the bridge recently mentioned and for miles beyond, the water is deeper than it looks from the road, holding Yellowstones of surprising size, especially in rocky, shaded portions of pools and smack up against grassy banks. Hoppers, large attractors, and Buggers work well here attached to a 4X tippet on a nine-foot leader. If the timing is right, sometime in June or July the salmonflies are out. The fish go nuts as they do whenever and wherever these huge stoneflies are found. Sofa Pillows, Stimulators, and the like turn the trick.

I live within an hour of the park yet do not fish here more than a few times each year, a mistake I intend to eliminate in the future. There is so much quality water in Yellowstone that is relatively unfished, especially if a flyfisher hikes a couple of miles away from the road that a pristine angling experience is easy to find. I've fished the famed stretches of rivers like the Firehole and the Madison in the park. This is worthwhile, but always too crowded these days for my preferences. And Slough

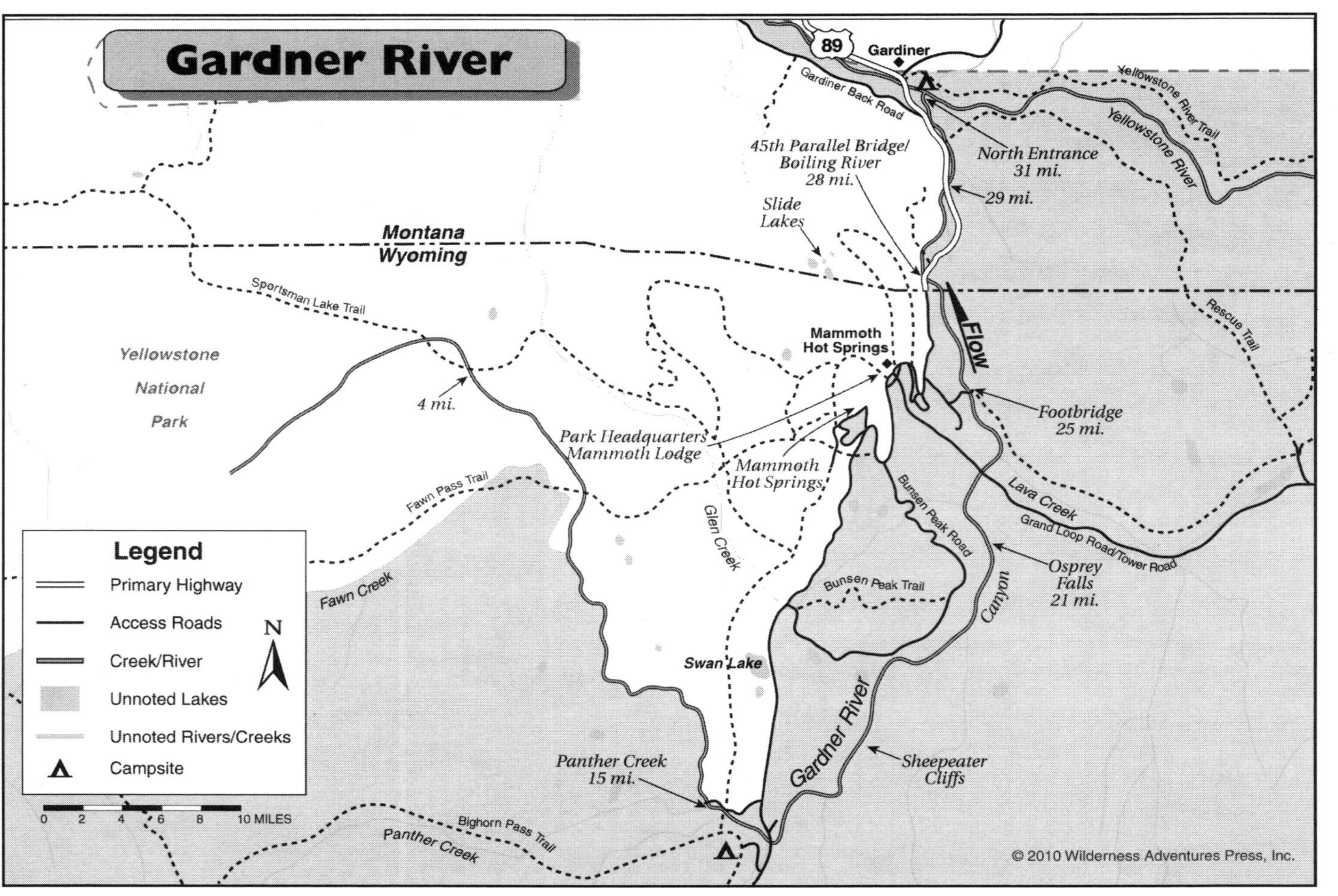
Gardner River
89
Gardiner
Gardiner Back Road
Yellowstone River Trail
Yellowstone River
45th Parallel Bridge/
Boiling River
28 mi.
North Entrance
31 mi.
29 mi.
Slide Lakes
Montana
Wyoming
Rescue Trail
Sportsman Lake Trail
Flow
Mammoth Hot Springs
Footbridge
25 mi.
Yellowstone
National
Park
4 mi.
Park Headquarters
Mammoth Lodge
Mammoth Hot Springs
Lava Creek
Grand Loop Road/Tower Road
Fawn Pass Trail
Glen Creek
Bunsen Peak Road
Bunsen Peak Trail
Canyon
Osprey Falls
21 mi.
Fawn Creek
Swan Lake
Gardner River
Legend
Primary Highway
Access Roads
Creek/River
Unnoted Lakes
Unnoted Rivers/Creeks
Campsite
N
Panther Creek
15 mi.
Sheepeater Cliffs
0   2   4   6   8   10 MILES
Bighorn Pass Trail
Panther Creek
© 2010 Wilderness Adventures Press, Inc.

Creek's upper meadows have become a flyfishing in-thing madhouse. Too bad. I remember not so far back when few people made the hike. A little exploring will turn anyone on to lesser known waters offering private wilderness experiences; of course sometimes including grizzlies, moose, and elk in a variety of combinations and numbers. Even in the populated Lamar drainage a little hiking past the bison and away from the road will produce delightful fishing for mid-sized to small trout in wild surroundings. The Lamar along the road to Cooke City is suburban angling in wilderness surroundings with cars, trucks, and campers parked all over the place and individuals casting every 30 or less feet. Pebble Creek Campground looks like a refuge for the piscatorial damned with sullen anglers slouched in chairs working on beers and *de rigeur* cigars while various types of music whine from sordid vehicles of all condition and description. I've spent evenings in county jugs that seem more pleasant upon brief reflection, but I'm digressing again.

There are some waters that I reserve for my bamboo fly rods. They are small spring creeks, or hallowed rivers in someplace eastern like Vermont and also a few western waters, among them the Gardner. I don't always use cane when fishing this water. There are times when I hammer weighted Woolly Buggers tight to grassy banks on windy days where an errant cast, something I'm completely capable of executing with the best of them, would splinter the fine wood. I'd rather wreck a graphite rod of far lesser intrinsic worth than risk harming what is a work of art skillfully and lovingly made by a craftsman. On calm days and when I'm in the mood, nothing will do but the feel of bamboo and perhaps a lame rhyme or two.

Some years ago, back in the days of its relative anonymity, flyfishing was considered an arcane art practiced by mildly addled, eccentric cranks. Few people even knew what flyfishing was. Guides, the few that existed, were normally cantankerous, rarely sober, and usually showed up in a battered pick-up truck featuring a cracked windshield and a bed filled with empty beer and oil cans, a chainsaw, and a hunting dog. Equipment was not easy to find. Graphite fly rods were far off in the technological distance and garishly-colored bonefish scrubs were not around. Rivers were not crowded and the living was good.

Now flyfishing is big business hustled by corporations, not to mention travel agencies and state tourism departments. The guiding business is booming to the extent that competition for prime runs on now-famous rivers often resembles a traffic jam or war zone. Those among us who feel the absurd need to be a part of anything ahead of the curve have taken to flyfishing like religious zealots. The once contemplative pursuit has become in most places – even out-of-the-way locations such as Tierra del Fuego, Siberia, and Mongolia – a dysfunctional madhouse.

Thirty-five million Americans fish to some extent. Flyfishers have long considered themselves to be the aristocracy of the sport. And a few thousand of these anglers insist upon using one fashion of device in the pursuit of their passion – the handcrafted split bamboo fly rod. Meeting this demand for perfection are the inheritors of a unique art form, one that venerates tradition while bucking obvious economic sense. The crafting of the rods reaches back through time and includes Theodore Roosevelt, Thoreau, and the grand statesmen Herbert Hoover.

I always assumed that the making of bamboo rods originated in England, but the true originators and innovators were from the US, mainly in the northeast. This was spurred on by the growing amount of leisure time Americans were gaining in the late 19th century and the burgeoning interest in outdoor recreation including flyfishing in Maine – the Rangely Lakes region in particular. The first split bamboo fly rods were developed by Pennsylvania gunsmith and violin maker Samuel Phillippe, his son Solon, and craftsmen Charles Murphy and Ebenezer Green from 1845 to 1865. Henry David Thoreau met Hiram Leonard in Maine in 1857 and perhaps this inspired Leonard to make his first rod 14 years later in 1871.

Leonard was at the very least an exceptional, if not eccentric based on this passage uncovered in George Black's book, *Casting a Spell - The Bamboo Fly Rod and the American Pursuit of Perfection* :

> *"In the woods he always carried his flute with him and played it well. Many is the night I hear him wake the wilderness with 'Nellie Gray,' 'The Irish Washerwoman,' 'Old Kentucky Home,' and other tunes now seldom heard.*
>
> *Mr. Leonard's powers of endurance were beyond belief, judging from appearances. He never seemed tired and would tramp all day through the forest, returning at night seemingly fresh.*
>
> *The men are scarce who could carry as heavy a load as long a distance as he could. In 1856 he carried a quarter of moose weighing 135 pounds from Little Spencer Pond to Lobster Lake, a distance of seven miles."*

Like Leonard, most of the bamboo rod makers were and are men of diverse character and talents. From Ed Payne to Walton Powell to Sam Carlson to Per Brandon, they were men who sought perfection in their craft, though most denied this, at the expense of making a decent living and often at the expense of relationships and their health. They were carpenters, engineers, and artists, to name a few occupations. Hoagy Carmichael, Junior (yes, that one) is considered to be one of the premier craftsman and his back-orders can run as long as two years.

Obviously, the meticulous work involved with designing a properly tapered rod, beveling the four or six strips that are glued together to form the device and even obtaining the best bamboo that grows only in a specific region in China was a labor of love and sometimes manic devotion.

The Latin name for this unique species of grass is *Arundinaria amabilis* – the lovely reed. In Wade-Giles Chinese, it is *tsing li*; in Cantonese, *cha kan chuk*, the tea stick. But in the trade it also acquired a lay name, albeit one that is totally inaccurate – Tonkin cane. As Black wonders, "Whether someone actually thought it came from the Gulf of Tonkin, or whether the folks at Montague (Rod and Reel Company) just thought the name would have exotic appeal in the market place, who knows? But it stuck."

I have many fly rods, most say far too many. Most of them are made of the modern fiber, graphite. The best of them are wonders to cast – powerful, accurate, and easy on the arm and shoulder. But on those occasions when I turn to my cane rods for special times on special, secluded waters, working a fly line with a bamboo rod reinforces in me the intrinsic beauty and innate qualities of bamboo that return flyfishing to a delicate, sensuous, contemplative activity. There is a feel of nature strength and response that seems, and is in my eyes, alive. No high tech fiber can duplicate this.

A number of flyfishers have become collectors of bamboo rods. As a result prices for works by the old, and new, masters have gone through the roof – $2,000, $3,000, more than $10,000. Still, I keep my eyes open for good buys. I turned up a Payne in near mint condition in a second hand store in eastern Montana for fifty bucks and another in similar condition by Wes Jordan, one of the best, in northern Alberta for $100. And that is the one I often turn to when I fish the Gardner and other rivers in Yellowstone Park. The cane rod just feels right for the place.

Its October now and much of the traffic is gone from the park. I pull over by the Gardner where the river begins to widen and slow down some as it sweeps in wide, lazy curves across a gravel valley. The banks are still covered with thick grass, though instead of the luminous green of summer the shades are brown, grey, and yellow-gold. The water is a little lower despite September's rains, and snow has crept down the mountains to a few hundred feet above the river. I can hear elk bugling back and forth in the hills above me in the direction of Mammoth. The day is warm for this time of year, near 60 but the wind cutting down from the high country is sharp, cold, smelling of snow. I tie on the ubiquitous Cree Bugger and begin to work the thing through aquamarine pools and tight to banks. Within minutes a brown slams the fly and thrashes in silver spray along a shallow riffle downstream of me. He, I can see the kype, leaps several times, runs towards an undercut bank and then comes grudgingly to me. Twenty inches at least and lit up with spawning intensity with blood reds, honey browns, and shades of olive. I release this one, stand up and look around. Little traffic and no one pays any attention to me fishing a couple of hundred yards from the road. Truly big browns over five pounds are often seen in the pocket water downstream, portions of which are closed for spawning. Even if I did hook one of the hefty ones down there, landing it would be near impossible in the tight quarters and rushing water. I spend the next couple of hours working up to the bridge where earlier in the year a crowd had gathered to watch me fish. I connected with several more browns and a pair of Yellowstone cutthroat. The fish averaged a solid 16 inches and I was pleased. Relatively easy casting, except when the wind gusted, and straight-forward wading. A half-dozen strong trout and the water to myself. The Gardner has always treated me well and I resolved once again to make the run from Livingston more often next year.

TRIP INFORMATION

Timing: The fishing season begins the Saturday of Memorial Day weekend (usually the last weekend in May) and extends through and includes the first Sunday in November. Any time is good, though the warm weather makes things that much nicer.

Where: The road between Gardiner and Mammoth Hot Springs provides easy access for much of this section, while a hiking trail follows the river into Gardner Canyon.

Hub: Gardiner is everything you'd expect a town on the edge of a national park to be, both good and bad, though not in the same sellout league as West Yellowstone and Jackson. Groceries, gas, etc. available. Parks Fly Shop is a good one and has everything an angler might need – PO Box 196, 202 Second Street South (US 89), 406-848-7314, richard@parksflyshop.com. Sawtooth Deli and Restaurant has good sandwiches for the road – 220 Park St, 406-848-7600. The Blue Goose Saloon is a slammer's bar of the first order. Riverside Cottages offer an interesting alternative to chain motel boredom – Highway 89 & 2nd Street, 521 Scott Street West, P.O. Box 677, 877-774-2836, riversidecottages@wispwest.net. Depending on season and the unit, anywhere from $50 to $180.

Appropriate Gear: Four- to 6-weight rods to eight foot, six inches. Can be windy. Hip waders.

Favorite Patterns: Parachute Adams, Beetle, Woolly Bugger, Elk Hair Caddis, Hare's Ear nymph, Stimulator, Royal Wulff or Humpy, Colorado King, Goddard Caddis, Montana Nymph, Sofa Pillow, Grouse and Green, Partridge and Orange wet flies.

Special Regulations: A Yellowstone National Park Fishing Permit is required to fish in the park. Anglers 16 years of age and older are required to purchase either a $15 three-day permit, a $20 seven-day permit, or a $35 season permit. Children 11 years of age or younger may fish with worms as bait.

Bitch Creek Nymph

Hook: Nymph; Eagle Claw L063, Mustad 9671, Tiemco 5262, Daiichi 1710

Tail: Two black, brown or olive hackle tips, usually from spade hackles

Body: Black, brown or olive chenille

Wing case: Chenille, an extension of the body chenille

Thorax: Yellow, orange or olive chenille

Hackle: Black, brown or olive neck hackle. Soft hackle is preferred

Thread: 6/0 or 3/0, color to match body or black

Chapter Ten

Little Blackfoot River

One of my favorite streams, a favorite of many Montanans and those from far-flung elsewhere, is the Little Blackfoot River. The stream is not too hard to wade despite its strong current, and some of its best water up from its junction with the Clark Fork at Garrison is readily accessible from Hwy 12 for about 14 miles up to Avon. After that, access is more problematic than realistic until the stream cuts south into the timbered mountains in the Helena National Forest. This stretch features long, deep runs over colorful coppery-gold gravels; runs that give way to deep, shadowy pools beneath willows, cottonwoods, alders, and thick bunches of grass and thorn brush. In the warmth of a summer afternoon a hopper pattern cast dead tight beneath all of the leafy branches will produce steadily. In late July evenings a few weeks after the winter runoff has mostly subsided, there is a heavy hatch of pale evening duns. A #14 Light Cahill can and often does produce splendid surface action from near dusk until the mayfly activity ceases. In the hills a Griffith's Gnat or small attractor like a Royal Wulff turns plenty of small, brilliantly colored brook trout, a few westslope cutthroat, and even fewer browns. It's small creek pocket fishing in the stillness of deep forest. But most of us come primarily for the brown trout. In the summer many of the state's rivers produce larger fish, but the Little B is beautiful, fun, and a challenge to fish. In the autumn, some truly large browns move up from the Clark Fork. Hooking these is not usually the problem. Playing and landing them in the tight, overgrown surroundings is.

The water bubbles and glides soft and cool along the far bank. It is the first week of August and the tall grass is still bright green. Normally it would be shades of dry brown. It has been a wet year and this is the first time Jim and I have fished the Little B or any other stream for that matter. The water has been too high to wade and the big fish have been holding out of reach, not actively feeding. The two of us usually fish together every other week or so in warm weather and then into the golden crispness of late October and finally the bleak but rewarding frigid gray monotones of early November. The unusual conditions have altered our behavior, too. Normally the flow in this river is down to sedate levels by the first of July, but this season lots of winter snow and spring rain have kept levels elevated, too high for our delicate sensibilities. Even the fields are too wet in some places for them to get their machinery in for cutting hay. Instead of skulking around in dark holes like outlaw thugs, eating the occasional stray mottled sculpin or caddis nymph, large, hungry brown trout are rising all over the place, holding close to the willowy and grassy banks near the surface waiting for breeze-blown grasshoppers to come their way. And this is a banner season for the bulky bugs. Banging the hopper patterns, often skipping them with sidearm casts beneath the thick tangle of branches next to the sheltering holds of undercut banks. We've been fishing for less than an hour and we've already landed a half-dozen trout between 15 and 17 inches. Lost a few flies in the process, also. We always release these fantastic fish, but the urge to kill a couple is, while somewhat buried by generations of so-called civilized living, instinctive and calls strongly at times. We are launching a ragged pattern of Jim's own design, a tragic combination of sage grouse feathers, antelope hair, rusty gold Antron dubbing and a sprig of red cut from an old flannel shirt of his. The hopper looks like hell, but it works. As Jim often said, "Artistic flies catch small, cute fish, if any. Big, ratty bugs take big, ugly browns. Take your pick." We both like big, ugly browns.

My friend is casting a beautiful Winston. A seven-foot six-inch, 4-weight matched to a battered Solitude reel. I've seen Jim go silent for days after one of his cherished rods blows up while bending gracefully against the force and weight of a large, angry brown, but as he said, "they are made to be fished, not hidden away in the basement like a demented in-law". We both have experience with this species. I watch as Jim easily drops the ungainly fly 40 feet away and about ten feet up from the tail of a long, deep run, just ahead of a large trout. While doing so, he makes a slight reach upstream that imparts a slight mend in the line in just the right place to cheat drag from the current, all this while the cast is whistling through the air for brief seconds. Beautiful. Someday I'd buy a couple – a nice four like Jim's and a wind-cheating 7-weight. And Jim is one of the finest casters I've seen – in Montana, in Iceland, Tasmania – anywhere. He fishes like he lives, according to one of our more cherished dictums: "Think like an outlaw", or in other words "Keep a low profile and try and stay below the radar". We've both found that life is a little bit less difficult if we practice those three words. We both like people and enjoy being around them, but we are also loners at heart preferring our own company for days on end at times. Then we become lonely for the madness of our species and jump back into the fray. Parts of Montana are still open enough and honest enough to let those of us who need and thrive under such a routine have our curious ways. The Little Blackfoot is such country.

A brown attacks the hopper within three feet of drift, raising a watery ruckus underneath the willows. Jim sets the hook, plays the fish as it sounds to hold along the bronze-colored cobble. The fish rattles its head in anger and then reaches for the sky in a series of silver-spray leaps. Each time the brown goes to the air, Jim maintains

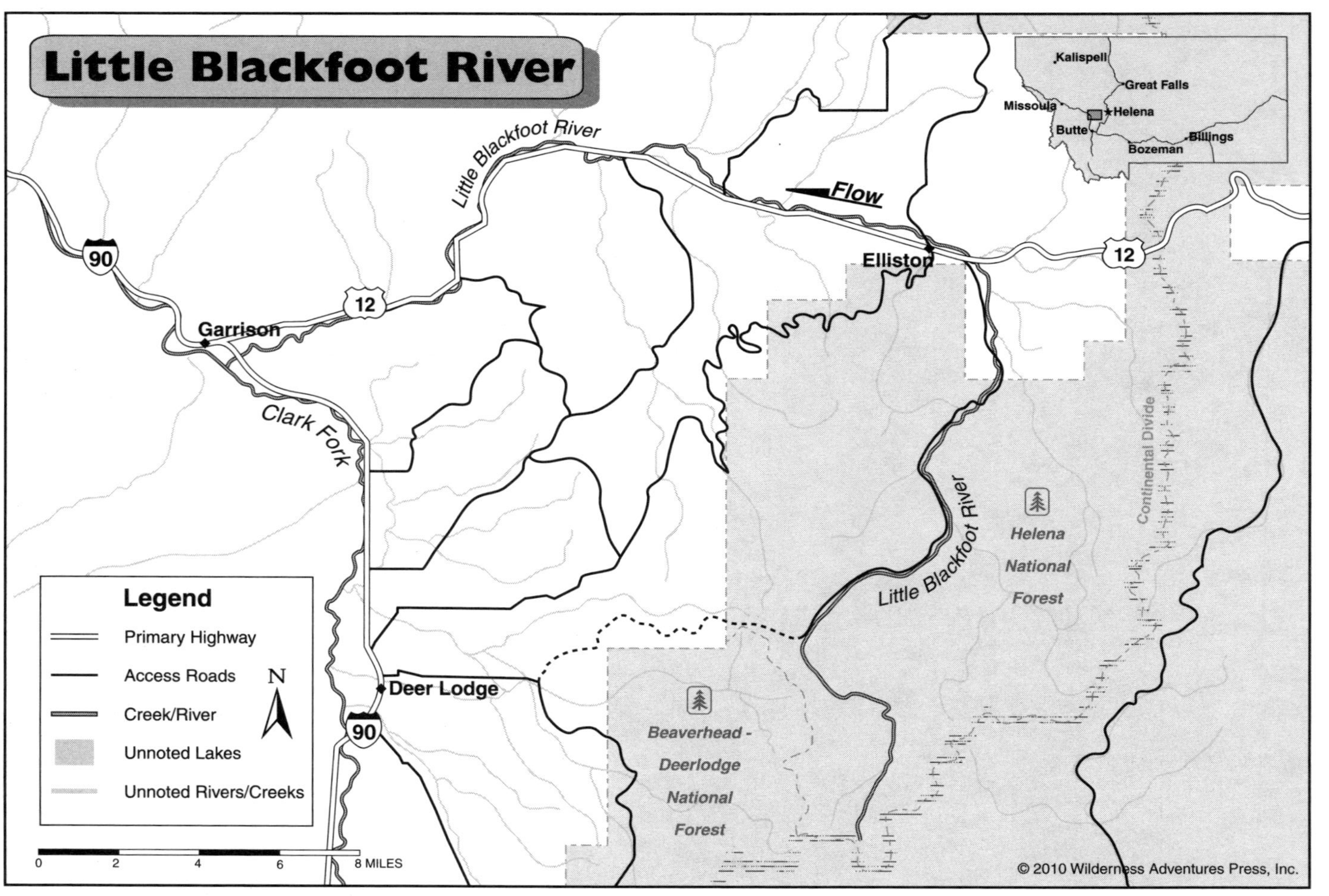
Little Blackfoot River
Little Blackfoot River
Flow
Kalispell
Great Falls
Missoula
Helena
Butte
Billings
Bozeman
Elliston
Garrison
Clark Fork
Little Blackfoot River
Helena National Forest
Continental Divide
Deer Lodge
Beaverhead - Deerlodge National Forest
Legend
Primary Highway
Access Roads
Creek/River
Unnoted Lakes
Unnoted Rivers/Creeks
N
0   2   4   6   8 MILES
© 2010 Wilderness Adventures Press, Inc.

a firm connection with the fish and backs downstream a step or two. By the time the three-pound trout comes to his feet, both angler and fish are well below the run and the other browns are still feeding. Jim is modest about all aspects of his life but one. His fishing ability. Put aside the fact that he is a fine artist on canvas, on the water he is a master. As he told me once after a few belts of scotch, "I can take trout where others can't even see a damn fish. That comes from many years of working water, staring at water and being fortunate to fish with the really good ones – Charles Brooks, LaFontaine (the first time I fished with Gary was on this water), lonesome Jack Gartside, Boston George, and some of the old-timers around here who've sadly all died off. I value the time I've spent with those men as much as anything in this life." From what I'd observed a number of times, he wasn't boasting. Jim has a form of radar that separates flyfishermen into at least two groups – those that are so good it's spooky and those who are merely skillful. Some days I've watched him work a Woolly Bugger well below the surface, watched him bounce the weighted thing along the bottom and then swiftly raise his rod. Then I'd stare in amazement as a 20-inch brown would come flying through the water and way up above the river, shaking its colorful body in stunned rage at the audacity that any human could have found it hiding beneath a tangle of submerged roots in the dark waters. Jim plays the fish fairly and quickly, admires the almost spectral gold, bronze, copper, black, white, and red that large wild browns carry with them through life, and then he turns the fish loose, smiling and laughing – a strong, yet muted sound. He'll turn to me, eyes glowing, and say, "That's what it's all about John, my man," and he'll move a bit upriver and take another fish. How, I'll never know. I can't see him doing anything different from me and I never see what triggers his strike – no subtle shift in line movement, no shadowy flash from below. Nothing. His intuition, no his artistry, is a mystery to me. A joyful fascination. He takes three more trout of the same size or larger from the run, then walks over and sits beside me on a dead cottonwood that rests along the smooth, rock bank like a large, stately, gray scarecrow. Or something like that. Maybe Jim will paint the scene in his own way someday.

We prefer to work subtle, sophisticated water that requires stealth, patience, and vision; the stuff that fails to catch the superficial interest of the newcomer pretenders. Small rivers that look like a little bit of nothing to the inexperienced. Like this one, where getting a fly through the brush to the fish is what counts. That's one of the reasons I like the guy. No bullshit. We spend time sitting on the bank observing several browns feeding along a crease in the river above us. The big trout are keyed to the sound of the grasshoppers "splatting" on the water's surface, homing in like wolves and crunching down on the insects. Then they return to their holding spots. Efficient. Businesslike. Predacious. I love brown trout.

The talk turns to the upcoming bird season and I mention an outing with a mutual friend, saying that I shot some Huns with him last fall on the bench country below the Sweet Grass Hills for a couple of days. You know, when we had those not too cool, overcast days and the birds were all over the place?..."

"He shot the Huns. You made a lot of noise from what I heard. Filled the sky with lead as they say in the hook-and-bullet rags. Give up that damn Beretta and buy that sixteen Darne of mine. You'll knock down birds with that gun. Take my word on this. Bird hunting is a hell of a lot more fun when you hit something once in awhile."

"Our friendship is special, Jim, sort of like what I have going with my ex-wife."

"Don't get me started on that."

We both laugh and resume watching the browns go about their noisy, voracious ways.

Eventually we stand up and stretch, then work our way up to within casting distance of the working trout. We fish some more, until dark, and catch plenty more browns. Big, bright ones. A nice afternoon.

I've fished the river mostly with Ginny and a couple of times with Gary LaFontaine. Twice I've encountered a young woman on the river who must live nearby. The first time I was wading upriver, fishing my way towards more open water when I caught sight of her sunbathing naked on a Hudson Bay blanket spread out on a sandy bar along the Little B. I did your basic male triple, she was tanned and appeared in excellent shape with dark brown hair, take then as quietly as possible turned around and fished my way back to where I'd begun. The second time was a couple of years later...

...The river flows quietly down here, drifting below cut banks of rock and clay. Sounds of traffic racing between Helena and Missoula are muted if not lost entirely. Long trains hauling heavy freight rumble by, their horns sounding at crossings with long-short-long-long wails that add a sense of aloneness to the fishing. Dry, powdery-green grasses, roots exposed along ragged edges of the dry soil above the water, grow above as do stands of Ponderosa pine. Small bands of deer, three, five, seven, browse among wildflowers now fading in the growing heat of summer. None of this matters to the river of course. It just runs on down to its meeting with the Clark Fork around Garrison. There, the two waters mingle, mixing in a wavering line a person could see from the interstate if he bothers to look. The river's clear aquamarine ridges against the deeper green of the Clark Fork for a hundred yards until the two blend into a subtle shade that is a mixture of each of them – another river, mildly different, but still the same. But back up here the current works its way patiently as it slides under the banks, gliding over and around smooth boulders, across sandy flats or bubbles among stretches of coppery-colored rocky streambed. Large brown trout hide in the darkness provided by thick bunches of overhanging willow and grass. The trout hold steady, slipping briefly into the light to snatch a grasshopper that plops on the river's surface or to crush a minnow that makes a careless move. Rainbows, tails up and flashing in the sunlight, nose among the rocks in shallow water, kicking up mayfly and caddis fly nymphs. Easy pickings for the trout. This is the way it will be until the clouds, rains, and finally heavy snows come in October and November. The rhythm is constant and changes only with the appearance of brief thunderstorms that raise and cloud the river. The hatching of insects varies by species as the days move along, but the trout and some silvery mountain whitefish never stop feeding. They don't care about time any more than the river does. They're aware of only the need to eat and avoid being eaten. The fish feed on whatever is prevalent and easiest to kill.

The river is just the river, not a conscious entity like you or me. The river doesn't care about anything. No worries, just water moving down hill doing gravity's bidding.

Upstream below a slight bend, a dark-haired woman stands at the edge of a deep glide. The day is already hot, mid-80s. She's wearing nothing more than cutoffs, rubber sandals, and a white T-shirt. A slight breeze pushes the careless grasshoppers above the swaying grasses and out over the water. The browns are lined up like wolves waiting for them. Nothing delicate about this. Slashing, pouncing, smacking of toothy jaws. Perhaps she imagines that she can hear the trout's teeth crashing together as they grind down on the crunchy carapaces of the insects. She works 50 feet of line back and forth enjoying the sight of the water vaporizing into fine spray as it merges with the light, creating miniature rainbows. The rod appears to be made of cane from the Tonkin region of southeast Asia, an old rod that her father probably gave

her when she was a kid. (I discover later that this is indeed almost exactly the case, though grandfather instead of father.) One made by a true artist in the arcane art of constructing bamboo fly rods that are not tools but rather extensions of the flyfisher's arm and mind. The wood glows with a red-brown grain and matching silk windings. A wonderful example of vanishing craftsmanship that took hundreds of hours to make. For years she rarely used the rod, afraid of breaking the precious instrument on an errant back cast or a large trout. She brought it out only on some small spring creeks near her home, taking little cutthroat and rainbows.

I saw this person years ago when I drove up from Missoula to fish this water. When I worked my way quietly up to her, she turned and smiled and we talked for a bit. She fished a lot, she said, and for years had been afraid to use the cane rod that was made by Wes Jordan, afraid that she'd break it on a bad cast or playing a large brown.

"The damn thing was meant to be fished," Dad said to me one day. "Better to blow it up on a cannibal brown. Fish with it. Don't drag it out once or twice a year and stare at it like it's some painting hanging on a wall in a museum. Fish with it. Let it show you what casting really can be."

So she took his advice and now fishes almost exclusively with the cane rod. Except when she uses a little six-and-a-half-foot Paul H. Young Little Giant bamboo rod she discovered in a second hand store down in Broadus in the southeast corner of the state several years ago. She was looking through old books, searching for a first edition, first printing of anything for her library when she spotted the dark leather-covered rod case gathering dust in a dark corner. Twenty dollars was all she paid. The rod was probably worth close to $4,000 considering its near-mint condition.

As for her graceful, pinpoint casting: "Takes concentration not to concentrate," she said to me.

When she cast with the rod, it truly was a part of her, an extension of her arm and she laughed out loud while standing in the river, out loud with the joy of being alive and standing in the river doing what she obviously loved.

She snapped a quick haul on the line as it loaded on the back cast and sent the bug sailing up and across the river's surface on a slight downward arc propelling the hopper crashing into the water where it ricocheted a few feet to land above a large brown she's watched feeding for some time up against a bank next to a hay field; an old beaverslide that will do heavy duty stacking hay later this month was visible in the distance. The raucous touchdown caught the trout's eye. The fish charged ahead, leaving a widening wake as it moved quickly against the current. She could see the fish's white mouth open and swallow the fly. No need to set the hook, the brown took care of that with its vicious take. It thrashed the surface at the first bite of the point and barb. She said that she dislikes barbless hooks along with most of the arrogance and pretension that often surfaces around the concept of catch-and-release fishing. She wants to make sure that she lands what she connects with. The woman wants to drop to her knees in the river and hold the trout, feel its cold, smooth wildness. She likes the predatory nature of fishing, especially hunting browns. Being a predator is at once violent, secretive and alive. Life and death.

"So, the hell with it," she said. "Let it slide. Enjoy the rush."

The brown was well into her backing, the line taut but bowed slightly over distance in the river. The rod bent towards the water, throbbing up and down. "Nothing sensual here, either," she said to the curious whitetails. Line was slowly regained and then the brown lay spent in the shallow water at her feet. Stooping down she twisted the hook from the trout's jaw, drawing blood that mixed with some of her own as it dripped bright red from a clean slice along her thumb ripped by the fish's teeth. She lifted the creature in her hands and pushed it towards the sun, laughing joyfully as she does so. Deep browns, rich yellows, black and crimson spots, burnished coppers, hard silvers and the white mouth glow against the blue sky. She held the trout in the air a long time before she killed it by whacking its head on a rock. She enjoys eating trout sometimes and killing the fish this way is swift and harshly merciful. This also preserves the quality of the flesh for cooking instead of having the meat fill with lactic acid from stress.

"Thank you for this fish," she said quietly to the land, head shaking slowly back and forth. "Just plain nuts, I guess."

All of this was at once strangely beautiful, a little horrifying and again, dreamlike.

"This brown, me, all of us bleed in our own ways in this one," she said. The last words I heard her speak as she nodded and walked out of the river and across a field holding the brown by the gill in one hand and her cane rod in the other. Never saw her again. I wonder from the distance of over 30 years if I ever saw her at all.

The river does not mind. Doesn't care. How can it, being nothing more than a combination of water, silt, fish, and insects mixed among flashes of light and dark? Be realistic here. A river is just a river and this one is not changed by her intrusion. One less brown trout is all.

Rusted-out tailgating splendor along a western Montana stream brings back memories of misspent youth on similar waters that also had their banks reinforced with the remains of demolition derby 1953 Studebaker Commanders, whiskey-running 1939 DeSoto Coupes, bank-robbing 1940 Packard Super Eights, and the remains of other long-gone vehicles. Big trout like to hang out in the submerged remains of these old wrecks. This little beat is no exception, having yielded a bunch of surly browns over the years to fender-tight casts of cree-hackled Woolly Buggers. The Clark Fork just above Missoula used to have a classy run of rust outs, but sadly they went the way of developers and their cookie cutter condos. There's still a nice bunch of battered clunkers jammed into an earthen bank over around Birney where the smallmouths are doing just fine. So how does the Ghostland Observatory figure into this trout chasing experience? Hard to say except that perhaps a derelict hipster has stared through a few too many window panes into the bright white light of flyfishing truth and come to the slightly addled conclusion that the two GLO freaks making music in Austin aren't all that different from an old freak chasing browns in Montana...

TRIP INFORMATION

Timing: Runoff can begin anywhere from late April and last well into June depending on the amount of snowpack and the spring weather. Otherwise the river is fine all year.

Where: Hwy 12 runs along the river 24 miles at the western end of MacDonald Pass all the way to the Little Blackfoot's junction with the Clark Fork at Garrison Junction. Two miles east of Elliston, Road 5 follows the upper Little Blackfoot to its headwaters near the Continental Divide. A campground is nestled in the forest right by the stream.

Hub: Helena is the closest town. Everything you need is here. It's the state capital. Rooms, food, groceries, liquor, flyfishing gear. Crosscurrents has everything a fly fisher needs at 326 N. Jackson Street, Helena, 406-449-2292, 1-888-434-7468. Brewhouse Pub & Grill has good beer and good food. Their amber Tumbleweed IPA is a winner – 939 1/2 Getchell Street, 406-457-9390. For lodging, take your pick. All major chains and price ranges are here. I normally camp when I'm staying around the Little B, or stay at the Last Chance Motel in Elliston. The place is clean, quiet, relatively cheap, and the owners are friendly. It's right on the south side of Hwy 12 – #26 US Highway 12 East, Elliston, 406-492-7250.

Appropriate Gear: In warm months I wade wet. Hip waders at other times. I use a seven-foot-six 4-weight, but 2- to 5-weights will do, up to eight-foot-six.

Favorite Patterns: Griffith's Gnat, Olive Tear Drop, Grey and Bright Green Emergent Sparkle Pupa, Light Cahill, Elk Hair Caddis, hopper pattern of choice, Hare's Ear nymph, Woolly Bugger.

Special Regulations: Open third Saturday in May through November 30. Mainstem river – Extended whitefish season and catch-and-release for trout open December 1 to third Saturday in May with artificial lures and/or maggot (love those maggots) only. Catch-and-release for cutthroat trout.

Griffith's Gnat

Hook: TMC 100BL   **Hackle:** Grizzly, palmered
Thread: Black   throughout length
Body: Peacock herl

Chapter Eleven

Sun River

"What's that awful sound, John?"

"Out To Lunch by Eric Dolphy."

"Very strange. Is the whole CD like this? Where's the melody?"

"It's in there somewhere and, yes, it is." I smiled at my companion who looked at me and decided to let the matter drop. Sixties alto sax. Discordant harmonies. Inverted rhythmic phrases. Admittedly Dolphy lacks the stylistic sophistication of the prodigiously talented Kenny G, but then our fishing trips never come close to reaching the rarefied levels of nuance and sophistication as do those delicate, foreign-wines-for-lunch, pampered float trips offered in the glitz ads that are scattered throughout the major flyfishing magazines like dead carp along a muddy bank – the excursions where you absolutely must wear 14,000 bucks of clothing draped with zirconium-encrusted hemostats, stomach pumps, thermometers, and don ball caps plastered with catchy phrases like "I fish, therefore I am".

Perhaps that's an unfair, even harsh, line of thought, especially as we slide out of Augusta up a dusty road towards a place we like to fish and camp along the Sun River. After all, we aren't running down esoteric central Montana trout water in my old beater pickup anymore, either. We sold out a couple of years back and bought an expensive Sports Utility Vehicle with leather seats and a real nice sound system. The Tahoe is now our only tangible asset, unless you figure in 200 fly rods, camera gear, a .357 magnum and a bunch of jazz CDs. At least the rig's windshield is cracked and chipped, the body has a dent or two and the interior reeks of damp waders and soggy Triscuits creating an ambiance approaching that of the Fort Peck Inn, a lofty vision in itself. None of this really matters, which is why I'm writing about it. The idea of the whole unplanned, undisciplined journey, the shaky premise we use to justify our inability to hold regular jobs or our very real need to get away from daily interactions with people, is that we live for good country and whatever is found there. And that by photographing and writing about our experiences with intensity and insight we can share the free-form energy and arcane experiences we encounter with others. And we can earn lots of money.

Just another line of silliness we run by ourselves and scores of unwitting victims from Forsyth to the Port of Del Bonita in a vague attempt to legitimize the insanely good times we have out here in the middle of everywhere doing whatever zips into our heads.

Standing in the wetness of the cool Sun, tossing a shredded hopper pattern out into the center of the river with a rhythm turned moronic through a deleterious combination of heat and repetitious casting is scintillating. To be sure, the casting is at once brilliant and artful with the line unfurling from its tight loop with unerring accuracy 15, 20 feet distant, but this is still repetitious, when out of the clear blue water comes a large chunk of determined silver, white mouth wide open. The fly is gone and the line on the reel is going, too. A rainbow leaps 50 yards from us, very large, and then falls back to the river and steals more line. The trout leaps again, as far above the water's surface as I've ever seen a freshwater fish go. And this time when the rainbow comes down, it does not drop down into the current, but, instead, flexes its tail flat on the top of the river and thrashes through a hot breeze fast away from me. Lifting gradually backwards on the rod to take up the slack I hear a sound that is a combination of crumpling Saran Wrap and breaking stick matches. Something isn't right. I've lost control of the situation. A new experience. Nothing I do with the rod helps and then I look at the pricey piece of graphite. Broken. Shattered just above the handle. Four-hundred bucks of junk and the trout throws the hook with bored disdain. The very large rainbow gleefully arcs through the light, jumping over and over as it heads down river. Pretty to watch. Tough to take, even at this advanced, broken-down stage in the life-long proceedings.

"Nice job, John," she says.

"Not my fault. The damn rod blew up. Damn good fish down the tubes."

"That's what you always say."

"What do you mean 'always'?"

"That makes five you've wrecked so far and it's not even August. Thank God for Uncle Orvis. (This was back when I was still in the good graces of the Orvis Company and they actually believed that sending me gear was good for their business. They finally came to their senses and disinherited me, but not after years of much needed and appreciated largess)."

"Thank God, nothing. I think I've been disinherited."

"What'd you do this time, darlin?"

"I quit drinking and they don't like the way I dress," and I torched a cigar to ease the pain.

"What's wrong with the way you dress?"

There is nothing like the support and compassion of a good woman to steer you through tough times. I begin to trudge back to camp to grab another rod, her laughter rings in my always ringing ears. I start to laugh. Hell, the things have a lifetime guarantee and there are at least 14 more in the back of the car. Break one. String up another. Onward and upward.

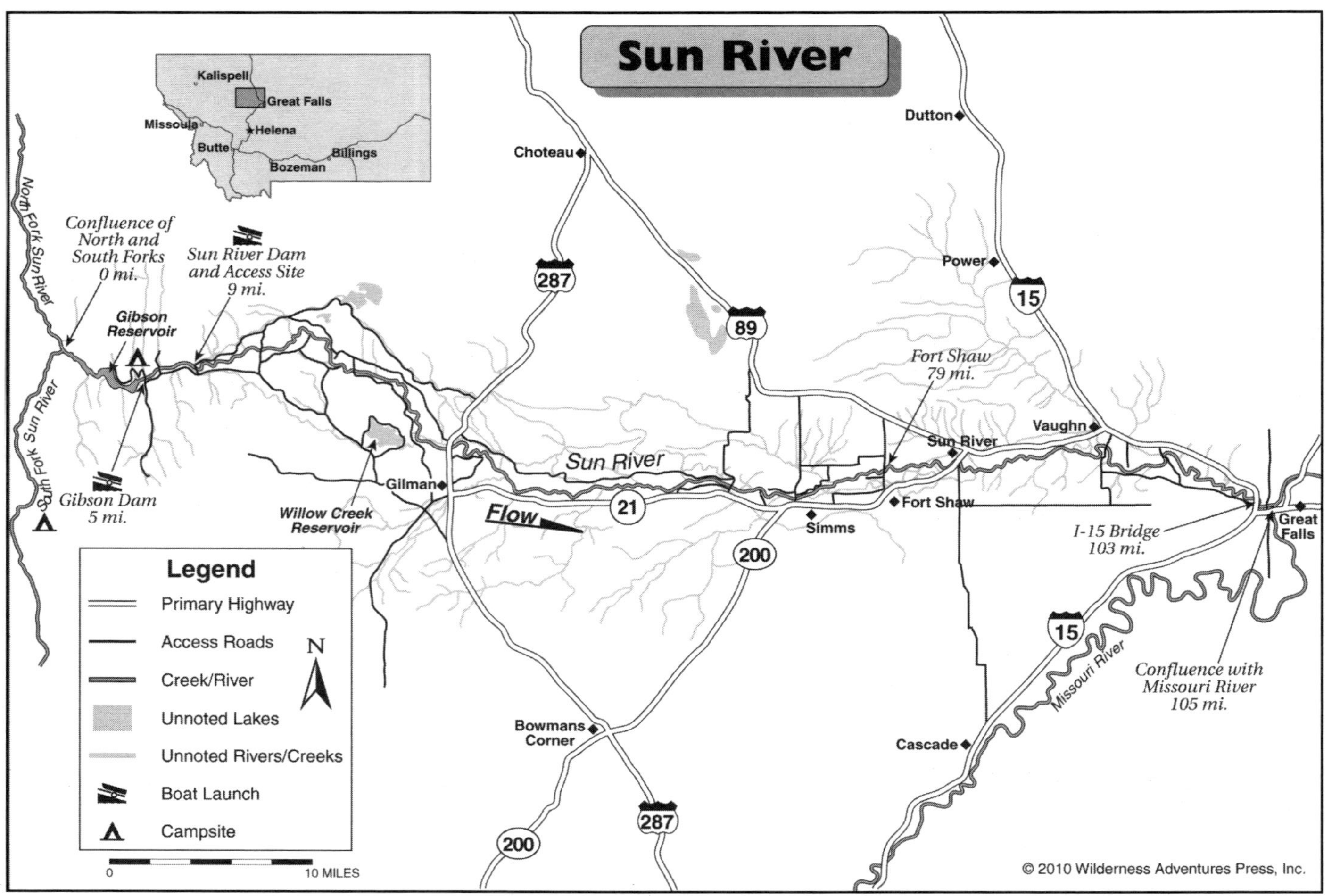
Sun River
Kalispell
Great Falls
Missoula
Helena
Butte
Billings
Bozeman
Dutton
Choteau
Power
North Fork Sun River
Confluence of North and South Forks 0 mi.
Sun River Dam and Access Site 9 mi.
287
89
15
Fort Shaw 79 mi.
Gibson Reservoir
South Fork Sun River
Vaughn
Sun River
Gilman
Sun River
Fort Shaw
Gibson Dam 5 mi.
Willow Creek Reservoir
Flow
21
Simms
I-15 Bridge 103 mi.
Great Falls
200
Legend
Primary Highway
Access Roads
Creek/River
Unnoted Lakes
Unnoted Rivers/Creeks
Boat Launch
Campsite
N
15
Missouri River
Confluence with Missouri River 105 mi.
Bowmans Corner
Cascade
287
200
0
10 MILES
© 2010 Wilderness Adventures Press, Inc.

Speaking of which, I look upriver and pray that the ancient, leaking concrete structure lyrically known as Gibson Dam (the main structure of the Sun River Project was built from 1926-29 and is a concrete arch dam and contains 167,500 cubic yards of concrete. The reservoir, with 1,296 surface acres and 15 miles of shoreline, offers fair fishing for rainbow trout, cutthroat trout, and brown trout), a decrepit edifice that blocks the Sun a couple of miles away hangs on for at least another few days. The idea of being washed away by billions of gallons of unleashed reservoir water, the two of us entwined in a confused jumble of sleeping bags and impaled by tent stakes, all this as we plummet 150 feet over the diversion dam roaring a quarter-mile just below us, the image holds little wonder or excitement for me. A couple of divorces, several addictions, numerous intriguing conversations with law enforcement officials and an awfully clear awareness that big money ain't in my future are all the thrills I want for this ride. Then again...if I were killed in such a dramatic mishap...maybe my books would sell.

Mid-morning a few days later and the Rocky Mountain Front screams at us from 50 miles away. The outraged mountains dominate our vision with a barrage of intense purple, white, salmon, slate grey, and forest green. The small stream we are now fishing flows through a deep cut in the high plains not far below the Alberta border on wide open tribal land. A friend of ours has given us access to this seldom-fished stretch of water, a couple of miles of lunatic perfection we reach first by highway outside of Browning, a road that diminishes to two-track then finally gives up all pretension of purpose and turns into a chaotic ride across a plowed field of rock and boulders. We park on a cut bank above the water, work our way downstream and start casting the hoppers, always the hoppers for us this time of year.

Over the years, I've criticized the Montana Department of Fish, Wildlife and Parks for a number of things they do that I strongly disagree with but where the Sun is concerned, the department is doing a solid job of rehabilitating and improving the quality of fishing. Low water from irrigation drawdown and drought, diversion dams, and riparian habitat destruction by cattle have led to lower than expected trout populations over the years. The Sun reminds me a lot of Alberta's classy Oldman and Castle Rivers, flows that offer wonderful fishing for cutthroat.

According to information on the FWP website:

> *"To make better progress on the goals of the Watershed Group, five workgroups were set up to work on problems related to weeds, agriculture, water quality, water management, and fisheries. The Fisheries Workgroup is made up of representatives from the Montana Department of Fish, Wildlife and Parks (FWP), Trout Unlimited, the U.S. Bureau of Reclamation, the U.S. Fish and Wildlife Service, Missouri River Fly Fishers Club, and others. Their goal is to improve*

the fisheries in the Sun River and its feeder streams. To do this, the group plans to find ways to:

- *Reduce fish losses in irrigation canals.*
- *Improve in-stream flows and water temperatures in the river and tributaries.*
- *Improve fish habitat in the river and tributaries, and*
- *Raise public awareness of the status of fisheries in the watershed."*

Regarding low flows:

"One promising approach is to reduce the losses of water in the irrigation canal system and use the saved water to improve river flow. For example, Muddy Creek near Vaughn receives an excessive amount of irrigation wastewater. Though a number of improvements have been made, the creek still often flows two to five times higher than some sections of the main stem Sun River during the summer irrigation season. Maybe some of this excess water could be intercepted before it reaches Muddy Creek and then pumped back up to fields that are currently irrigated with Sun River water. In that way, less water would be taken from the Sun River, and river flows would improve.

Many irrigation canals cross gravelly soils, and substantial amounts of water can be lost by percolation into the ground. Leaky ditches can be lined or sealed to reduce seepage losses and saved water could be left in the river. A one-mile test section of a large irrigation ditch near Fairfield was sprayed with a special sealing compound in 2003. This was a cooperative project involving the Greenfields Irrigation District and the Fish, Wildlife and Parks Department.

Another possibility is to put fish screens on the main irrigation ditches to prevent loss of fish from the river. Screening large canals is expensive, often costing hundreds of thousands of dollars, but is possible. The U.S. Bureau of Reclamation has been studying fish losses in the Fort Shaw irrigation canal, and hopefully either a screen or a low-voltage electric barrier will be installed in the future."

It's easy to see that fish and game, sportsman and conservation groups have a long-term task ahead of them, but like any good river, the Sun is worth the effort.

One thing many of us take for granted is Montana's stream access law which allows anglers access to recreational access (like flyfishing) on all waters below their ordinary high water lines. This means that you can fish rivers and streams flowing through private property by accessing them from public roads or bridges providing you don't walk above the mark left by high water meaning "the line that water impresses on land by covering it for sufficient periods to cause physical characteristics that distinguish the area below the line from the area above it".

When this law was first passed it was upheld by the Montana State Supreme Court in 1984. The bridge access portion of this law was reaffirmed by the state assembly in 2009 despite intense lobbying and enormous spending by mainly out-of-state opponents who have been buying large tracts of the state for decades trying to lock up prime land for their personal use.

You know who these clowns are. They own TV networks, or used to read the news on these networks, or made killings on junk bonds, Ponzi schemes, and other shenanigans on Wall Street at our expense, or are has-been pop music stars who have attempted to deny access to creeks used by children, a female talk show host closing off lake access in northwest Montana, or a few of them make more millions off developments with cutesy names that run along the lines of the Animal Farm or Rusted Horse or Tin Bow Club, exclusive and private reserves for the rich that often feature designer golf courses that suck up water and pollute stream courses with fertilizers and other chemicals, and pricey homes built to conform to brain-dead covenants so they resemble multi-million dollar versions of what Malvina Reynolds described in her 1962 song *Little Boxes:* "...and they're all made out of ticky-tacky, and they all look just the same".

And the walls closing off still more land from the great unwashed such as myself grow longer and larger. "Let them eat squawfish" seems to be their operating dictum.

They are legion and they are dark inside. Their pockets are deep. They are relentless. They are patient as only the soulless can be. They don't care about, or for, the rest of us. So, please, whenever you have a chance to donate time and money to the cause of keeping the access law alive, do so. Without it, fishing in Montana as we know it now is dead like a bloated mountain whitefish stinking on the bank beneath a hot summer sun.

Here endeth the epistle.

In the summer and fall, fishing upstream from the bridge on Highway 287 about five miles north of Augusta – site of what used to be (things have calmed down for tourist purposes) an authentic and very untamed rodeo and attendant craziness including gunfire, horses in bars, topless women, lots of fistfights, plenty of cops making sure no one got in or out once the festivities began, and general non-family fun – can be entertaining.

The water runs through a wide valley marked by steep cliffs, cottonwoods, and fields. The rock is sandy, tan and the browns which run to 20 inches or so are more blonde than brown, a protective coloration adaptation to better blend in with the streambed. The wading is easy and a 4- or 5-weight, eight-foot-six works fine provided the wind is done. If not, all bets are off. It blows out here. Crystalline sapphire pools, pocket water, deep runs, down trees, snags, grassy and willow-choked banks, even rainbows tailing in riffles is the angling order of the day.

One late August afternoon, I worked large Elk Hair Caddis, maybe #10, to every piece of water working back and forth across the streambed wearing Teva sandals, cutoffs, shirt, hat, and sunglasses. An aging derelict on the run from society and himself launching cast after cast over the river's surface. The possibility of escape now turned temporarily real. Upper 80s. Passing cumulus clouds providing transitory shade and brown trout mixed with some rainbows and cutthroat – all of them sleek, strong, and energetic as they leaped, thrashed, often in inches-deep water, and ran with gay abandon. From 10 inches to 18 and not one with hook scars or torn jaws, even after my eager efforts. Finally I reached a north-turning bend lined with cottonwoods. I could see the Front running into Canada framed by the silvery green leaves that whispered in the soft air. Deer grazed in a field. A red-winged blackbird whistled electrically from some cattails in a marshy depression nearby. This was plenty. More than enough. I was grateful for the action and the tranquility. The needed solitude. I decided to head back. No bridge in sight. No impressive structure spanning the river gorge. How far had I wandered? Ninety minutes later, I reached the Suburban. About four miles, a little more, I figured. Hot, exhausted, sweaty, thirsty. River intoxication had carried me far upstream. No regrets, though, as I drank down a couple of bottles of iced tea and ate a bunch of Flathead cherries. Looking west the towering silver, grey-blue reefs of the Rocky Mountain Front ran the gamut of the skyline looking like a series of ancient battlements, castles, and spires housing lunatic alchemists or perhaps demon musicians. Red-tails worked the ridges in pairs. A group of semi-retired pelicans played pinochle on a gravel bar. The birds' languid motions indicated that a casual game was in progress. Swallows swooped down on caddis and lesser insects. Western meadowlarks talked back and forth in the tall, browning fields behind me. A rancher motored by on a tractor pulling a manure spreader, a wooden green one. He waved and laughed. So did I. Good day going down out here. Never get enough of these.

Rainbow trout race to the surface every time the flies hit the water. As soon as the terrestrial imitations land near a midstream obstruction or along an undercut rocky shelf or above a splashing riffle, the fish tag the bugs. All of them are leapers and all of them are healthy fish. Strong, silvery trout that haven't been bothered in years, as our friend laughingly assured us earlier in the day. He finds us amusing and is amazed as he says that we "are allowed loose without adult supervision." Knowing how to go invisible helps, helps a lot.

A flat-out amazing stream dancing through arid, empty land. The only sign of humans is an old wooden house, windows broken out, roof long blown away, side boards weathered a wind-battered grey. If there was a road that led to a bridge that crossed this stream, which there isn't, and if you looked down into the pure water, you'd say "Too shallow and trout don't swim in this kind of country anyway". But the stream is deeper than it looks. Swift runs over bright gravels look skinny when standing on a grassy bank 50 feet above the water. Once in the stream, the flow pushes against our stomachs with chilly friendliness as we work upstream. Blue-green pools are 10 feet deep or more, the streambed hidden in darkness.

Four hours of easy fishing makes us believe we have a grip on what we're doing, but we know better. Un-fished, unspoiled, damn good water always makes us feel this way. Put us on a pretentious spring creek and we start crying within 30 minutes. Fifteen-foot, 6X leaders. Size 22 patterns. Skillful presentations. Entomological insights. Educated salmonids. Forget it. Size 6 hoppers and 3X tippet are our speed, especially when coupled with wild, cooperative trout.

Much later in the season we stop in at the Cleveland Bar, an aging wooden joint hiding out in the Bears Paw Mountains. It's Sunday morning. Earlier we fished brush-choked Peoples Creek with tiny dries for little brook trout. Now we are on our way back to the Sun for one last splash before winter shows up. My friend walks into the old, vine-covered place for a quick drink. I stand outside in the breeze, smoking and looking at mountains that appear gentle at first touch, but the more I look the tougher they become. Good country. We could disappear without effort back in here. Raucous laughter ricochets through the screen door and open windows.

"I thought for sure you were from New Hampshire. Live free or die!" roars a deep voice.

"You don't know shit, Tim," this time a feminine one. "Anyone can tell she's from Minnesota. It's in her eyes. Look at them."

I smoke my way through this conversation, riding the wind up a brushy draw, through a grove of aspen and on up to a rocky ridge. Time disappears until my companion exits laughing and shouting over her shoulder, "It's in my eyes".

With an inept sense of the appropriate, I put on "Low Life" by Donald Bird and we wander off towards the Sun and our campsite several hours away to the west. This time we listen to the music all the way through and I begin to think there is at least a small ray of hope for us. And later after pasta with invisible sauce, and grilled vegetables, we sit around the fire watching stars come out and out and out. But we eventually get cold feet and go to sleep.

The wind is insane by the time we crawl out for coffee. Snow, sleet, rain, hail – all of it is coming down, but out of some desperate need to prove to myself and to her that I still am the crazy, take-it-as-it-comes angler of the past, I string the line through the guides and tie on a fat, brown Woolly Bugger. Even 0X tippet is elusive in the cold. I settle for a lame clinch knot. The whole thing probably takes 20 minutes and I look around. She's gone. Where now? I wonder. Looking towards the river for the hell of it and there she is standing in the water up to her hips casting into the teeth of a harsh wind. I can see her laughing and can imagine the sound ringing once again in my ears. Way ahead of me as usual.

The hell with "Out To Lunch".

It's high time for Ornette Coleman's "Snowflakes and Sunshine".

TRIP INFORMATION

Timing: Hitting the river before runoff is tricky due to winter snow levels and spring weather. Late April to mid-May sometimes plays well. After runoff in July (often late July) the water is low and clear through autumn.

Where: About an hour west of Great Falls on Highway 200 then Hwy 21 to Augusta and either Hwy 287 for several miles to access at the bridge or farther west out of Augusta on a hard gravel and dirt road well-marked into spectacular country on the edge of the Bob Marshall Wilderness, about a 30 mile drive.

Hub: Augusta, population somewhere around 600, has a motel, restaurants, gas station, great second-hand store, and an old-time general store. The Bunkhouse Inn – 406-562-3387. Mel's Diner has good food including some wild game – 121 Main Street, 406-406-562-3408.

Appropriate Gear: The usual suspects for western flyfishing. A 5-weight, eight-foot-six rod is the pick. Chest waders, shades, hat, etc.

Favorite Patterns: Hoppers, Yellow, Red, Green Humpy, Buggers, Muddlers, Montana Nymphs, Hare's Ear nymph, wet flies swinging through the current.

Special Regulations: Open third Saturday in May through November 30.

Yellow Humpy

Hook: Standard dry fly size 8-18
Thread: Yellow 8/0 or 6/0
Body: Yellow floss

Tail: Deer hair
Hackle: Mixed grizzly and brown
Wing: Deer hair

Back: Long deer hair folded over for the back and used for the wings

CHAPTER TWELVE

Mission Mountains

When I see the Mission Mountains blasting up from the river corridor right through the sky in the Swan Valley, I trip back to a time when Missoula wasn't a jive-ass rat race (that's what the place has become so no death threats, please, ala poor George Webber and his home town of Libya Hill in North Carolina – see parenthetical note on Thomas Wolfe below), but rather an amalgam of straight business owners, loggers, railroad workers, crazed hipsters and college students. Some of them including me were far more interested in passing the time wading streams like Rock Creek, the Bitterroot, Blackfoot, Nine Mile, or hiking way up in the Missions to rarely-visited mountain jewels filled with heavily-spotted westslope cutthroat, or rainbows or stunted brook trout or sometimes goldens.

I heard about lakes that had been planted via bucket biology by old-timers in the 1930s and 1940s; this told to me by a slightly-mad county deputy that could have been 65 or 90 – big Norwegian guy with hands the size of a first baseman's mitt – who had pulled me over in my Toyota Landcruiser for doing 92. The speed limit back then was safe-and-prudent much like open range or high noon in Tombstone (following the passing of this politically correct, nuisance law the number of deaths on the state's Interstate rose 111 percent from 27 to 56 in the following 12-month period). He told me to be careful up ahead because he'd seen a cow moose grazing along Condon Creek near the highway. Slamming into nearly a ton of moose at any speed would be ugly, at my speed, deadly. I thanked him for the warning. Being stopped by the man was a badge of honor. He was famous for pulling over a governor of Montana (Forrest H. Anderson?) who was weaving about in his limo and issuing a citation for reckless driving. I got out and we stood along the back of my rig talking about trout. I offered him a beer from my cooler in the back and he accepted – how I miss the old days when cops were human, Montana seemed still wild, little land was posted, and all of the streams seemed to fish like the sweetest of sweet dreams. Land's posted these days. Few cops are like this antique Scandinavian, but the fishing is good or better in a bunch of places as you shall see if you wade through this book. Over the course of 45 minutes, I learned where he and some of his buddies had hauled in goldens to unnamed lakes. The same story with westslope cutthroat. He made me promise not to tell and I haven't, but he said it was okay to suggest a general direction like "up over that ridge, down around the bog you'll find and beyond the next ridge".

Fair enough. The spots he told me have yielded nearly black-backed cutthroat to six pounds, goldens of two and three pounds in a deep pocket no more than two acres that avoids freeze-out because of an underwater spring near a cliff face that bubbles the whole emerald beauty like a hot tub. Woolly Worms cast out from shore, allowed to sink for a few seconds then slowly retrieved,with brief pauses, turned the trick on both species of trout. This method works almost anywhere, particularly with a Bigg's Special (aka Sheep Creek). I was unaware of this pattern back then so the Woolly Worm had to do and it did fine.

This was back in the late 60s and early 70s when not that many people knew about Montana, about those sedate little blow-outs called the Aber Day Kegger of 1972-77 with the likes of Doug Kershaw wailing away on his fiddle, bow strings flying in the wind, Bonnie Raitt being Bonnie Raitt, and of course the Mission Mountain Wood Band. They were the home team, our band. This was a period of sail-away years when posting the highest score on the Circus pinball machine at the long gone real Eddie's Club earned a thirsty soul a case of beer. Pin Larson owned the Stockman's on Front Street. He used to greet me with a "What's up, buddy?" and snare French fries from my plate while I drained icy mugs of beer and ate my cheeseburger. When my tab got too high, Pin would have me work it off cleaning up all of the empty beer bottles dropped through a chute and deposited in the basement on Sunday mornings. Lost Highway played at the Top Hat on the other side of Front. My blonde-haired girlfriend (a story not for now or the faint of heart) worked at Garden City News selling good books, newspapers and magazines on one side while a beer-drinking friend of mine manned the other side of the store moving material of a more adventurous nature to Missoula's more discriminating readers. Glenn West ran a small fly shop alongside the Clark Fork near a bowling alley and the Holiday Inn. It was called Grizzly Hackle. There's an outfit by the same name operating in town today, but it's not the same deal. Not even close – much like trying to compare a 2009 Chevy Impala to a 1964 Morgan Plus 4 LeMans. At the old place, I'd wander in and learn about entomology from the late Harmon Henkin who always seemed to be there when I was, how to tie a small butterfly from Glenn, the virtues of Tonkin cane and other arcane aspects of flyfishing from both of them. Life seemed easy back then just like it finally seems once again right here and now.

When I hike up to Island Lake, losing the trail and bushwhacking the last few hundred yards like always, and I eventually drop down over a small rocky crest to gratefully see that my aloof friends, the goldens, are still swimming around in a stoned-out blissful isolation life instantaneous – no back then or maybe sometime later. Only right now ripped in the Mission Mountains. Water pours from snowfields in long, arcing, rainbow curves. Rocks are clattering down cliffs and scree slopes – the sound echoing round and round. Marmots whistle back and forth, high pitched, pure calls. A warm wind is whipping confused grasshoppers up thousands of feet from the

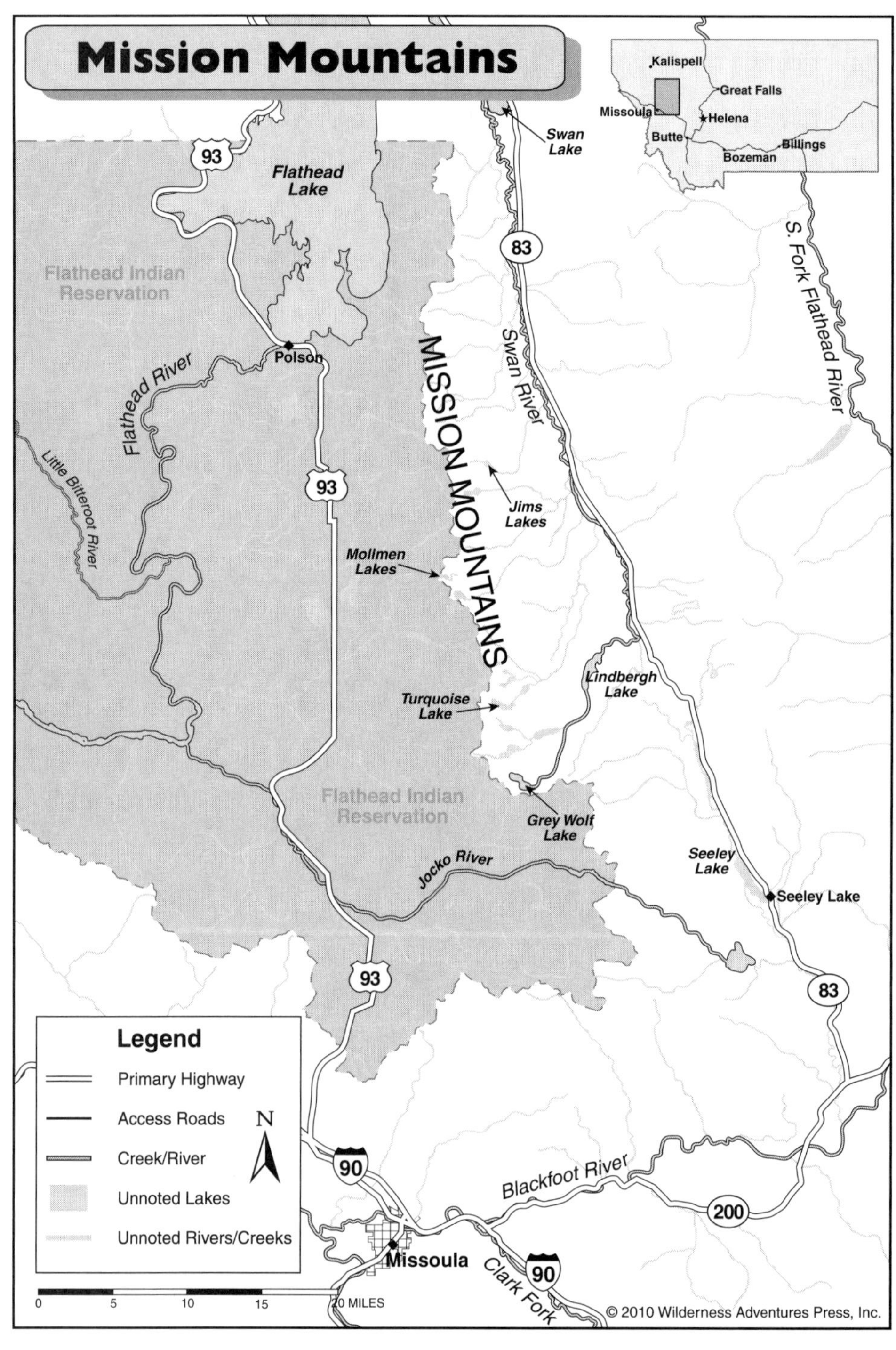

Mission Mountains
Kalispell
Great Falls
Missoula
Helena
Butte
Billings
Bozeman
Flathead Lake
93
Swan Lake
83
S. Fork Flathead River
Flathead Indian Reservation
Flathead River
Polson
Little Bitterroot River
93
Swan River
MISSION MOUNTAINS
Jims Lakes
Mollmen Lakes
Turquoise Lake
Lindbergh Lake
Grey Wolf Lake
Seeley Lake
Seeley Lake
Flathead Indian Reservation
Jocko River
93
Legend
Primary Highway
Access Roads
Creek/River
Unnoted Lakes
Unnoted Rivers/Creeks
N
90
Blackfoot River
200
Missoula
Clark Fork
90
83
0   5   10   15   20 MILES
© 2010 Wilderness Adventures Press, Inc.

verdant Swan Valley, the creatures probably wondering in their insect minds about the abrupt change in altitude and locale. Grizzly tracks – this time old ones – mark a sandy shore and lead off down to a mossy break where the lake's outlet rushes down to Heart then Crescent Lake then way down to Glacier Creek cascading through a dense forest of pine and fir. No one's around but me. So when Thomas Wolfe wrote the novel *You Can't Go Home Again* set in Libya Hill (actually someone at Harpers dug out enough words from *October Fair* to publish a couple of separate books including the above and *The Web and the Rock* after Wolfe's death in 1938, but this acquires only the most tangential relationship to flyfishing by expanding the lead for this chapter), I look around me, youthful memories swirling this glacial cirque as real as today, and I say out loud, "You got that one wrong, buddy".

The Kraft Creek Road, a little north of the Holland Lake turnoff, heads west into the mountains passing over the Swan River, along a number of ponds and then finally alongside Glacier Creek until dead-ending less than a mile from Glacier Lake. Both the creek and lake have some cutthroat, brook trout, and rainbows in them, but they are few. A Royal Wulff or other attractor pattern will take some trout in the eight- to twelve-inch range. I usually head here in early October after most of the hikers have retreated to lower elevation pursuits. The hike to Island Lake is about six steep miles into remote, above tree line, rocky landscape. I often made this trip with my old friend, Rupert, an Australian shepherd who enjoyed numerous relatively uncommon scents of moose, grizzly, beaver, and ruffed and spruce grouse he encountered along the trail. He'd often blast off into the underbrush flushing the grouse up into nearby pines. I'd always have a .22 pistol and I'd take two or three for the evening's meal. The birds wouldn't move, thinking that motionlessness equated to invisibility, even as their companions were plinked off the limb next to them, roasted on a spit over the fire, basted with olive oil after seasoning with salt, pepper and a little garlic powder. The dog and I lived the good life under the stars. He'd then curl up by the fire while I sipped Courvoisier – a tradition of sorts on those hikes of years ago.

In the morning, we'd work our way up to a narrow saddle that gave way to a view of diamond and sapphire lakes, sharp-edged, snowy peaks, immense snowfields, dwindling glaciers, and streams of melt water shooting far out into space before plummeting a couple of thousand feet to a hidden valley we called our own. I snacked on mixed nuts, apricots, and cold water. Rupert had some Purina dog chow. We were content. By mid-afternoon we dropped back down to camp to play with the goldens.

Rupert enjoyed leaping off a cliff and landing on top of the fish, a terrifying event in the trout's mind as small chunks of bright gold flashed off in all directions. The dog would stalk the bank above the lake and harass the trout in this fashion for a good half hour while I sipped a Rainer and smoked a cigar. Tired of the action, he'd find a warm rock sheltered from the breeze and collapse for a snooze until dinner. The goldens regrouped within minutes, wild fish are rarely bothered by intruders. By then, I'd have my 5-weight rigged with an olive Woolly Worm at the end of a 12-foot leader tapered to 6X. The largest golden I've ever taken here was two pounds and the species is not a fighter like a brown or a rainbow, so light tippets are fine (no pun intended).

Golden trout have always fascinated me with their cartoon-intense coloration and the fact that they swim in only the highest, purest and most difficult lakes to reach in North America. As the years passed in Montana, I learned about more and more waters that held these unique salmonid that have been long since been transplanted from their native waters in California's high Sierra country. I've caught large ones of five pounds or more in Wyoming's Bridger Wilderness and in some lakes in the Beartooth Mountains of south-central Montana. And again some large specimens that I stumbled upon in an unnamed lake in the Whitefish Range, though they were frozen out some years back. But my favorite place to look for these curiosities is in a way-up-there lake in the Mission Mountains of northwest Montana. The fish don't grow large, but I'll always remember the first time a lady friend of mine and I, along with my Irish wolfhound Bonzo Dhogge (named after a bizarre Irish band of the time), staggered into this water after slogging through many feet of melting snow under a wicked late July sun. The water was dead calm and the goldens were lazily circling around like gold ingots as they sipped very small bugs. We set up a modest camp, caught a few, kept a few for dinner. We fried them whole with the heads on in butter and seasoned them with sea salt, black pepper, and some lemon juice. They were excellent. Then we spent the evening sipping Rich & Rare around a small fire as we watched the stars come out and meteors flare overhead. I haven't seen the lady in many years. Heard she'd become a psychiatrist practicing her bizarre craft somewhere in the Midwest. Glad to have survived that one...

...I was beginning to wonder, to talk out loud to myself, to answer my own questions. Were my friends right? Was I really crazy?

People had told me that the hike into this high Mission Mountain lake was a death march under the best of conditions and when they heard that I was going to make my third trip here in less than a month, they just stared, mouths open, or they turned away, too embarrassed for me to comment.

Why was I up here in these mountains in the chill of mid-October?

Spectacular scenery, solitude, and the joy of self-sufficiency that comes with backpacking were all part of the attraction. But the real reason the steep 10-mile hike seemed inconsequential was right in front of me, swirling in the emerald waters, flashing in the clear light.

Golden trout, a lot of them, were casually dining on a hatch of small caddis flies. I was here to try and catch one, to admire its beauty and rarity. There are not many of these fish around and not many anglers have ever seen one, let alone felt one struggling at the end of the line. I was the last of the very few, if any, people who made it up here to see this lake before the rough winter winds and deep snows closed the trail for eight months.

A light puff of breeze pushed my small fly a few feet from its intended target and as the fluff hit the lake's surface, a 12-inch piece of gold rose up and sucked in the offering. The strength of the fish surprised me – quick, strong runs punctuated with vigorous waggings of the head, then brief soundings on the bottom. The fish came haltingly to shore, partially on its side, the fly hooked in the roof of its mouth. The body glowed in the sunshine. A bright crimson band ran the length of the fish through 11 bronze parr marks. Black spots covered its back and tail. The fins were orange tipped with white. A magic blending of yellows, reds, greens, and black in perfect proportion.

The golden's appearance was stunning. The killer hikes were worth the sweaty, lung-burning effort. This was the most brilliant of trout caught in primitive surroundings – the rugged mountains of Montana.

To help understand this fish's allure, an explanation of its life and history is required.

Goldens originated in the Kern River drainage in the Sierra Mountains of central California. Golden stock was exported to Colorado, Idaho, Montana, Oregon, Utah, Washington, Wyoming, and as far away as England until 1939 when California passed legislation prohibiting the shipping of eggs and fish out of state. (The trout I just

caught was the offspring of fish planted in the late 1920s by a now old friend of mine.) The golden became California's state fish in 1947. Idaho, Washington, Montana, and Wyoming still carry on stocking programs on a limited basis. Small populations remain in the Uinta Mountains of Utah and the Pincher Creek area of Alberta. Goldens may be holding out in the isolated lakes of Colorado and Oregon.

Goldens need their own secure water. One of the main problems with establishing a fishery is that goldens will hybridize with other trout and lose their hold on a lake or stream. This was brought home last summer when, after catching several westslope cutthroat with yellow-tinted gill covers and a distinct golden hue on their sides, I remembered hearing that this particular isolated chain of lakes had been planted with goldens in the 1930s. A call to Fish, Wildlife and Parks a few days later confirmed this and also revealed that the lake had been recently stocked with cutthroat. It is obvious that cutthroats are taking over the lake and in a few more generations almost all visible traces of goldens will be gone.

The desirability of goldens to anglers probably led to a number of the colorful trout being transported "in coffee cans" from their original waters in California to neighboring lakes and streams during the 1870s by cattlemen who wanted goldens swimming in streams near where they tended their stock. One story has it that in 1876, a Colonel Stevens lugged a dozen of the fish from Mulkey Creek in the Sierras over a crest and dumped them in Cottonwood Creek. The Colonel operated a sawmill in the area and the goldens no doubt occupied his spare time quite nicely.

In 1918, the California Department of Fish and Game began raising goldens in the Cottonwood Lakes at an elevation of 11,000 feet. Today eggs are still gathered there and transported to the Mount Whitney hatchery before wilderness plantings.

Most people believe that the fish can only survive in lakes of high altitude. Goldens have been successfully transplanted as low as 3,000 feet, and in a number of lakes between 5,000 and 7,000 feet.

Most of the goldens caught today are technically known as *Salmo agua bonita* and are originally from the South Fork of the Kern River. Several other species of goldens exist in California. Among them are: *Salmo whitei* and *Salmo gilberti* of Coyote Creek; *Salmo roosevelti* of Volcano Creek; and *Salmo rosei* of the Culver Lake drainage. All of these trout are distinguished through minor variations in coloring and marking, but as Robert H. Smith states in his book *Trout of North America,* trying to compare them is "like trying to compare two sunsets".

Nobody knows for sure the evolutionary history of goldens, but some experts believe the trout may be descendents of redband trout, of which rare members include the Gila, Apache, and Mexican.

How did goldens evolve into the brightly-colored creatures they are today? There are several theories.

First, their colors tend to mirror the environment of their native range, the reds and other brightly-colored gravels of the Kern Basin, making the fish difficult for predators to spot, even though there are few predators at the altitude where they exist. An interesting idea is that the intense light, unfiltered at high altitudes, produces deadly levels of radiation, and the colors of goldens may be a form of protection from this harsh light. Some credence is given to this by the fact that the trout lose their color intensity after prolonged stays in lakes at lower elevations.

Goldens can reach an impressive size, although the days of 11-pounders being taken from Cooks Lake in Wyoming are long past. A five-pound fish would be a truly large one. Today 12-inch fish are common, and in streams five to seven inches is average. Exceptions exist, but lakes that hold big fish are hard to find and get to. And once there, the angler may find the goldens extremely selective (trout on English chalk streams have nothing on goldens in this respect).

The trout grow rapidly for the first three years, sometimes reaching 15 inches and more than a pound. After this, things slow down and a golden that is eight years old is an old golden.

So what does the flyfisher do if he wants to try his luck with these rare fish? Prepare to suffer. Ninety-nine percent of the water holding goldens is fished by less than one percent of the seekers of this gold. The reason for this is simple: Golden waters are remote and difficult to reach. Steep climbs (literally) are to be expected. And even with a good map, some golden lakes are almost impossible to find. Chasing these fish takes preparation and patience. Someone who is not willing to go the extra mile had better look to other trout for recreation.

There are specific tactics for goldens – most of the time this means using small dry flies or nymphs. Aquatic insects are the most important food, especially caddis flies and midges. Shrimp and terrestrials (ants, beetles and grasshoppers) are also a key part of the diet. When the air heats up as the day progresses, winds sweep up ridges dragging with them helpless insects that live down below – a natural artificial hatch the angler should watch for.

One hot August afternoon, warm winds from well below the lake I was fishing snarled my lines, but also swept hundreds of small hoppers onto the water's surface. Goldens went crazy, racing along the surface like surfers as they competed with each other for the unexpected gourmet offering. A quick switch to a #10 Joe's Hopper provided memorable fishing between tangled, eye-threatening casts.

To be safe, the prudent angler packs in an assortment of caddis and midge imitations, among them: Elk Hair Caddis, Goddard Caddis, Adams and Bucktail Caddis in #14 and smaller. The Hare's Ear nymph in the same sizes is also a good choice. Some patterns to try when the fish are acting selective are Muddler Minnows and Spruce Flies in #8 and smaller. The ever-faithful Woolly Bugger, especially in olive, can be a life saver.

Presentation must be extremely cautious. A light, delicate cast that gently delivers the fly is needed. The slightest disturbance and a golden trout stampede with Bonanza overtones will result. Keep low and use whatever cover is available. Remember, these fish are *spooky* and you just risked a coronary to find them, so take your time and do things right. Almost all success with dry flies or nymphs and the goldens involves waiting – minutes at a time. Let the fly adjust to its water-borne situation for as long as five minutes (shorter with nymphs). This is the *key* to catching the trout when they are being selective. After an agonizing wait, give the fly a slight flick. This often draws the ardent response of one or more greedy goldens for a solid take.

So what does the intrepid angler do when none of this works? Switch to the Spruce or the Muddler and cast near drop-offs and submerged boulders. Let the streamer rest a minute, then retrieve it in slow, short strips, with a couple of seconds between each strip. If this fails to work, shift to Woolly Buggers or shrimp imitations using the above technique.

Still unsuccessful? Go back to camp, have a cocktail, drink in the scenery and try again later. High mountain fishing, especially for goldens, is never a sure thing. A number of trips I've made were slight excuses to indulge masochistic tendencies.

Fishing for goldens that October afternoon stayed good and special until dark, when I put my rod down and enjoyed a simple meal over a warm fire. Millions of stars came out as the wind disappeared over a snowy ridge. Another good year of fishing was over. When I went back down to the valley in the morning, living seemed right and good. The way it should after chasing these golden fish way back in the mountains.

Obviously, I'm obsessed with goldens, and westslope cutthroat and bull trout and brook trout and on and on, but to suggest that this narrow slice of mountainous paradise in northwest Montana is only for those seeking gold would be wrong. Bull trout, cutts, brookies, mountain whitefish, and a few rainbows abound in cutthroat lakes like Turquoise and Gray Wolf – on well-marked and good but steep and long trails; Lace Lake just below Turquoise, Mollman Lakes – Woodard Lakes, Jim Lakes (except the lower ones that Plum Creek destroyed through clearcutting), Cold Lakes and High Park Lake. All are reached by hikes of several miles or more and are for backpackers in good shape. Topo maps are a must. The tributaries flowing down to the Swan River contain all of the above species including nice bull trout beginning in late August (which are illegal to target except in Swan Lake, Lake Koocanusa, Hungry Horse Reservoir, and the South Fork of the Flathead). If any of the above-mentioned fish are sighted on redds, enjoy the spectacle and forgo the fishing.

The Mission Mountains are true, pure Montana magic. Whenever I'm in them, I become a kid again. Not all that many places can do that for me.

TRIP INFORMATION

Timing: Most of the high country will not be open until mid-July at the earliest. Deep banks of snow and ice-covered lakes will be the norm. Down in the Swan Valley floor, the streams will be thick with runoff from mid-May through late June or later. From ice-out through early October, when early winter storms show up, the hiking and fishing is fine.

Where: Take Highway 200 about eight miles east of Missoula for half an hour to Clearwater Junction, then take a left on Highway 83 running north-south between Seeley Lake and Swan Lake. This is the best way into this country. Forest service roads like Kraft Creek head west and wind their way to trailheads up and down the range.

Hub: Whitefish, about 70 minutes northwest of Swan Lake, is a resort town filled with summer and winter homes and condos, many restaurants, bars, and motels. Grouse Mountain is a bit pricey but has good rooms and dining facilities – 1205 US Highway 93 West, 406-862-3000, 1-800-321-8822. Central Avenue is filled with restaurants and bars including The Great Northern, Tupelo Grill, Truby's Wood Fired Pizza, Serrano's Mexican Restaurant, and so on. Stumptown Anglers has everything needed to fish the Missions and other area waters – 5790 Highway 97 South, Whitefish, 877-906-9949, www.stumptownangler.com

Appropriate Gear: Even in summer, the nights can be autumn-cool so plan accordingly. Lightweight chest or hip waders are needed. Bear spray. Mosquito repellent. Lightweight camping and fishing gear.

Favorite Patterns: Attractor patterns for the streams – Goofus Bugs, Wulffs, Adams, Goddard Caddis, Elk Hairs, Hare's Ear nymphs, Soft Hackles work at times, even in the lakes (especially orange-bodied), Woolly Worm.

Special Regulations: On the east side of the divide (marked on state highway and DeLorme maps) of the Missions, a Montana license does the trick. Over into the Flathead Reservation, a tribal permit is needed. License fees and types can be found here – www.cskt.org.

Woolly Worm

Hook: 2X-long wet #6-12
Thread: Black

Body: Chenille in brown, olive or black
Tail: Red wool or died red hackle

Hackle: Grizzly, palmered through body

Chapter Thirteen

Middle Fork of the Flathead River

Except for the watery, psychotic, orange glow from a farmyard light across the river, things were pretty dark out and damn cold. My fingers passed being numb and went to warm as they sometimes do when my circulatory system panics. A wolf howls in the mountains to the north. A long, chilling wail. Then another. Talking back and forth with forever wildness as another day approaches. Perhaps these are offspring from the Magic Pack that roams far up the North Fork of the Flathead River along the Canadian border – animals that have worked their way down towards humans and their domesticated animals. After each cast, the ice in the guides needs to be punched out with thumb and forefinger. Late November well before dawn, maybe 5:30 and several dozen casts quartering upstream towards the Blankenship Bridge at the confluence of the Middle and North Forks have produced nothing. No bumps, takes, swirls, or anything else related to successful angling. When all of these conditions are factored together, there seems a clear indication that it is time to trudge up to the Suburban, drink more hot coffee from another thermos (the first one lies empty on the bank gathering frost), and head back to where it is dry and warm – especially warm. But I think, what the hell, I'm here and a few more casts can't hurt.

About four launches into this last futile set of insanity the rod jerks, hard, then line whips off the reel as something large tears downstream. At first the fish is even with me out in the middle of the flow, then the line knifes through the dark, roiling surface 30, 50, 70 yards down river. The fish stops, holds in a deep eddy that I remember from brighter and warmer times on the river. Line is regained as I move over the cobbled shoreline stumbling into big rocks, driftwood, something that smells dead even in this cold (perhaps a logger or a moose). Based on the angle of the line, the fish has burrowed through the chill water to the bottom that is maybe 15 feet in this pool. I'm finally even with the fish once again. Just me and the trout in the darkness of a northwestern Montana winter morning. Surprisingly, the fish gives up the fight putting up only token resistance as I reel in the remaining line. The big ones often do this, like they've seen too much of life to waste energy on futile struggles. I set the

8-weight rod on the stones and slide my fingerless-gloved hand down the thick leader that measures seven feet and tapers to a dainty 20-pound tippet. There is some light from the false dawn, the stars, and that yard light. My eyes are pretty well adjusted to the dark after an hour. The air smells of snow, the dead animal, the frigid river, and the big fish beneath me. I can see the trout on its side shining faintly silver as small waves from the current lap over its thick side. I slip my fore and middle fingers under the gill plate and lift the fish in the air.

This is a nice one, indeed, close to 20 pounds. The largest I've ever taken from the river that is the setting for this annual run of lake trout (*Salvelinus namaycush*) up from Flathead Lake, perhaps to spawn but more likely to feed on smaller specimens of bull trout, dropping back down to the huge lake after spawning themselves in wilderness tributaries. Lake trout are related to bull trout, Arctic char, Dolly Varden, and brook trout. So in a way, these trout feeding on their cousins are cannibals of a sort.

I've chased for these fish since the 1970s. Now that I live in Livingston I rarely take the time or make the effort to drive 350 miles over the Continental Divide into the Flathead Valley to pursue the fish. I shouldn't be so lazy. One lake trout like this one makes the trip, the cold, the slightly eerie darkness, all worthwhile. The pattern I'm using is of my own design – long streamer hook, lots of white and dyed-green marabou, silver tinsel body weighted with 0.30 wire and a black thread tapered head. Lots of fun to cast, but predawn hours are normally calm so my head and back are spared painful shots due to bad casting. To look at the pattern (and I'm being generous here) is to look at a clumsily tied conglomeration of materials that looks like a miniature feather duster when dry but when in the water and stripped in retrieve accurately mimics a five- or six-inch bull trout. If it works, I could care less what it looks like, lying like a dead bird on my tying bench.

This one lake trout is enough for the morning. I kill it quickly with a blow to the top of its head. The Department of Fish, Wildlife and Parks encourages keeping all lake trout here to cut down on the species voracious predation on the bull trout, much the same as this is encouraged in Yellowstone Park to help populations of native Yellowstone cutthroat. I'm doing my part here, arm in arm with FWP. Sometimes fishing makes strange bedfellows. Walking back to my rig I think about how good steaks cut from this fish will taste after being seasoned with black pepper and sea salt, grilled and then dipped in lemon-lime butter.

We'd become accustomed to being stared at by the tourists that ambled about Apgar Village hard on the western shores of scenic Lake McDonald in Glacier National Park. After all, these were visitors of sophistication and distinction, individuals dressed in brown silk knee-high socks and sandals – often brightly-colored plastic items, Bermuda shorts of even brighter pigmentation, shirts stretched tight over protruding bellies – even so with the men in the peripatetic throngs, large square-lensed sunglasses and wool Tam O'Shanter hats of sedate hue. We were, to be honest,

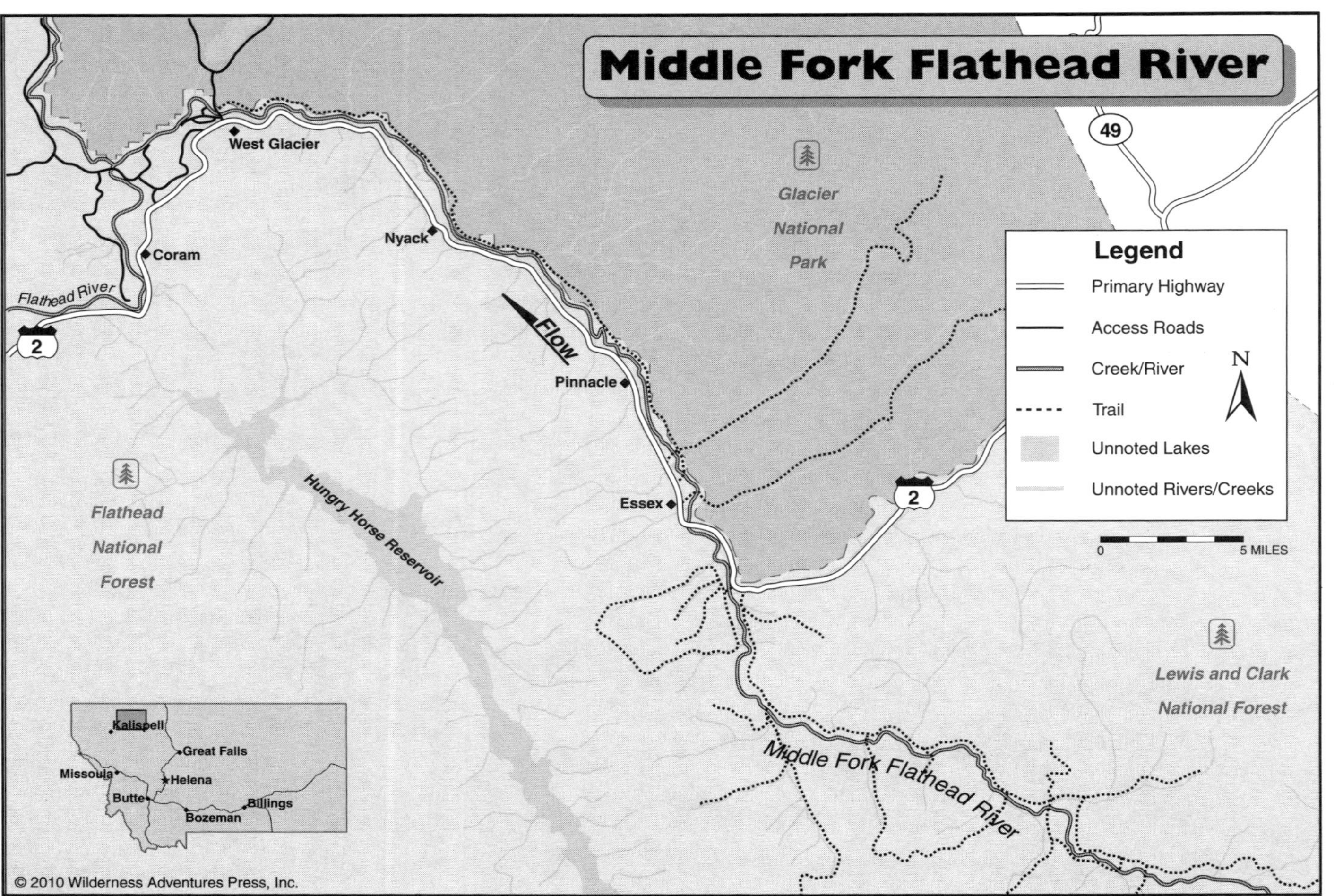

Middle Fork Flathead River
49
West Glacier
Coram
Flathead River
2
Nyack
Flow
Glacier National Park
Pinnacle
Essex
2
Legend
Primary Highway
Access Roads
Creek/River
Trail
Unnoted Lakes
Unnoted Rivers/Creeks
N
0
5 MILES
Flathead National Forest
Hungry Horse Reservoir
Middle Fork Flathead River
Lewis and Clark National Forest
Kalispell
Great Falls
Missoula
Helena
Butte
Billings
Bozeman
© 2010 Wilderness Adventures Press, Inc.

merely a couple of bozos inflating a rubber raft on the pebbled beach, rigging fly rods, loading oars, cooler and vest – certainly arcane behavior in the eyes of these travelers. Ours was not an activity or visual wonder delineated in park brochures, so we were something of an oddity and curiosity. The large number of cameras pointed in our direction and clicking steadily appeared to verify this observation. Finally set up, we paddled away from the madding crowd and worked around the point that was at the end of the village limits and were soon in the grasp of McDonald Creek. We spun and glided beneath a roadway bridge as more curious onlookers peered at us from one side then raced across the road as tires screeched and horns blared to watch us slide out of view behind a pine forested bend. My friend manned the oars. I began to cast on water that was so much wilderness despite being in the midst of tens of thousands of July-hatched tourists, that the whole incongruity of the experience was initially unsettling and exhilarating. Hell, a grizzly bear could take us out and yet we were within hailing distance of broad Buicks, teetering Winnebagos and Prowlers, and vicious SUVs of all descriptions and price ranges. We had several miles of excellent trout water to ourselves all the way to the Middle Fork not far from West Glacier View, a location of exotic ice cream emporiums, gas stations charging fantastic rates for fuel, rafting companies eager to float you down wild rivers for huge expense, gewgaw and gimcrack shops selling wonders painfully crafted in the Orient and, most magical of all, a copper-domed tourism center, I believe for the noble province of Alberta. We were fishing in the Land of Oz. We first explored this stretch in the mid-80s and over the years (this was up into the mid-90s) had never seen any other anglers, only a stray and usually lost camera-bedecked hiker. Nowadays some people work the creek, but not many.

Cast after cast turned westslope cutthroat and a few mountain whitefish. The trout rose eagerly, near vertically from the sandy bottom, mouths wide open to take Humpies, Wulffs, Hoppers, Adams, whatever. Then they'd run in circles or plough to the depths in search of sanctuary before giving in to the inevitable act of being briefly admired and released. Some went to 15 inches, the whitefish often larger. The farther down we went the larger the fish until an 18-inch specimen was more common than not. We'd see blue herons, kingfishers, grizzlies, bald eagles, white-tailed deer, black bear, a cougar once, western tanagers – a wild, unspoiled place.

Some of the water was deep, pouring over long-submerged deadfalls, places big trout would hold. They seldom rose to dries, but would chase Buggers and Muddlers that we sunk with split shot. On the first or second strip, the fat trout would charge from shadowy cover and slam the fly, impaling themselves on the hook as they did so. A tricky fight ensued where the intrepid angler had to do a balancing act between firm resistance to keep the angry cutthroat from lethal limbs that guarded his hideout and also allowing enough freedom of play to avoid snapping a 4X leader, the largest we used. Often the fish won, providing an element of surprise and sport to our intrusive behavior. When we emerged victorious the cutthroat was normally 20 or more inches and brightly colored despite the lightly-shaded nature of the streambed. We'd often pull over along this penultimate stretch to work all of the holding spots. We'd pass an hour doing this before heading down to the confluence with the Middle Fork.

We alternated on each trip for the first river stretch between rowing and fishing because where McDonald Creek mixed its waters with those of the Middle Fork produced a boiling seam of perhaps 200 yards loaded with cutthroat and rainbows, often over 20 inches. The first cast of a #12 Wulff or a #6 Sofa Pillow slightly ahead and to the north bank always turned several large trout. The rush of seeing 15 to 20 pounds of fish flying to the fly was enormous. Once hooked, the trout would all dive and head downstream before turning sideways in the strong flow and sending angry shudderings up the line. Whoever was rowing pushed hard against the current and worked to quieter water on the shore opposite Glacier Park. The fish would be brought to net, truly appreciated, released, and then gear was realigned, the raft moved out to the current and the process repeated three, perhaps four times on a good day. My friend once estimated that we'd take between 12 and 15 pounds of trout in those 20 minutes or so.

From here down to our takeout at the Blankenship Bridge, the Middle Fork offered every type of water we could desire – deep pools of more than 20 feet, quick runs, bankside eddies nestled against timbered and grassy banks, graveled drop-offs, and shallow runs that held tailing trout that were easy prey for our Hare's Ear nymphs. Most of the trout were in the 10- to 14-inch range, but a 20-inch fish would surprise a Joe's Hopper drifting quietly over a cool, deep run. Some of the river traveled through narrow gorges, the color of the water the bluest sapphire and very deep. We could see enormous trout holding far down among the gravel, stone, and boulders. Some had to be over 20 pounds and were most likely bull trout waiting to make their autumn spawning run up into remote tributaries of the North Fork. High water marks lined the grey rock 15 feet or more above us, telling tales of ferocious spring runoff. Dead lodgepole pine were wrecked and wedged into the rock and forest well above us. These corridors were magnificent and awe inspiring like some type of natural world cathedral where our silence and respect was not asked for but subliminally demanded. We rarely took trout here, because we rarely cast a line in these small canyons. We'd just drift and stare.

The last quarter mile was a fast, rapids rush to the takeout, water that most anglers thought was fishless, but we'd learned differently over the years and by accident. I was looking to the landing and dragging a Yellow Humpy up against a gravel, sand, and stone bank that was collapsing from the rushing water as we past when suddenly my rod was nearly jerked into the river and a good-sized rainbow leaped over and over downstream. We steadied in the large pool formed by the merger of the Middle Fork with the North Fork and brought the fish to net. Stunned, we weighed it on our Chatillon scale – 3.2 pounds. From that point on we always hammered the bank with rapid fire casts, taking one, two, three trout.

From there we would float towards a sandy beach, unload our gear, heft the raft onto the truck, and sip cold drinks until we were ready to run up to Apgar to fetch the other truck. Every time I float this stretch of water the experience is good.

Over the years, but not as much now as then, one of the simpler pleasures of wandering around Montana fishing my way through the seasons and good country is after a long, often hot, day of maybe catching some trout, I finally pull up to a local bar. Not the ones with the plastic, suicide-inducing atmosphere of those homogenous atrocities found at major motels, the ones with some hapless bar band staggering listlessly through a tragic cover of *Proud Mary*. No, not those places. The bars I like are filled with ranchers, area residents, local crazies, and even a flyfisherman or two. These establishments usually have a juke box with ancient country music, a 12-pound brown trout (or in one case an 18-pound, slightly-singed dolphin minus fins) mounted on the wall, a fish that was caught sometime before Lewis and Clark passed through the state, enough mounted deer, antelope, and elk heads to make the place seem packed when it isn't, and maybe there's the chance to order some decent food. I like these places – the ones where the fishing information is often spurious at best. Along the lines of, "Hell yes I know a good spot. Take a left on Spurgin Road just out of town. After eight miles take that two-track running off towards Benders Bluff for 347 miles until to see the river. You can't miss it. Lots of good water up that way and plenty of fish. Big ones and no people." The truth usually boils down to a muddy trickle and no people, but what the hell?

With that in mind here are six bars that come quickly to mind out of dozens of good ones. Most of these take credit cards. They all take cash, even Canadian currency. The list runs from the northwest corner of Montana out to the high plains of Livingston where I live.

These first two work well not only for the Middle Fork, but also the Swan River and the Mission Mountains. Point of Rocks is at mile marker 154 on Hwy 93 halfway between Eureka and Whitefish. Whether you're coming back from fishing the Elk River in Fernie, B.C. or working the many small mountain streams in the Whitefish Range, this is worth the stop. A semi-rustic structure is set beneath tall pine and larch. There's a good selection of beers, some wines, and the drinks are reasonable and robust. The food isn't bad either. One evening a friend and I stopped in after catching a few bull trout and westslope cutthroat. We had some bourbon ditches at the bar, then went upstairs and ordered rib eye steaks. They were so good we ordered two more and some more drinks and two more. Great meal at a nice place, though we were a bit full at the end of the proceedings. Phone: 406-881-2752. U.S. Hwy 93, PO Box 66, Olney, MT 59927.

Down in my old hometown of Whitefish there is the Great Northern Bar & Grill. This one is centrally located with several other bars within walking distance, as in across the street. The bar is comfortable, the drinks are good, there are 15 micro brews on tap and the food isn't too bad – barbecue, seafood, Italian, Mexican, burgers, steaks. Four nights a week there's real rock and roll which attracts the local wildlife as it did when I used to stroll in. I remember many great days of floating either the North, South, Middle, or main stem of the Flathead River or fishing in Glacier Park, and catching lots of rainbows and cutts, then spending time in the Northern sipping a few drinks with friends before drifting over to the Palace bar for some more fun. Phone: 406-862-2816. 27 Central Avenue, Whitefish, MT 59937.

Two-and-a-half hours down the road is Missoula, the town many fly into when heading north to the Flathead Valley. This is the scene of much of my misspent college career. There is an abundance of fishing in the area – Rock Creek, the Clark Fork, and the Bitterroot to name a few. If you have some hours to kill before driving or flying north, strike out for the Oxford Bar & Café. This venerable, 100-year-old institution serves good, basic drinks, beer and a bit of wine. There's a café, billiards, poker and keno. I've spent many an evening here knocking off shots of whiskey with beer chasers and having a burger or two. Bankers, loggers, stock brokers, town derelicts, college students, and senators show up. Years ago I wrote a poem about a twisted day in the valley that ended this way: "When the music stopped, we climbed in a pickup for the ride back to town. Four wheel drive this time and over the top of a Cadillac, its roof now crushed down. We kept going to a bar that was late and fluorescent bright. Scrambled eggs and fried brains, shots of whiskey and another rodeo down the drain." I actually sold this sucker and that's the Oxford. Phone: 406-549-0117. 337 North Higgins, Missoula, MT 59802.

I can think of many more, but space mercifully precludes my prattling on, still there is the Mint here in Livingston, the Mint in White Sulphur Springs and the Mint down in Sheridan, Wyoming and the ...

That's some of the personality that I associate with the Middle Fork, though there are several others, all of them worth getting to know a little bit and each mood and facet of this river is as intriguing, devilish, and illusory as the next. While the tour rafting companies may hammer the river during the warm weather months, the struggle to avoid these venal clowns is worth the effort. Like all fine rivers, the Middle Fork is too tough to be destroyed, even by venal rafting outfits who consider the river their cash cow.

TRIP INFORMATION

Timing: Runoff is usually in force by Glacier's opening day and this often lasts into the first part of July. From then on the water is excellent.

Where: From West Glacier, US 2 follows the river up to where Bear Creek enters, then trails follow the river to its headwaters in both the Bob Marshall and Great Bear Wilderness. To reach McDonald Creek, enter Yellowstone Park at West Glacier and drive the few miles to Apgar Village.

Bonus Feature: All three forks of the Flathead River are beautiful rivers, good fishing (especially in the Bob Marshall Wilderness Area for the Middle and South Forks). I've had some intriguing days on the South Fork, including late summer 2009 when my brother-in-law and I caught numerous westslope cutthroat to 17 inches on dries that included Elk Hairs and Humpies, and this was right near a campground. The fishing farther up and away from a Kelly-humped (blocked by dirt and rock berm) logging road has always been fantastic. With this in mind I include the following:

Nearly 40 years ago, I backpacked far into the 1,000,000-acre Bob Marshall Wilderness in northwest Montana. My destination was the South Fork of the Flathead River. I put myself through the arcane torture of lugging a 60-pound pack because I had heard rumors that the river was filled with native westslope cutthroat trout that ran to several pounds and pounced on any dry fly tossed their way. It took me four days to reach the river and once I'd caught my breath, I rigged up an old Fenwick red glass 6-weight with #12 Royal Coachman. This was the height of my angling sophistication back then and things haven't progressed all that much to this day. I cast 30 feet out into the river and before the fly had drifted more than a foot an 18-inch trout slammed the pattern. I landed the fish, admired its beautiful coloring and jet-black spots, then released and cast again. Same thing. This went on cast after cast until dark and for the next two weeks I worked my way upriver fishing the main flow and numerous tributaries. The fishing was spectacular on a crystal clear river that flowed through open grassy flats, across wide gravel bars, or through thick pine forest. Mountain peaks spiked the sky everywhere.

That country and that water is still as good today as it was in the halcyon days of my youth. For those who would like to experience this without dragging a pack along, there is Spotted Bear Ranch. Located above Hungry Horse Reservoir 55 miles from the nearest highway, this respected, quality operation owned by Kirk Gentry offers wonderful wilderness horse pack and float flyfishing expeditions or there are lodge-based packages. And you will catch fish. The lodge is included in the books *Luxury Fishing Resorts* and *Fly Fishing North America*. The lodge and all cabins are rustic structures settled beneath a canopy of large pines. While rustic, they contain most modern amenities.

The following are condensed versions of two of the many possible itineraries.

This sample itinerary is one of several offered by Spotted Bear and was recognized by Orvis as "2001 Orvis Endorsed Expedition of the Year". All trips are limited to six to eight anglers. This one is five days and four nights.

> **Friday:** *Arrive in the Flathead Valley/Kalispell area at Glacier International Airport and spend the night at a local lodging facility.*
> **Saturday:** *Arrive at Spotted Bear Ranch between 8:00 and 9:00am. Have breakfast at the lodge. Those renting a car should plan on a 2.5 hour drive.*
> *A pre-arranged shuttle is also available at $80/person roundtrip. A 25-minute drive to the outfitters roost follows. Hit the trail around noon on horseback and arrive at the Black Bear area four to six hours later (8 to 10 miles). While camp is set up and dinner prepared there will be plenty of time for fishing.*
> **Sunday:** *After a camp breakfast, there is another four- to six-hour ride to Salmon Forks with more fishing in late afternoon and evening.*
> **Monday:** *Breakfast, then spend the day hiking and fishing along the South Fork, Big Salmon Lake or other small streams (Author's note: this is the area I backpacked into described at the head of this report.) Spend another night at this location.*
> **Tuesday:** *After breakfast the rafts are loaded. The day is spent float and wade fishing for 11 miles down to Hodag Creek. A large shore lunch is prepared along the way.*
> **Wednesday:** *Float and fish to the take-out point, approximately six miles. The pack staff meets the anglers with necessary stock for the two-mile ride (or you can hike) around the Gorge and back to Outfitters Roost. Drive back to lodge, clean up then have a western BBQ. After supper, head back to Kalispell.*
> **Thursday:** *Depart from Kalispell.*

In these five days, an angler will pass through some of the finest, unspoiled country in the lower 48 and catch a hell of a lot of cutts, and maybe even a bull trout in the process. On the several trips that I've made into the Bob Marshall, in addition to the fishing, I've seen elk, deer, moose, grizzly and black bears, coyotes, eagles, martens, and lots of grouse.

For those who would prefer to hang around the ranch with its comfortable, well-maintained cabins the following is a five-day/six-night sample, where you fish Monday through Friday.

Typically, you arrive at the lodge Sunday around 5:00pm in time for the evening meal. Guided activities are Monday through Friday with a Saturday morning departure.

Monday-Tuesday: *Your guide delivers a morning beverage to your private cabin at a pre-arranged time. Breakfast is served at 8:00am. A 10-mile float on the South Fork with a shore lunch concludes with hors d'oeuvres and dinner.*
Wednesday: *Walk/wade fish the main river or tributaries that include Cedar Creek, Forest Creek, Canyon Creek, Wounded Buck Creek or many others.*
Thursday: *Take a horseback ride or hike to Spotted Bear Lake to fish from a raft or float tube for cutthroat trout. The lake is 10 acres.*
Friday: *Fish favorite stretch of water or make arrangements with your guide to fish another stretch of the river.*

When I lived in the Whitefish area, I got to know this beautiful portion of the world quite well, so I would humbly suggest to your guide that you'd like to take a crack at the Spotted Bear River. The stream is gorgeous and fun and holds its own with other waters in the region.

There is an Orvis Fly Fishing Shop on the premises. From the standpoint of equipment I would recommend both hip and chest waders, a 5- or 6-weight rod with some guts for the main river, a 2- or 3- weight of less than eight feet for the creeks, and nine-foot leaders tapered to 3X or 4X with spools of 4X and 5X tippet material. A selection of attractor patterns, Elk Hairs, and perhaps some Sofa Pillows or Stimulators will cover most needs. Sunscreen and insect repellant should be included.

The ranch may be contacted at: Spotted Bear Ranch, 115 Lake Blaine Drive, Kalispell, 800-223-4333, www.spottedbear.com. They offer wild Montana at its best. And I'm not on the take with these guys. They don't even know I'm writing this or, for that matter, that I exist is my guess.

Hub: Whitefish, about 70 minutes northwest of Swan is the best hub for this river as it is for the Mission Mountains. Grouse Mountain is a bit pricey but has good rooms and dining facilities – 1205 US Highway 93 W, Whitefish, 406-862-3000, 1-800-321-8822. Central Avenue is filled with restaurants and bars including The Great Northern, Tupelo Grill, Truby's Wood Fired Pizza, Serrano's Mexican Restaurant and so on. Stumptown Anglers has everything needed to fish the Flathead's forks and other area waters – 5790 Highway 97 South, Whitefish, 877-906-9949, www.stumptownangler.com.

Appropriate Gear: The Middle Fork is windy at times and reasonably large water. Five- through 7-weights with either weight-forward or double-taper. Nine-foot leaders tapered to 4X. Hip or chest waders or wade wet in summer. Insect repellent and sunscreen.

Favorite Patterns: I've had luck with a Stimulator all through the year as well as Tan or Grey Elk Hair Caddis and attractors like Wulffs or Humpies. Hoppers work well in the warmer months. Buggers, Muddlers, sculpin patterns. Montana, Hare's Ear, Bitch Creek nymphs. I prefer weight to bead heads but that's purely selective on my part, a slight matter of the confidence factor surfacing in an addled brain.

Special Regulations: Open third Saturday in May through November 30. Closed to angling June 1 through August 31 within a 100-yard radius of the Bear Creek stream mouth. Extended whitefish season and catch-and-release for trout open December 1 to third Saturday in May with artificial lures only. Catch-and-release for cutthroat trout.

Montana/Glacier National Park boundary is the ordinary high water mark on the park side of the river.

Stimulator

Hook: 200R, sizes 6-10
Thread: Fire orange
Tail: Golden-brown elk hair
Rib: Copper or gold wire

Wing: Golden-brown elk hair
Thorax: Fire orange Antron
Hackle: Furnace

Abdomen: Blend of gold, ginger, amber, yellow goat with golden-brown Haretron. Palmer with blue dun hackle

Chapter Fourteen

Spring on the Blackfeet Rez

Spring Fishing on the Blackfeet Rez is:

The only truth is wind. Alberta Clipper cold. Chinook warm. Strong. Blustery. Often from the north. Always.

The fish are big. The fish are small. Not around. Surfing gale-generated waves. Hard to catch. Easy to catch. Schooled up by the hundreds, thousands. Rainbows. Cutts. Hybrid variations. Then gone again. Nowhere to be seen.

The weather always wins. The landscape is staggering. Surreal. Lonesome. It will snow. It will rain. The sun will blast down. Browning is depressing. East Glacier is a tourist ghost town even in July. Freight trains rumble over Marias Pass. Tiny nymphs work as well as large streamers.

After 25 years doing this early-season stuff, I've learned that I know next to nothing about the angling, the country, or the people that live here. I've always been an outsider despite childish pretensions otherwise, thinking I was a friend while being pimped for PR. That's how it goes. No big deal. The return my way has been fair. Money for stories or book chapters. Wild country. Huge fish. A touch of freedom. Unexplained visuals that spin around bluffs or race along ridges. Blue-light-glows arcing from the tops of buttes. Extraordinary howlings. Unusual footprints. The usual suspects.

I've caught trout over 10 pounds a few times on waters called Mission, Duck, Goose, Kipp, Twin. Brook. Cutthroat. Rainbow. Brown. Hybrid. A rogue bull.

But I don't know anything up this alien way. Alien to my soft, white mind. Rhythms, techniques, dictions all beyond me.

Summer. Autumn. A bit calmer, vaguely familiar, feeling safer.

Spring means hardball. All the juice turned loose after a dark winter's frozen dormancy. Moving along muddy two-tracks next to Cut Bank Creek. Opening, closing rusting barbed wire gates. Spending a ghostly night in an abandoned radar base barracks eating canned beef stew. Drinking whiskey. Smoking a lot of Camel straights. Listening to my fear creaking through twisted, corroded beams and rotted window frames. Even the pigeons don't spend the night in this place. Coyotes howl near daybreak, saying "Thank God" to the sunrise and looking left across the border into Alberta before catching a couple of big fish in a nearby creek. Whitetails running at my motion. Crop duster in his beater biplane just over my head, then landing on a red dust road in front of me. Eagles soaring with more grace higher up the sky, looking for rabbits, mice, voles.

Vicious winds tear down from the Front blowing everything ahead of their course. Russian thistle, clumps of sage brush, license plates, cigarette packs, beer cans, crop land, ball caps, large rips of plastic that used to masquerade as storm windows, all of this sucked along in a swirling wake of confused detritus.

The Blackfeet.

Yeah I know them. Quite well. You bet. Not at all. Never will. How could I?

Browning. Heart Butte. Blackfoot. Government housing. Abject poverty. A sense of humor that mocks me with no hope of entrance. Long-time tribal acquaintances seeing me as a means to an end. In the schools, on the streets, riding in cars – too much booze, too many drugs, just like everywhere, but way different on the Rez – poison taken to a badland nomadic death trip. High-plains wanderers fenced in by the inevitability of modern change. Happens to all of us, but true murder for these people.

The great American pastime crashing head on where the Front is obvious. Not running down buffalo and not looking for images in ice water or wandering after scapegoat seasons. Not a hack, movie-actor's wannabe film trip. A lot of green thunderbirds discarded and smashed along dusty roadsides. Dead men gasping with whitewashed education draining from torn ears that could not bank on truth. Reservations not honored around chinookville. Sliding along on fusel oil and ancient dreams. Kicked aside by forgotten collisions with rotted pickups. The breeze drinks it all bone dry.

And even with all these imagined memories and images rattling around in my head, I've always come back here in the spring. Ice-out April. Paradise May. Wet June. Mountains running madly. Green grasses waving ocean visions. Wildflowers exploding. Rafts of cloud racing the sky.

Waters here flow down from all over the place and wind up in different seas. Mountain streams from southeastern Glacier Park run into the Middle Fork of the Flathead and eventually the Pacific. The St. Mary drifts across the border into Alberta running north before turning to go way east to Hudson Bay. Cut Bank Creek, Milk River, and others slide off across the high plains to join the Missouri and eventually the Gulf of Mexico. Everything liquid swirling, foaming, rushing in all directions like the wind.

Magnificent in its isolation despite its desolation.

And the fish. The times of hundreds of rainbows cruising at my feet. Enormous, dark silhouettes of 20 pounds. Mouths whitely agape in sexual excitement or maybe eating nymphs. Crimsons, purples, silvers. Fluorescent. Life lit up like a natural Vegas strip. Trout obsessed with false spawn. An illusion of procreation that can't be met in closed systems. Enormous rainbows that blast off and blow up a 5-weight. Or dog

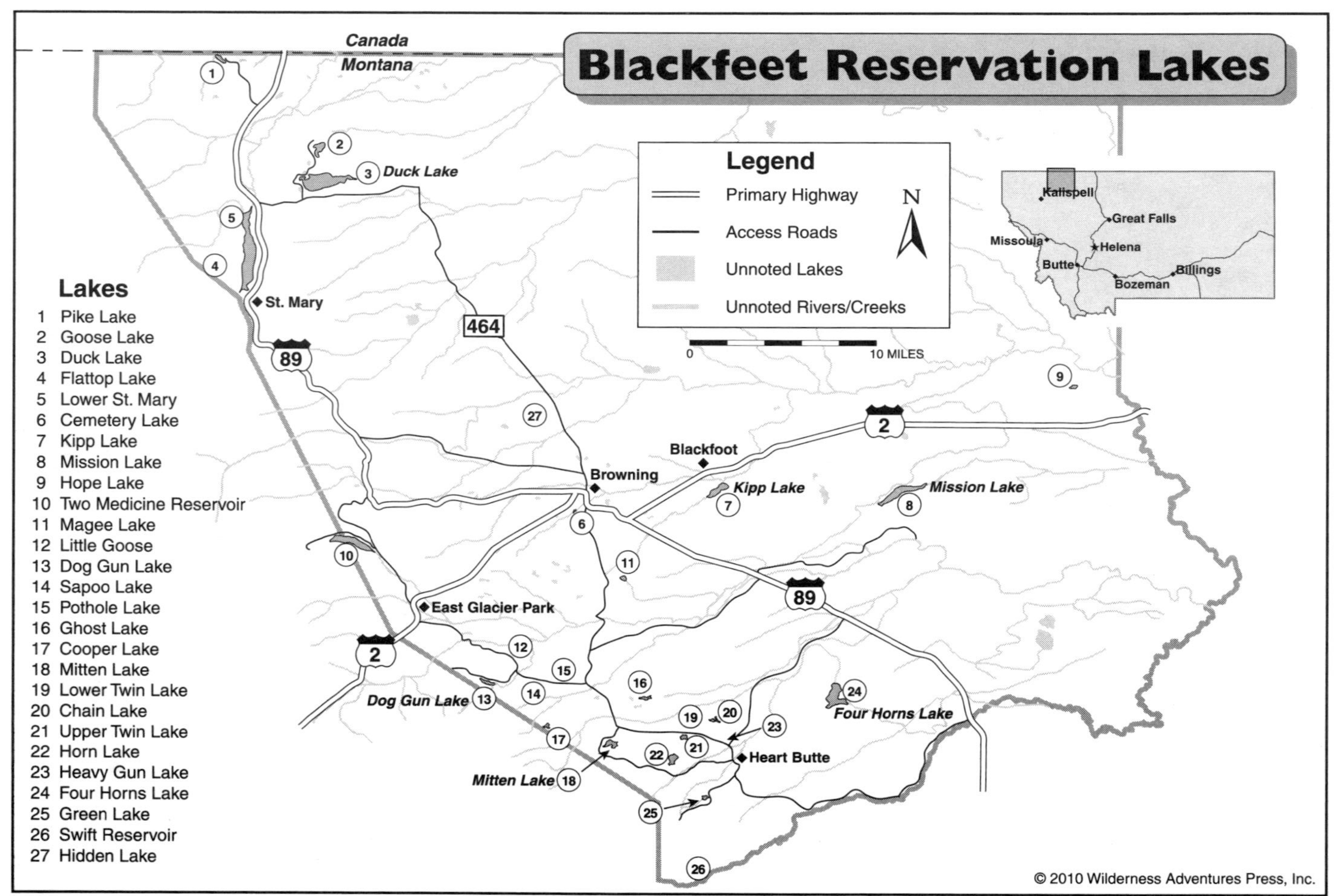
Blackfeet Reservation Lakes

Canada
Montana

Legend
Primary Highway
Access Roads
Unnoted Lakes
Unnoted Rivers/Creeks
N
0   10 MILES

Kalispell
Great Falls
Missoula
Helena
Butte
Bozeman
Billings

Duck Lake
St. Mary
464
89
2
27
Browning
Blackfoot
Kipp Lake
Mission Lake
Hope Lake
Two Medicine Reservoir
East Glacier Park
Dog Gun Lake
Mitten Lake
Four Horns Lake
Heart Butte
89
2

Lakes
1   Pike Lake
2   Goose Lake
3   Duck Lake
4   Flattop Lake
5   Lower St. Mary
6   Cemetery Lake
7   Kipp Lake
8   Mission Lake
9   Hope Lake
10 Two Medicine Reservoir
11 Magee Lake
12 Little Goose
13 Dog Gun Lake
14 Sapoo Lake
15 Pothole Lake
16 Ghost Lake
17 Cooper Lake
18 Mitten Lake
19 Lower Twin Lake
20 Chain Lake
21 Upper Twin Lake
22 Horn Lake
23 Heavy Gun Lake
24 Four Horns Lake
25 Green Lake
26 Swift Reservoir
27 Hidden Lake

a wind-cheating eight down deep until the game is up and the sullen fish is pulled defeated to shore. Only to be released. To pretend to breed some more. Metaphor for nothing.

I haven't been up to the Rez in a few years. I want to give the place one more shot to see if good memories, high times from my Flathead Valley days remained. Does any of the crazed, somewhat demoralized magic remain or have I hammered through too many years and too many arcane mistakes to see anything up this way?

Was any of the illusion left?

About 20 years ago I was fishing with Rich Landers, the outdoor editor of the *Spokesman Review*. We were out on a lonely, windswept pond on the eastern edge of the Blackfeet Reservation with our friend Joe Kipp. The water wasn't much to look at. Relatively shallow, grass, reeds, and brush dead brown in early April, a rancher's faded-blue pickup stuck in the mud nearby, telephone wires wailing in the wind. But on his third cast, Landers connected with the biggest rainbow-cutthroat hybrid I'd ever seen. The fish severely arced the 8-weight rod as it powered back and forth in the knee-deep water, last year's dead weeds piling up on the leader. Eventually Rich brought the exhausted fish to him where he held it with both hands just beneath the water's surface.

"Is this a good one, John?" he asked. "Seems pretty big."

"Yeah, Rich, it's a good one," I said thinking all the while, damn big fish. Seven, eight, nine pounds. Something like that.

We took pictures and then let it go. The trout swam off into the relative depths of the pond, leaving a huge wake as it disappeared.

A fine way to begin three days of fishing, except in those ensuing, wind-blown 60 hours we caught only three more trout. Three. Rainbows of two to four pounds. Nice, but something of a letdown after the riotous beginning.

That's Blackfeet Reservation fishing, too. A small piece of water can be packed with trout, big fat ones, but for whatever reasons – the weather, the time of day, their own capricious moods – they can play invisible, making a pond appear lifeless from an angling point of view.

And I've had times where an imitation damselfly dry has taken fish after fish on calm days near reeds growing out of sand and silt lake bottom. Hundreds of the real thing flitted and buzzed just above the mirrored surface of Dog Gun Lake while big trout bulged and broke the water nearby as I cast my gaudy forgery among them. Cruising rainbows up to six pounds sucked the thing in. Big hard-silver fish with luminous red bands and diaphanous waves Prussian blue along their backs. After an hour my arm was tired, the damsel pattern was a shredded blue mess and all seemed right in the world.

Or there is always casting nymphs onto the receding ice in late April with Chief Mountain standing alone in the eerie light of a spring sunset, a serious presence of sacred proportions. The weighted pattern clicks on the rotting ice as I drag it slowly towards the water. It drops over the edge and before sinking six inches, the

Gold-ribbed Hare's Ear is tagged by a rainbow that has been following the sound of the nymph from beneath the frozen crust of Duck Lake. The trout key to the sounds of bugs skittering and bouncing on the ice in the warming air of a new season.

In the shallow bays on the eastern side of Duck Lake, I've sight-fished for large rainbows using a orange-pink scud on 4X (way too thin to hold the big ones) and cast 50, 60 feet ahead with a 6-weight in the still air of a new day. The fly is visible drifting down through the water that is as clear as air, atmosphere that holds thick, heavy rainbows that storm the scud with white open mouths. Set the hook, hold on as the reel whines and sometimes the trout are checked, sometimes they pop the tippet with a sharp "ping." Tie on a new scud and cast again. There's no shortage of salmonid targets up from the chill depths feeding and participating in the false spawning act driven by internal drives in a closed system that doesn't provide inlet or outlet streams and vital spawning gravels. Illusion everywhere in this country.

A take-what-comes-your-way attitude works best here and, I guess, anywhere else.

Summer fishing on the Blackfeet Rez is:

Dead calm. Really hot. One-hundred-and-five degrees and a hotter wind with relations in the Sahara. Flies buzzing around your head. Sometimes cruising fish sipping mayflies. Slashing wayfaring grasshoppers. Splashing after electric blue damsel flies. Thunderstorms crashing out onto the plains. Black, dark blue boiling crazy then racing off east towards Conrad or Galata. Star-packed deep purple skies. Full moons hanging on illusion. Coyotes tagging along for the mirror ride.

Over southeast in Blackfeet Country where the land is even more spread out and lonesome tricks are played. Rolling magically upwards with my foot off the accelerator on a stretch of road my friends and I named "Zero Gravity Hill" years ago. Still more illusion in country driven by tilted horizon. I marvel at a ridge of cloud that stretches far into Canada and well to the south of Augusta behind me. The wall of moisture spins back on itself as it is torn between the updraft of the Front and a desire to roll on eastward across the high plains towards the Dakotas. I watch all this while keeping an eye on the highway largely empty of traffic today except for a random semi or pickup. I turn left on a lesser paved road, then right on another. Within a few miles I cut left on a dirt road that winds up into the foothills and mountains. A beautiful, familiar and sometimes-fished stream sparkles alongside the serpentine, now rutted road as I drift through aspen only beginning to leaf out and through dense stands of old pine that are intense green with a new year's exuberance. The creek is flowing at a perfect level, its flow not yet marred by the riotous gushings of snow-melt and heavy spring rains. Caddis rise off the surface in the warming air. Clumsy, whirring flight unlike the delicate liftings of mayflies or the workmanlike efforts of stoneflies. A few rise forms mark the surface of long deep glides. This is one of the prettiest streams I've ever fished. Eagles, grizzly, elk, deer, moose, badger, marten, mountain chickadees, swallowtail butterflies later, and a few trout, mostly around a foot long, live in this drainage that seems to be little changed over the past 50 years. I always catch westslope cutthroat trout here on Elk Hairs and Royal Wulffs and Humpies with a light 4-weight and a slight tippet. Maybe a Hare's Ear nymph down below. The biggest was taken a half-dozen years back. Sixteen inches and a leaper. A cutthroat rarity. If the fish only ran to four inches I'd still hold this water, this undeveloped valley and canyon, close. A perfect place or nearly so, and that's enough these days.

In land like this, memories ride in like young bucks returning from a rite of passage in some far away enemy territory, maybe down Mexico way raising hell with Apache or N'de. Knowing what's seen, the visual side of things on the rez can be confusing until you reach a point where you say, "The hell with it" and sail away on the image stream. I've spent time here and many other places on the improbable landscape or maybe dreamscape that is the rez with Joe Kipp. When we both drank,

we used to bump along two-tracks or roll cross country with the pickups trailing dust and the clatter of empty Budweiser cans in the metal bed marking our progress. Joe's shown me a lot, certainly more than I can absorb or ever understand. He's a good guy, making a solid go of it in tough country.

I drop down what's left of a rocky track and park out of sight beneath a thick copse of aspen. Pull on hip waders. Assemble a rod with a #16 Wulff at the tip. At the edge of the stream I stand and watch as a bunch of trout rise to caddis that are close to the size of the bug on my line. The trout work steadily in splashing, carefree takes that is this species' trademark. The hell with death. There's food about. Line is stripped off the reel. A quick cast below the fish to measure distance and then a quartering shot above the cutthroat holding lowest in the chain. A nice drift on the inside edge of

the current seam and a take. A quick struggle and a 10-inch westslope – bright, black spotted, orange-red slashes below the jaw. Released, it shoots for cover below its kind 30 feet away. Another cast. Another trout. Thirteen inches. Maybe. Same coloring. Nice. Working upstream to runs, glides, deep pools. Always fish. As good or better than remembered. In shallow riffles, I shift to the nymph and take cutthroat running about 14 inches that are nosing the small gravels dredging caddis pupae.

In a few hours I look and see that I'm well above the canyon that marks the entrance into the mountains. Through the narrow view upstream snow-covered peaks glisten as snow begins to melt in the afternoon warmth. The sky is blue shading to silver-white in the hot light. A pair of redtails works a ridge on my right. Sharp cries slice the stillness and mix with the talking water. Bending down on my knees, I drop my mouth to the surface and drink the water that tastes of snow, gravel, and tannin. The walk back takes awhile but seems like nothing. Tossing the gear in the back of the Suburban, I open the cooler, grab a beer, light a cigar, and enjoy what's left of the light. I'll find a motel room – TV, lousy pizza, neon, slamming car doors, whiskey, little sleep – in the dark, in Cut Bank. Later.

This day's been good. Tomorrow. Who knows? Maybe a lake or two. Possibly another stream like this one. The rez has more than one. A couple more days alone. Ideal after a bad trip earlier this month, one riddled with commercialism and too much booze, melancholy. All this will be pleasant, peaceful, but honestly now after a couple of decades of lying to myself, despite the fantastic country and the fish and all of this, the rez is largely a sad experience. That's my problem, but a real one. Poverty. Hopelessness. Future oil and gas development. Guiding hucksterism. As a late friend used to say, "It's all going or gone." Feels that way here. Hopefully I'm wrong. The gut says I'm not. But then…

…out where it's empty, wind talks. Rain is an uncommon friend. There are some strange people blown away by the electric hum of nothing, running small stores, growing weeds in the dust. Real drunk. Linked together by the white light express that ties all of us in a twisted knot. Mountains blast out of nowhere, screaming in the sky. Large creatures wander fearless disrupting the current with their curious buzz. Snow and ice sweep down. Cattle freeze. Minds vanish. The beating moves in constant time and is hard to disguise, but the trick to this is to skip off to oblivion and enjoy the view.

Yeah it's weird and sad up here, and I'll always feel like a stranger, but the land is beyond believing and the fishing can be great, so in a decade or so when I'm well into my 60s, I'll more than likely wander back here in the spring or maybe some late-summer afternoon much sooner than expected.

Fishing on the Blackfeet Rez is:

False expectations. Enormous fish that come and go like the wind. St. Elmo's Fire racing around buttes in the warm night. Unreal visions within the land flickering truth. A world not quite familiar.

Trout insanity.

TRIP INFORMATION

Timing: Ice-out in late April, depending on the winter and spring weather, is by far the best time for really large rainbows that are up in the shallows going through their false spawning ritual. Various hatches like *callibaetis* in warm weather can trigger the big trout and early fall is a fine time with clear skies and cooler temperatures. The wind can and often does blow hard any time of the year. Lakes open all year. Streams open third Saturday in May through November 30.

Where: The Blackfeet Reservation is bisected by U.S. Highway 2 in northwestern Montana. It is about two hours from Great Falls to the east, southeast and about the same distance from Kalispell in the west.

Hub: Cut Bank is on the eastern edge of the reservation on Highway 2. Browning is the main town on the rez, located on Highway 2 about 15 minutes east of East Glacier on the edge of Glacier National Park. The Corner Motel is reasonable and pleasant – 1201 East Main Street, Cut Bank, 406-873-5588, 800-851-5541. A very good outfitter for fishing (also bird and big game hunting) on the Blackfeet Reservation is Morning Star Outfitters run by Joe and Kathy Kipp. Joe knows the ins and outs of this country better than anyone. P.O. Box 968, Browning, 406-338-2785. A good place to eat is on the west side of the rez, called the Summit Station. Great views. Good food. Summit Station is located on Highway 2 at Marias Pass, 10 miles west of East Glacier Park, 406-226-9171.

Appropriate Gear: The water in the lakes and streams is cold, so chest waders are recommended. Rods of eight-foot-six, 5-weight and up are needed for the big water and the wind. Maybe 3- or 4-weights for the streams.

Favorite Patterns: Scuds, Hare's Ears, Woolly Buggers, BWO, hoppers, beetles, ants, Callibaetis Sparkle Dun, Pheasant Tail, damselfly imitations, CDC Comparadun.

Special regulations: You'll need a Blackfeet tribal fishing permit. Permit types and fees: Daily Fishing Permit – $20 (valid for purchase day only); Three Day Fishing Permit – $30 (valid for three consecutive days only); Season Fishing Permit – $65 (valid April 1-March 31). Blackfeet Fish and Wildlife, contact: info@ blackfeetfishandwildlife.com. 406-338-7207.

Callibaetis Emerger

Hook: 1X Fine wire, standard shank, turned-down eye; like a TMC 100; sizes 12-18

Thread: Gray
Tail: Tan or light gray Z-lon or hen hackle tip cut with v-notch at rear

Body: Gray or tan turkey biot
Thorax: Gray rabbit
Wing: Tan deer hair
Hackle: Grizzly

Damselfly Dry

Hook: 2X-long dry fly hook, sizes 12 to 8
Thread: Gray 8/0
Abdomen: Micro chenille in a color to match the natural insect

Thorax: D-fly dubbing in a color to match the abdomen
Thorax covering: Closed-cell foam in a color to match the thorax dubbing

Wings: Flashabou and two gray cock neck feathers
Legs: Black deer hair

CHAPTER FIFTEEN

Marias River

After too many years venerating too many bad habits, the simple process of knowing where I am during any given moment of linear time is often an intriguing mystery. Right now crystal clear water, only slightly cool, drifts over gold and copper rocks and pebbles. A warm breeze puffs along between tall, bone dry grey and ochre cliffs and bluffs. The moving air rustling the intense green leaves of tall trees, bushes, and grasses. I mean this could be a wide bend in the Rio Grande or even a saltwater flat along some backcountry island in the gulf. But I'm pretty sure it isn't. The Montana State Highway Map shows this to be the Marias River, about a mile below the Tiber Dam that is holding back huge Lake Elwell. Again, this setting reminds me of Mexico but the map says the towns of Lothair and Chester along U.S. 2 and the Hi-Line are only a few air miles north. A line a bit farther up the map, about two inches, says Canada. Even in my addled state, the surety that Mexico is way down south someplace and not here rises to the surface, much like the fish that are casually working ahead of me in a thin run of nearly invisible water.

Adding to the confusion is this sight fishing for these two- to three-pound silvery fish that are schooled up and working the shallow riffles and slightly deeper dips in the gravels. Hundreds of them. Could this be a bonefish flat someplace off of Belize? Looks similar. They race to take my fly, an adroitly-tied Elk Hair Caddis.

I launch another frozen rope effort into the wind. The fly skips sideways on the surface and then two of the bright, shining fish race towards the bug from equidistant locations. They collide head-on with a soft thump, then dizzily retreat while a third one nabs the drenched pattern. I set the hook, the fish thrashes the surface in a silver dazzle highlighted by hard sunlight, then runs downstream, creates some more wet racket before turning on its side. I retrieve line as I slosh down to it, bend over and admire its 18 inches of length and couple of pounds of silvery, scaled flanks before turning the fish loose with a quick twist of the hook. A Rocky Mountain whitefish. Gorgeous, as it flashes away across the river that shimmers the blue of the sky. A native unlike the revered and respected interloping browns, rainbows, and brook trout. Whitefish. Scorned by most artful anglers as they wander most of the state's rivers in numbers that exceed these classy salmonid species by seven, even eight, to one.

I like whitefish. Their eagerness to take a fly. The fact that they're natives like grayling, red bands, and bull trout. Their lack of popularity with the flyfishing artistes, and the way they taste after being smoked over cherry or hickory, cooled on ice, and served with pepper and lemon. Good fish, every one of them.

In a couple of hours I catch dozens of whitefish and every now and then a rainbow that sweeps up from the turquoise depths of a languid pool and out hustles the others for my fly. The rainbows leap across the surface scattering the schools of whitefish in little groups that quickly reform into the basic larger unit. The rainbows are not large, up to 15 inches, silvery with lots of black spots and muted crimson bands along their flanks.

The Marias River always grabs my attention as I wander back and forth, north and south around north central Montana for 125 miles before joining the Missouri River at Vimy Ridge near Loma. Back in June of 1805, the Lewis and Clark Expedition camped at the mouth of the river. Capt. Meriwether Lewis named the river in honor of his cousin Maria Wood – Maria's River. Over time the apostrophe faded into history and became Marias. The Blackfeet referred to the stream as "the river that scolds all others", the reason for this I've yet to discover. In 1806 Lewis, thinking that the river might be the main channel of the Missouri, and hoping that it would prove to be a viable waterway for commerce heading north, left the main party and went upstream as far as Cut Bank before giving up on his notion. In 1831, Fort Pigean, a trading post, was established at the mouth of the Marias by James Kipp for the American Fur Company. Kipp purchased 2,400 beaver pelts from Indians who came to his new fort. A year later, the post was abandoned, then razed by the Blackfeet.

Today the Marias has little to do with anything as it twists and turns beneath towering cliffs of sandstone or wanders lazily through immense fields of wheat or even canola. Red-tailed hawks, golden eagles, and turkey vultures soar high above, easily riding the thermals as they search for prey and carrion. Antelope, mule deer, white tails, fox, and even some beavers wander along the riverine corridor.

In July, with the sun cooking everything and the sky burned to a flat silver-white, this is hot country, often well over 100 degrees. Standing by a stretch of the river about 50 miles above Tiber Dam on such a day, a healthy wind blowing, it's hard not to sweat as dusty devil winds spin like maniac tops, bouncing among the swales or crashing into enormous cottonwoods. Looking out into a shallow stretch of the river, the blue water is roiled here and there by fat carp rooting around in the mud. I find a 5-weight rod in the back of a Suburban already rigged with a Hare's Ear nymph, so I launch casts above the feeding carp, drift the fly along the bottom of the stream and eventually into the mouth of one of the carp. I yank back, setting the hook, and the fish does nothing but continue turning rocks and silt until something trips in its brain that the current situation is not a good one. The 10-pound fish turns 180 degrees and powers downstream pulling line steadily from the reel. I try and check this run with no result. I try again with more force and the 4X tippet pops. Interesting. Strong fish. My carp fishing jones is now satisfied for another year or two.

I look back to the bank and spot a jackrabbit loping swiftly from the shelter of one clump of boulders to another. A rattlesnake lies comatose on a large slab of sandstone.

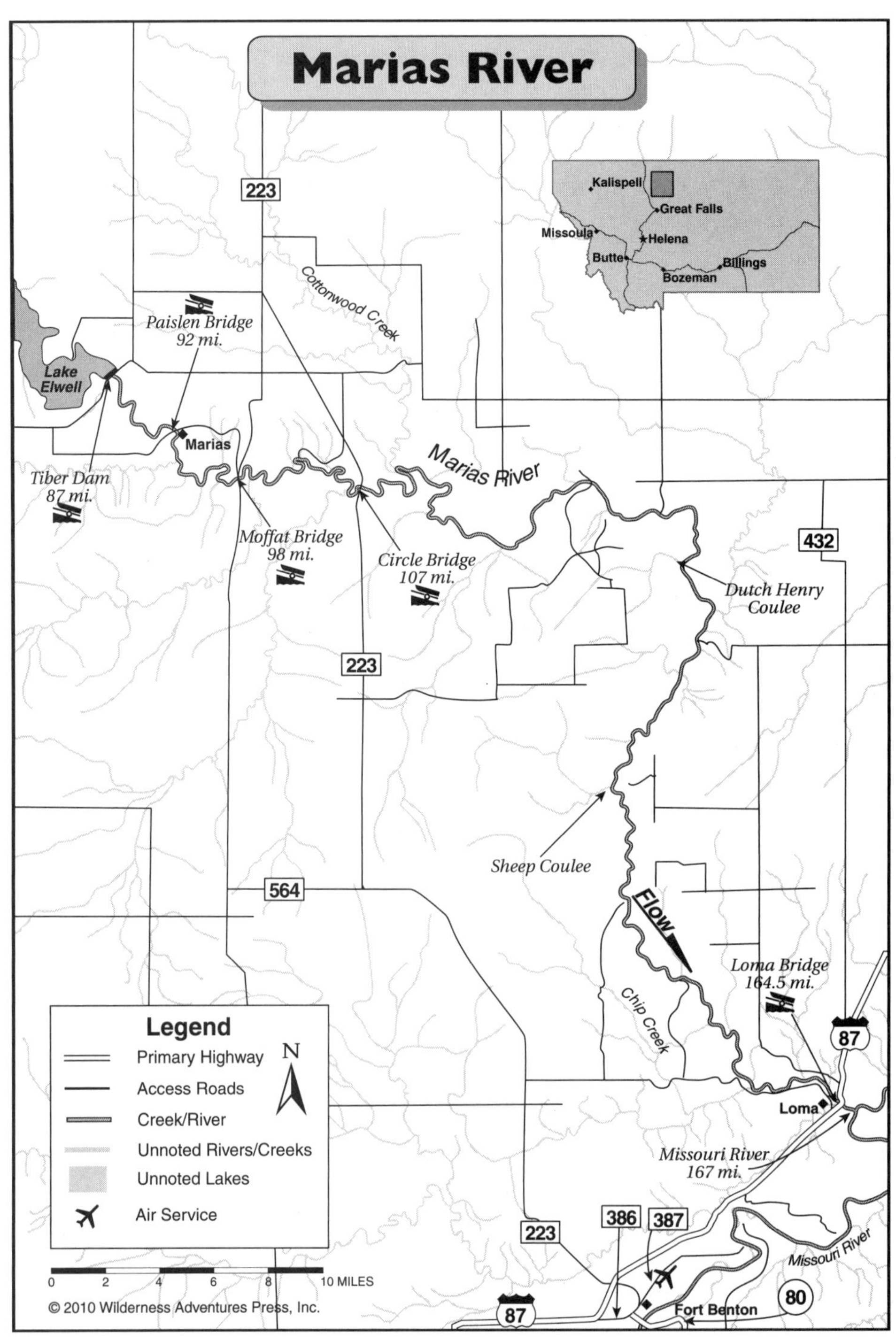
Marias River
223
Kalispell
Great Falls
Missoula
Helena
Butte
Billings
Bozeman
Cottonwood Creek
Paislen Bridge
92 mi.
Lake Elwell
Marias
Marias River
Tiber Dam
87 mi.
Moffat Bridge
98 mi.
Circle Bridge
107 mi.
432
Dutch Henry Coulee
223
Sheep Coulee
Flow
Loma Bridge
164.5 mi.
87
Chip Creek
564
Loma
Missouri River
167 mi.
Legend
N
Primary Highway
Access Roads
Creek/River
Unnoted Rivers/Creeks
Unnoted Lakes
Air Service
0   2   4   6   8   10 MILES
© 2010 Wilderness Adventures Press, Inc.
223
386
387
87
Fort Benton
80
Missouri River

Flies buzz around without any apparent enthusiasm for much of anything. The few mosquitoes that brave the breeze and try and suck my blood do so in a haphazard, listless fashion. I almost feel guilty when I swat them. About a half-mile away at the mouth of a ragged coulee that's clearly seen its share of flash floods, a band of antelope feed carelessly on native grasses. The buck rests on a slight slope above his harem, surveying his realm with natural indifference. This is peaceful country right now. Empty of humans. No planes or jets tear the sky overhead. The place is beautiful, serene but also a touch frightening in its lonesome isolation. I like that and I like the way the air shimmers from the heat that radiates from the tan bluffs and cliffs that define the coulee.

Good country here at the headwaters of the Marias about 30 minutes south of Cut Bank. Coming in from the south is the Two Medicine River laden with silt accumulated as it drifted through dry, clay-banked valleys and gorges. Flowing in from the northwest is Cut Bank Creek, the water clear and still cool. The two streams connect and flow double-banded downstream for hundreds of yards – milky brown on one side, dark and clear on the other. Eventually they mix, forming a turbid brown current that is the Marias. The river wanders through miles of fields, coulees, bluffs and cliffs before emptying into Lake Elwell, a massive reservoir covering thousands of acres. Brilliant turquoise water shimmers beneath sere sage hills and sandy rock outcroppings. Billions of gallons of water lying out in the middle of intense aridness. The place looks like Cabo down, once again, Mexico way.

Below Tiber Dam the water again runs clear and cool, cold in spring and fall. In the spring, large rainbows spawn in the clean gravels of the Marias, the well-oxygenated water providing perfect habitat for the incubating eggs and emerging fry. Come autumn, big browns move from their deep-water pocket pool downstream holding water. They run up into these gravels and build numerous enormous redds. Irregularly-shaped areas that the fish have cleared of all debris and silt with vigorous flappings and shiverings of their tails.

For the big-fish trout hunter, these two times of the season are significant. Anyone willing to brave the often wickedly cold, brutal winds that drive glass-like sleet and snow into the skin, anyone willing to cast weighted streamers like Marabou Muddlers and Woolly Buggers into the teeth of a sometimes, most times, gale has a legitimate opportunity to connect with a rainbow or brown of several pounds. The fish are aggressive at these times of breeding and fight like hell. Because the trout are approaching spawning velocity, I make a concerted effort at playing them quickly, before carefully releasing them to try and ensure their survival. And the following reveals some of my not always politically correct thoughts concerning the high art of catch-and-release.

Not large as brown trout go in this central Montana river. Perhaps 14 inches and plump. Perfect for the cast iron skillet tonight back at camp. So I grasped the fish around its belly and whacked its head on a streamside rock, the sound of the killing blow sounding like a muted "thwack" of a baseball bat making contact with a fastball grooved right down the pipe. The brown quivered spasmodically in my hand for brief seconds, then stilled, the body lifeless, bright yellow and walnut hues already starting to fade, eyes glazed in death.

My friend watched the scene and asked, "Why'd you kill it instead of putting it in the creel?"

"Ends the suffering and killing them this way preserves the flavor," and I placed the brown in an old wicker creel I had. "When they flop around and die slowly, lactic acid builds in the muscle tissues and sours the flesh. Sour meat isn't to my liking."

This friend and I had broken into the daily newspaper game long years ago and during his stretch as one of this country's last real newsmen, he'd covered the cops for a paper in Vegas, so he'd pretty much seen it all. Still, when I looked up at him I noticed a look of something approaching pained perplexity.

"What gives, man?"

"Hell Holt, I'm a Pollack. We live on meat," and he laughed as he drank his beer. "But it was almost like you enjoyed killing that brown…in a twisted way."

He'd nailed me and I had to think on that one for a bit. When catch-and-release fishing – the sometimes artful fooling of a fish with a fly and a skillful presentation, the playing of that fish and then its careful release back to its watery environment – first came into vogue over 20 years ago, I was all for it. I was in favor of anything that preserved and even enhanced any fishery. I went for almost five years without killing anything. Trout, bass, even carp, escaped the frying pan. I stopped hunting sharp-tailed grouse in the coulee-and-bluff country of southeastern Montana, land that I care for more than myself. And I preached the gospel according to Barbless Hook at (not "to," "at") anyone within earshot.

Catch and release was the only way. Anyone killing fish for the pan or a trophy was a sub-normal barbarian in my narrow-focused eyes.

Time passed and I assiduously turned free thousands of fish that I briefly captured from the many glorious rivers in Montana and Alberta and from the lakes of the interior of Iceland and the musky waters of Wisconsin. I'd become a zealot. When the fight with a truly large sporting fish lasted 10 minutes or more I would carefully unhook the fish and then very slowly move it back and forth in calm water, hoping to infuse oxygen into its gills and then its bloodstream. When a given fish finally quivered back to some semblance of life and would then swim slowly away sinking into the dark depths of a river or lake to sulk, a feeling passed through me of having done the right thing. I felt like a fine and good man. A one-man cult called Holt.

As the pursuit of fish with a fly passed from being something looked upon by other anglers (bait, spin, and what-not) as a harmless and often futile eccentricity and on into the horrible realm of big business, full-tilt marketeering that it is today, one of the big hooks for the recently-monied, youthful arbitrageurs was that they could catch their fish and release them alive, too. That glorious 22-inch rainbow that leaped and crashed its way down the Beaverhead on a blustery October afternoon would live to fight again. And the catcher of that fish could go on for eons claiming that not only was he a skilled angler, but he was also a true sportsman. He released his fish. Killing wasn't his style. He wasn't a slob spinfisher who caught a mess of bluegills for the family dinner. Or way down the angling chain, a lowly, boorish baitfisher who resorted to loathsome worms impaled on a hook. These cretins were and are swine in the eyes of the flyfishing purist.

Well, bullshit. It's all baitfishing. What in the hell do people think a trout takes a #22 BWO for? Does a five-pound brown (and I've never fully comprehended why such large fish make such fools of themselves delicately sipping a bug that may provide all of one calorie of food value) think that the tiny mélange of dubbing, hackle, and thread is a work of art deserving detailed examination. No. That fish is after food. Nothing more. Nothing less.

Bait is bait whether its feathers and yarn, earthworms, or dough balls. Fish aren't in any of this for the sport, and while I'm at it, neither are most of the guides anymore.

Used to be they were largely a surly, drunken and/or hungover cantankerous lot who loved to fish almost as much as they loved to slug cheap bourbon and remain ever surely unfaithful to their wives or girlfriends (now some of them have boyfriends, but this is too complicated a subject to deal with here). The new millennium version of a guide claims to be a skilled fisheries biologist, entomologist, consummate outdoorsman, and God's gift to flyfishing. Every one of them, everyone, truly believes deep down in his venal heart, that guys like Lee Wulff and A.J. McClane were hacks. That they, the new millennium model know it all and can cast like Renoir painted. And they are dressed to prove it with gaudy electric blues, reds, and greens in shades with names I refuse to mention. And they are holier-than-thou when it comes to returning the fish you just caught, though they think nothing of floating over the same piece of holding water 100 times a year and catching the same beleaguered fish countless times, the hapless creature hook scarred and emaciated come autumn.

How does this connect with killing and catch-and-release? Simple. The concept of releasing a fish after it was fooled, played and then played out was and still is a good one. Keeping one, ten or a hundred fish a day destroys even the best fishery in no time. But guides are now in the meat market business. They make their bucks, sometimes big ones in tips, on their reputations of putting their clients (I love this term) onto large numbers of large fish.

I live near the Yellowstone River. I watch as the armada of skilled and unskilled guides drift the swells downstream day after day in season. When I walk the banks of the river near evening after this onslaught, I often notice dead or dying trout floating belly up in slowing circling eddies or calm places near shore. Ten-inch rainbows. Fifteen-inch cutthroat. Twenty-inch browns. Often with bleeding gills and hook scars.

Sure, some of the released fish live to fight another day, but not 90 percent. Try 50 percent or 30.

I've watched baitfishers over the years and most of them kill only enough fish for a good dinner, maybe six or eight. True, some slaughter dozens, but they're in a minority. Let's say one of the artful anglers and his more artful guide float a Montana river and take 50 trout – browns, rainbows, brooks, whatever – and release all of them and 90 percent live. Well, that means five of the poor suckers died. Five fish. That's an optimistic scenario. Possibly half of those trout went belly up. Twenty-five. Pretty simple math here.

And that barely gets to the soul of the matter. The attraction of fishing is visceral and primal, genetic from way back in our hunter gatherer days when meat brought home to the cave meant living to fight another day. Forget all this artsy-fartsy nonsense about "I fish to experience the land and all its wonders. I love to fully experience the riparian corridor." I feel the same way about good country, but when I cast a Joe's Hopper tight to a bank above a feeding brown I want to connect with that wild fish, feel the rush that comes from its all-out-fight for survival. Every trout I return to the river I want to kill, at least a little bit. I'm a predator and a meat eater, and I've got the teeth to prove it.

I'm with the Inuits and the Dene of the Yukon and Northwest Territories on this one, on how they feel about this matter. To catch fish and not kill and eat any of them is both disrespectful to the fish and dishonest to an individual's being. Catch-and-release does help maintain a fishery in some overworked waters and in these situations it has its place. But to go through an entire angling life without killing a fish, taking responsibility for that life and eating that fish is a horribly tame, insane approach to flyfishing – a juiceless, arrogant, frightened way to go about connecting with nature.

So several years ago, I finally realized that I was fishing more and enjoying it less (sounds like an old pitch line from a cigarette commercial). I decided to keep a few fish to eat each season. In part because they're good to eat and also to get back in touch with the life-and-death aspects of the sport. I now fish less than I used to but have regained the enjoyment I'd lost in my righteous days. And every time I kill a fish I experience a sense of awe bordering on fear about how serious even the fun aspects really are. The best of life puts me online with how transitory and insignificant all of what I do is. Killing a brown trout on the Musselshell River as the Crazy Mountains look down at me is a humbling, valuable experience.

When I looked up from the fish I'd just killed, my friend was bringing a decent brown to shore. Sixteen inches I guessed. He dropped to his knees in the water, thrashed around trying to grab the thrashing trout, and struggled with pulling the hook from the brown's jaw. Then, holding this fish, he paused before turning to a slab of rock next to him. He raised that brown to shoulder height, and I watched the sunlight sparkle on the fish's radiant flanks, and then with both hands he brought its head down on the stone.

I saw it shiver and die.

He turned to me and his eyes were alive with sadness, the thrill that comes from killing, and the beginnings of a new awareness about what fishing can really be about. Life and death on the river mirrors the dance we stagger through everywhere else. Ending the life of that one brown changed things for my friend.

"Holt, killing them instead of putting them back isn't the same thing, is it?"

"No, it isn't."

But enough of my idiocy. I'm having far too much fun being a hypocrite and bothering these eager whitefish. No matter where I cast, a fish or maybe six or seven race to the fly and lay waste to it. I try to cast well away from the groups and schools, allowing the Elk Hair to bob and weave its high way down the river, but the slightest twitch or merest surface disturbance created by drag brings the wild fish running and I'm forced to endure a riotous take, a sterling display of dancing silver, the energy of the whitefish pulsing up the line, through the rod, along my arm and into me. I know we have many miles of driving to do today, but I can't resist standing in this water, feeling the warm breeze funneling through the river canyon and casting and casting and casting on Maria's River.

TRIP INFORMATION

Timing: The best times for the 12 miles below the dam are from the opening of the regular season on the third Saturday in May into June for the rainbows, and then September into November for browns. Hopper action can be excellent in July and August. The laughing whitefish are especially eager during the low-water months of summer.

Where: Access to the river below the dam is gained by Hwy 223 south for about a dozen miles south from Chester then right/west at a clearly marked gravel road to the recreation area. There is an excellent campground along the river nestled beneath large cottonwoods.

Hub: Chester sits astride U.S. Highway 2 along Montana's Hi-Line, 57 miles west of Havre. Ginny and I have stayed at the Wheat Sheaf Motel. The place has nine rooms, each with a kitchenette, television, showers, and phone. There's a lounge and pets are allowed, 406-759-5300. There's also a service station nearby. Sporting goods, groceries, and other gear can be found in Havre including: Countryside Bagel Café, 335 1st Street, Suite C, 406-265-4435; Siesta Motel Inc. 600 1st Street, 406-265-5863; there's no fly shop but a K-Mart on Hwy 2 has some gear and so does Master Sports, 301 First Street, 406-265-4712.

Appropriate Gear: Five- to 7-weights, eight- to nine-foot rods help cover the wide water in places and fight the wind coupled with 7.5- to 9-foot leaders and tippet material to 5X, most often 4X. When the weather is cool and due to cold water flows from the dam, chest waders are in order most of the time or at least hip waders.

Favorite Patterns: My favorite hopper pattern is a Joe's Hopper. Looks good, floats well, and the more ragged it gets, the better it works. Woolly Buggers, Marabou Muddlers, attractors like Humpies and Wulffs, Prince nymphs, Gold-ribbed Hare's Ear nymphs, Elk Hair Caddis.

Special Regulations: Open entire year downstream from the Hwy 223 Bridge. Open third Saturday in May through November 30 unless otherwise specified in district.

Joe's Hopper

Hook: TMC 5212 Sizes 4 through 16

Thread: Black or dark brown

Body: Yellow wool or chenille

Tail: Red hackle fibers or deer hair

Wing: Two matched turkey quill sections

Ribbing: Brown hackle

Hackle: Brown and grizzly mixed

Chapter Sixteen

Ranch Ponds:

Cameron Lake – Sweetgrass Hills

The last of the light was going, drifting away with an orange-gold edge that crept lazily up the cone-shaped butte while silently pulling purple and steel blues behind as the sun dropped away behind the Rocky Mountain Front one hundred miles to the west. In windy land that always seems to be blowing somewhere, strangely, the air was flat calm and so was the surface of the small lake – no ragged waves whipped white by 80-mile-an-hour gusts roaring across the prairie and shooting up the draws. Though in this uncommon stillness the water was far from lifeless. Countless rainbows dimpled the surface. Little ones of six inches, medium ones, and here and there, large fish of several pounds or more. Sippings, splashing, and slurpings – the sounds of fish eating without a worry in the world. They were casually feeding on some small bug of mayfly dimensions, probably some mutant *callibaetis* sub-species spawned by the incredible isolation and stark raving loneliness of this place. The last of the summer's heat was dying a peaceful mid-September death out here above Montana's Hi-Line not far below the Alberta border. The Sweet Grass Hills – West, Middle, East and the slightly lesser entities of Mount Lebanon and Haystack Butte. Middle towered above us, casting a serious reflection on the still water. The evening was turning cool. The trout seemed to take no notice of this or the fading light show. They just kept sipping away making their liquid, crystalline sounds. Soft music swiftly sucked dry by the waves of tan grama and buffalo grass holding motionless. Miles and miles of the stuff languidly fading into autumn.

I launched a cast of about 70 feet out ahead of a rise made by a worthy trout and got lucky when it sucked down the fly, setting the hook in its voracious vehemence. Feeling the bite of the point galvanized the rainbow into a series of leaps towards the far shore, water spraying in sheets. The fish crashed across the lake, putting down everything in its path except for a group of mallards that lifted immediately into the air with beating wings and disturbed "quacks". They were out of sight over a near ridge in seconds, bound for quieter doings in some other puddle. A Sheep Creek Special – olive chenille, brown hackle and little more with a small spilt shot at the head – is cast out among working trout, or just out on the water, allowed to sink for five or six seconds, then retrieved with a series of two or three six-inch strips only to sink a little more before repeating the process. Often a rainbow slams the nymph on the way down or right at the beginning of the second set of strips. This pattern and method has worked for me on similar lakes throughout Montana and places as far away as the Yukon or even the interior of Iceland.

The fishing went like this until deep dark and I kept a few smaller ones for dinner. I liked the taste of trout sautéed in olive oil and butter with a handful of slivered almonds thrown in. Salt, pepper, and a squeeze of lime juice and that was that. Walking up the rise from the lake shore I looked up and saw the sky filled with stars hanging in three-dimensional relief against the blackness. A crescent moon was showing itself silvery as it rose west of the far away lights of the railroad town of Shelby. Coyotes howled in acknowledgment from the tops of flattened hills. Ginny and I cooked the fish in a pan on a Coleman stove. No fires here. Too dry and no wood to speak of, except for wiry tangles of sage. No trees out here in the huge openness.

There really wasn't anything special to this place. Nothing much to it. A trio of volcanic-shaped buttes, three towering cones, standing alone together out here like a miniature mountain range. Cameron Lake is representative, a classic example, of a ranch pond and/or northern high plains pothole lake or reservoir. There are other, similar places we have spent time in, like the Missouri Breaks a few hours away where BLM maps and a little nosing around can produce similar results and include a bass or two. A place where the river flows large and silent. Where elk the size of draft horses rise up out of brushy cuts in the land around sunset. Where thunder and lightning appear from all directions all at once out of nowhere and pound the land with such intensity that praying for survival seems the natural thing to do. We'd had times there where even bouncing and lurching across a bone-dry dirt two-track required four-wheel drive if we were to reach a little-known lake filled with voracious three-inch largemouth bass. And there was the morning in that country when we woke to the sound of a pick-up truck slamming on its brakes near camp. A government biologist was heading out to the field. We were pulling an Avon raft we'd used to float the Missouri below Fort Peck Dam and other lesser flows. The anomalous sight of the craft out here made the woman driver look once. Drive off. Stop. Look again. Repeat the sequence then roar off to a plague-infested prairie dog town. She obviously preferred studying the Black Death to possibly dealing with lunatic flyfishers ensconced in the middle of a desert. Or there are all those lakes along the Front over by Augusta filled with overweight browns and just-as-fat rainbows. We've caught plenty of those with the rocky reefs of the mountains holding silently in the background.

So where we were now is no big deal, even if a Canadian mining company eventually has its way and tears the gold out of the butte rising above the lake we just fished.

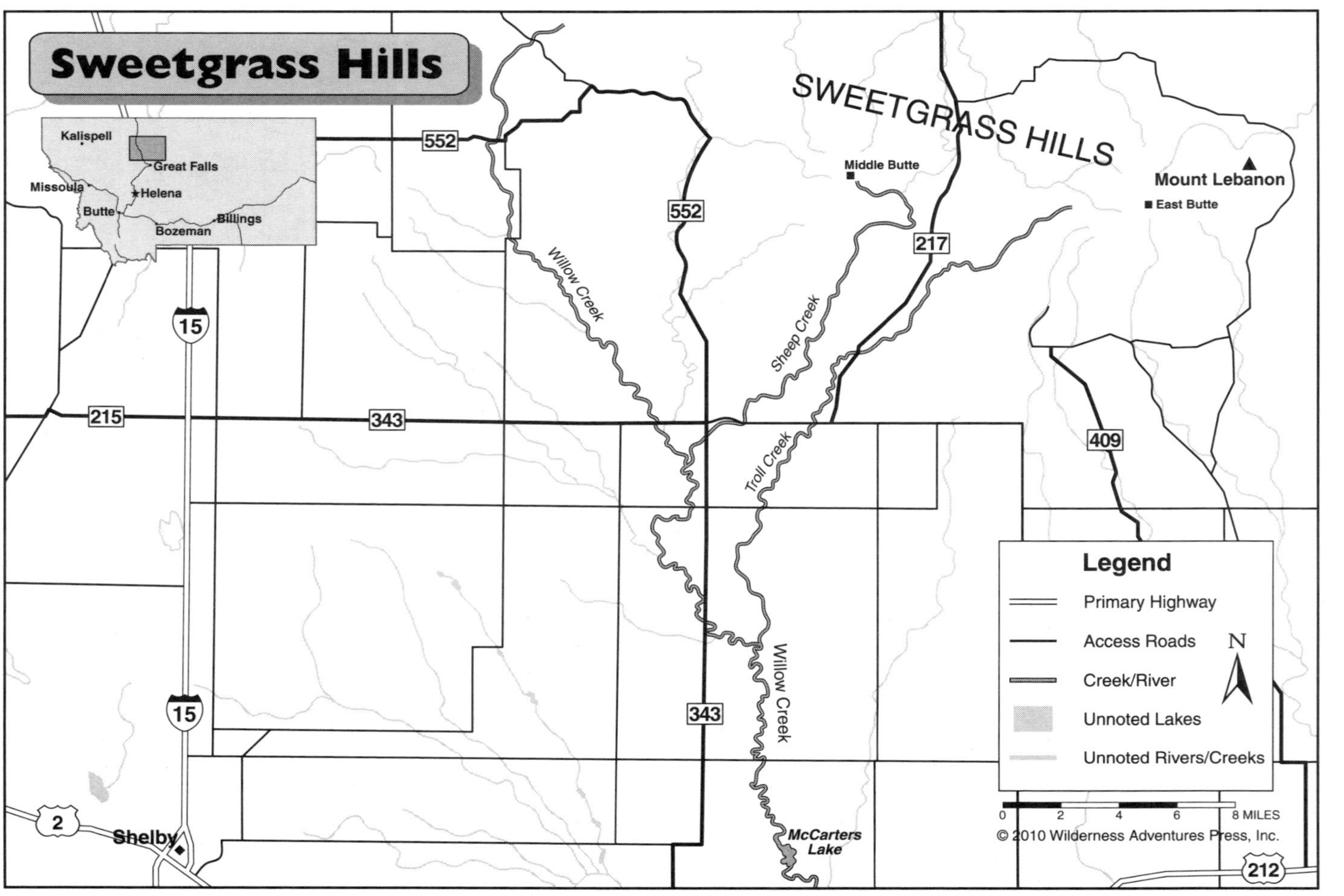
Sweetgrass Hills
SWEETGRASS HILLS
Kalispell
Great Falls
Missoula
Helena
Butte
Billings
Bozeman
Mount Lebanon
East Butte
Middle Butte
552
552
217
409
215
343
343
15
15
2
Shelby
Willow Creek
Sheep Creek
Troll Creek
Willow Creek
McCarters Lake
212
Legend
Primary Highway
Access Roads
Creek/River
Unnoted Lakes
Unnoted Rivers/Creeks
N
0   2   4   6   8 MILES
© 2010 Wilderness Adventures Press, Inc.

This lake is stocked with 4,000 rainbows of four to five inches each year and they grow very fast gorging on all of the insects, leeches, and so on in the fertile water. For being in the middle of nowhere, the place receives some attention, mainly from people living in and around Shelby. In 2007, days fished were given by the MFWP as 671, for a state rank of 305. Seems like a lot but compare this to 106,330 days fished on the stretch of the Madison River between Ennis Lake to Hebgen Dam, the number one location in Montana. The trout that make it through the first year and even into the third season are large, fat and strong, weighing several pounds.

We can go elsewhere and for that matter even come back here and catch these fish while we watch the butte being leveled with tons of explosives, and then see the blasted rock hauled away by a horde of massive earth-moving machines. It is all the same to us. As Annie Dillard said in an article for Harper's, "We arise from dirt and dwindle to dirt, and the might of the universe is arrayed against us."

After eating the rainbows, we stand in the star-bright darkness looking at the shadows we cast when far in the distance we spot headlights climbing and dipping, moving in our direction like a spastic searchlight. A car or truck is heading towards us on the only road in, a dusty job that wanders through wheat fields and range land. We watch as the car approaches. It stops every now and then to open and close a barbed-wire gate before moving ahead. Eventually we can hear the faint whine of its engine, the sound drifting unnaturally to us. The air is so clear up here that we can see ranch lights many miles away and the observed car's approach over a period of 30 minutes or so. We wonder if the vehicle is full of sex-crazed, carousing teenagers from nearby Sunburst or even worse, axe murderers looking for random victims like us. We've been random victims all our lives. In fact, we are quite good at it. I long for the .357 magnum I'd left on the kitchen table yesterday. Eventually the car, an old Japanese beater from the sounds of the muffler and the rotten exhaust smell, drives by us and stops nearby at the next gate in the road. We hear the muffled, bass booming of the sound system, not at all like the booming of night owls slicing through the air above us. Then the car backs up and turns around. "God. They're leaving," we think, but are wrong as usual. The car rolls by, pulls down to the water not far from us and stops.

All is quiet, even the car's music. Then the inside light flashes on and stays that way. Then goes off. Then on again. This continues for an hour or so. Ginny walks over to our rig and grabs a pair of binoculars. She creeps to within yards of the car and begins about spying on the car's occupants. I slip up behind her and take a look through the glasses. When the inside light goes on I could see a pair of guys, in their 20s, passing something back and forth. A cigarette lighter flickers on and off and clouds of smoke filled the interior. The image is so cloudy it looks like one of my photographs. This activity goes on well into the night. The moon, now a copper crescent, was dropping down towards the southeastern horizon. We finally give up and sneak back to camp reasonably assured that the two smokers of what obviously isn't pipe tobacco, a smell of something much more aromatic, herbal, reaches us on the slight evening breeze, aren't out this way to do us wrong.

"Well over 100 years of living between us and look at what we do for amusement," I laugh.

"It's pathetic, John," and we both laugh and then crawl into our cold sleeping bags. If the two in the car are indeed dope fiends, as a rule ruthless individuals every one of them, they are too well-tuned by now to bother us. If we have grievously slighted their character and they are merely axe murders, well, our lifeless, sightless heads will be looking out on wide, open Montana for eternity.

The intense light of a new day's sun flashing over the eastern hills wakes us. It is nippy out and there is frost on the ground, but at least our heads are still attached. Looking down to the lake, we notice that the car is gone and so are our un-met friends. Following a breakfast of thick Ethiopian coffee, Krusteez pancakes covered with butter and Vermont maple syrup, and some bananas, we head down to the water for a dip. Mid-morning and already 80 degrees. Another blown away gorgeous late-summer day. We strip and jump in the water. Definitely awake now. As we paddle around like confused springer spaniels, tiny trout nibble at the hairs on our bodies. I hope that the sun's intensity will keep much larger trout holding tight to the lake's bottom. After awhile we climb out and dry off in the warming air. Not a cloud in sight. Nothing. And then a small rise forms out in the middle. Little fish. Then more and more. Larger ripples. The wind is still a dead issue but the lake was dancing. Perhaps we'd chase the rainbows later, for now we prefer being voyeurs once again.

As time passes I find myself enjoying the straight-forward, relatively easy things in life more and more. Trying to clip the end off of my cigar without taking a piece of my index finger, pondering my choice in the presidential election (just determining that there was indeed the merest suggestion of a choice took weeks), or watching the Weather Channel as some slightly-crazed forecaster becomes apoplectic about the latest weather system off the west coast of Africa; all of this is great stuff, highly pleasurable and relatively risk free. But sometimes I need more. So rising rapidly to the top of this delightful list is ranch pond fishing. Twenty years ago I thought this was kids' stuff, not worthy of my articulate and very rugged angling attentions. What in the hell was the thrill in catching a bunch of dumb, planted rainbows, even if they're big, fat seven-pounders? Time changes most attitudes and casting to carefree fish casually cruising for damselflies and mayflies and orange garlic marshmallows now seems like a perfect way to spend an afternoon, an evening, or even a few months.

Perhaps 35 years ago when things concerning all things fishing were a little bit different, I had the opportunity to fish with a couple of senior gentlemen from the Hi-Line area and they took me to a pond of a rancher friend of theirs. Mid-October, clear, and as we pulled down a long, narrow dirt road in a battered Jeep Wagoneer, dust billowed in our wake while we bounced and lurched over ruts and rocks at about 50 mph. The high plains rolled off in all directions in their spectacular washed-out, sere, ochre dryness. Bands of antelope grazed warily in small coulees. Red-tailed hawks circled high above the sage- and grass-covered ridges. Jackrabbits bounded for cover. The ever-present wind of this country was strangely absent. The pond was perhaps 10 acres, deep and deep blue. Small beds of dying-back, dark green aquatic weeds ringed the shore.

The two guys unloaded a couple of five-gallon white buckets and old Fenwick red fiberglass fly rods with Pflueger reels (one of the best ever made). Two six-packs of Pabst and a pint of Kesslers also appeared along with a bag of chocolate, cream-filled donuts (these guys were pros). The outfits were already rigged with large patterns that resembled a cross between a leech and a huge dysfunctional sculpin. The "streamers", for lack of a better word, were launched far out across the water (both men were excellent casters) where the things landed with a resounding "splat". I figured that any rainbows hanging around here would be long gone following this fusillade, the trout hiding down deep until the barrage was over.

Quite wrong as usual.

A dozen of the biggest trout I'd seen in some time came from all directions and savaged the streamers-come-musky lures. Rods bent severely as a brace of rainbows fought for their very lives, racing, leaping, and crashing across the pond. In a minute or two they were brought to shore, hoisted from the water as they dangled from stout

leaders, smacked on the head with the flat side of an ax and dumped in the buckets. Each weighed seven or eight pounds at the least. Two more casts. The same routine.

One of the guys (both named Bob) looked at me, laughed and said, "The wife, she likes fish."

The other, laughing even harder, said, "She's a damn big woman and likes to eat."

They returned to their work and within 45 minutes must have had close to 25 pounds of trout in those buckets. Please remember, the wife "likes to eat", and ranch ponds are rarely bastions of the dreaded catch-and-release mania. During this onslaught I'd made two casts with a #4 long-shanked Woolly Bugger and taken a pair of rainbows of five pounds or so. My bugger seemed tiny, out of place, next to what these guys were using. Size 2 or larger hooks. This mayhem went on for a bit longer, all of us chain-smoking Camel straights, then each of the Bobs turned loose a large rainbow.

I was stunned. What weirdness was going on now?

"Always practice a little catch-and-release. Good for what ails you and shit like that," the other guy said.

I was wrong again.

"Damn straight," boomed a voice toned by years of whiskey and cigarettes. I turned around and the tall, sun-wind-burned elderly gent turned out to be the rancher who owned the pond. He examined the buckets and suggested we take some more. "Damn cannibal rainbows, eat every f*ckin' thing in sight. Can't plant any new blood, like them Kamloopers, in here 'til they're gone. Poison the bastards out. I think that's the damn answer."

We fished some more and then retired from our gentle pursuits. All of this took perhaps an hour. Most of the Pabst was gone, the empties lying in a ragged pile next to the buckets full of fish. The whiskey WAS gone. Time to go.

I still have the image of those white buckets being carried back to the rusted, hammered maroon and faux-wood-paneled Wagoneer. All those trout, their huge tails and heads draped over the sides, some of the fish still twitching in the purple-orange glow of a true Montana sunset. We thanked the rancher, who lit up at the idea of joining us at a local bar for a few blasts of bar whiskey and schooners of tap Grain Belt beer. He even offered to buy the beer nuts and Slim Jims for our dinner. We were living as only true derelict fishermen know how.

Three good guys and that afternoon-early-evening-turned-late evening remains one of the finest, and most blood thirsty, angling days of my life. Classic western madness.

Ah, ranch ponds, the stuff of delicate tippets, tiny flies, and excessive conservation. Never in my atavistic wanderings.

Early in October, Ginny and I drove 336 miles north to Cameron Lake just below the Canadian border. The fact that we'd taken large rainbows here had little to do with our decision. Damn straight.

When we started out from Livingston, the morning was already warm, quite sunny. By the time we passed Great Falls at great speed on the interstate, a thick dark band of clouds was sweeping down on us from up Alberta way. The air was turning cool – no, cold – and soon flakes of hard, dry snow were blowing sideways from northwest to southeast across the land. If timing is everything, we have it. Want a nice day to turn cold and rough, call us. This particular feat of magic is our specialty.

As I closed the last rusted, barbed-wire gate that led to the pond, the icy wind kicked up another notch. This was a gale now, with temperatures falling fast past freezing and heading with vehemence towards the teens. There were whitecaps on the little body of water. Thick piles of stiffening foam were piling up on the rocks. I could barely hear myself as I yelled to Ginny, "We've come this far. Have to give it a shot then we'll head back to town for a warm room and a good dinner."

She yelled something of her own, most likely along the lines of, "any day's a good day to fish".

I rigged up with frozen, bright red fingers, once again tying on the damselfly imitation called the Sheep Creek. Worked in summer, maybe it will play now. We trudged down to the water leaning at steep angles into the wind. My first cast blew back in my face. I worked along the shore and cast with the cool breeze. The fly landed 70 feet away, sank and then was yanked by a fish. I played it briefly and brought the rainbow to me. Twelve inches, filled with silvers, greens, crimsons, and indigos. Fat, healthy, gorgeous.

Ginny took photos and as I released it, the wind died. I mean died. The gale wasn't there anymore. Not a flicker of breeze. The clouds lifted a thousand feet. Sharp shafts of golden sunlight ripped through creases in the cover lighting up the land, turning on summer's last hints of green. The place looked like the Scottish Highlands. Muted emeralds, silvers, soft blues. And the surface of the pond was now dimpled with rise forms of hundreds of feeding fish. Rainbows from eight inches to a few pounds were sipping small mayflies, *callibaetis* no doubt. A few eager trout leaped free of the water in their enthusiasm, dropping back in quicksilver splashes. The temperature climbed up into the 50s and the vast rangeland glowed peacefully. This lasted for three hours and we caught and photographed dozens of fish. Our hands and feet were numb from the water, but who cared? We'd received a reprieve.

"We caught a break Ginny, let's head back now."

She agreed, and as we put away our gear the clouds lowered, the cold wind kicked up and the snow began flying its sideways dance once more. We hustled our chilled act back to town as the countryside disappeared beneath swirling clouds and sheets of snow. We got that warm room and had that good meal and thought that the day had been as fine as we could remember.

That, too, is ranch pond fishing.

Insane gluttony. A huge fish. Lots of smaller ones as winter bears down on Montana.

All of it.

TRIP INFORMATION

Timing: Mid-June through the end of the month when everything is brilliant green and the damselflies are all over the place, and again in September through early October before winter closes in on this country with serious intent. The rest of the summer months are extremely hot and fly-blown.

Where: Take I-15 north out of Shelby for 30 miles to the Sunburst turnoff then east on Oilmont Highway and after 15 miles, be on the lookout for Miners Coulee Road on heading north/left. Middle Butte dominates the horizon and after about five miles turn right onto Cameron Lake Road and follow your nose to the water. Be sure and close gates (or leave them as you found them) coming in and going out. The rancher has had problems with litter so has closed the place to camping these days. Making sure the place is spotless may help change this policy. Also, for those interested in exploring other places like the Missouri Breaks, in addition to the state highway map and Delorme Atlas Gazetteer I recommend checking out the Montana Bureau of Land Management state map center at http://plicmapcenter.org/MT/. The local BLM or Montana Dept. of Fish, Wildlife and Parks office are excellent places for current information.

Hub: Shelby is the main town in the area. The O'Haire Manor Hotel is good and $65 per night at 204 Second Street South, 406-434-5555. There's also the Lewis & Clark RV Park that is located north of Shelby (I-15) off Exit 364. The best place for food and drinks is the Frontier Bar & Supper Club located on Highway 2, ten miles east of Shelby. No sporting goods store or fly shop in the area. There are a couple of convenience stores in town.

Appropriate Gear: Five- to 6-weight, eight- to nine-foot rods with weight forward lines. Sink tips aren't necessary if you use weighted nymphs and a small split shot. Leaders of 9 to 12 feet tapered to 4X, even though the takes will be strong.

Favorite Patterns: #12-16 Hare's Ear, #-8-12 Sheep Creek Special, #10-12 Montana Nymph, #14-18 Elk Hair Caddis, 16-20 BWO.

Sheep Creek Special by George Biggs

Hook: TMC 5262, Sizes 8-16

Body: Dark olive chenille

Tail: Brown hackle wound on the shank as for a dry fly

Wing: Five to seven mallard flank fibers

Thread: Dark olive

Chapter Seventeen

Warm Springs Creek

For many years, flyfishing in Montana for me translated into chasing trout – westslope cutthroat, bull trout, browns, rainbows, brookies, Yellowstone cutts. If the fish was a member of the salmonid family, I hunted it. The mere thought of casting over northerns or smallmouth bass appalled my foolish sensibilities. Even just a dozen or so years ago, suggesting that an individual was planning on fishing for anything but trout in Montana would normally lead to an unpleasant situation whether it was in a fly shop or a local tavern. Over time, the angling process slowly evolved to include smallmouth and largemouth bass, northerns, goldeye, and the noble carp.

And time brings about strange and often fine changes in an individual. Over the past decade, I've found myself wandering about the state looking for those loathsome northern pike in remote creeks in the northeastern corner of the state, channel catfish down Broadus way, sunfish, bluegills, and crappie in some ponds scattered around the plains near the Dakotas, and last and rising swiftly up this non-salmonid list, smallmouth bass. The species fights like charged, angry steel when hooked, especially in moving water. On a 4-weight rod, a half-pound fish feels like a two-pound cutthroat, and I love cutthroat – westslope, Yellowstone, Snake River, et al.

More and more of my time is spent fishing for this bass. One of my favorite waters is Warm Springs Creek located 15 miles north of Lewistown in the Judith Basin dead center in the middle of Montana. The stream heads in the Judith Mountains and flows for 25 miles first through timbered mountains then open prairie ranchland and fields of wheat and barley to the Judith River near Denton. The spring that is the source of Warm Springs (also known as Warm Spring) Creek releases 58,000 gallons of 68-degree water per minute. The river is about 30 feet wide at the most and flows at an average of about six miles per hour, which is quite brisk. There is a state fishing access about six miles west on State Highway 81 which is a left off of Highway 191 heading north from Lewistown. I've found over the years that many ranchers will grant access to the stream on their land with a polite request. I always follow this up with a thank-you note and even a pint of bourbon. Money well-spent for the privilege of fishing fine water.

The Montana Department of Fish, Wildlife and Parks first introduced smallmouth to Warm Springs Creek in 1973. Since that time periodic plantings have helped to insure a healthy population of the species. I've run across the bass in isolated spring-fed ponds in the Bears Paw Mountains along the Hi-Line in the north central part of the state and in a few places along the Montana-North Dakota border. Locals and area biologists speak guardedly of bass over four pounds.

Years ago I stopped at a lower stretch of Warm Springs Creek and asked a rancher's wife for permission to fish. She readily agreed and even offered me a glass of lemonade on my way back to the car at the end of fishing. I had little luck because of the 100-degree temperatures and clear skies, but the water looked promising with deep runs, moss and grass beds, and bubbling riffles giving to aquamarine pools. The heat was brutal and my efforts produced a few bass from a quarter- to a half-pound. They fought well, but the only pleasure in this fishing was discovering new water and wet wading in the relatively cool water. The sun cooked the sky hot silver and burned my skin through its tan despite sunscreen. While walking along the shore and peering down into the water that deepens quickly in places along weed beds, I spotted smallmouths that were at least three pounds and probably larger. These fish swam slowly and with little fear, ghosting along in the shadows created by the dense aquatic plant growth. I knew that I'd return.

That first time on this water, I worked patterns that had worked for smallmouths in other parts of the country – Muddler Minnows, Marabou versions of the same, Bitch Creek nymphs, even some poppers that resembled dyspeptic frogs. I experienced marginal success but I felt like I was fishing for someone else, imagined, real or otherwise, instead of working water in ways that have always produced for me in the past.

So with this in mind, I switched to a Woolly Bugger of my own design the next time I traveled to Warm Springs. This one has a black marabou tail, brown body, and is palmered with cree hackle. I tie the thing thick, bushy, and ugly and weight it with some heavy wire (even fuse wire for large pools on the Yellowstone that flows through the town I live in) so that it bobs up and down through the water column as I retrieve it with short, varied, and quick strips. Over the years this iteration of the venerable Bugger has taken hundreds of large trout including many browns over 20 inches.

I remember fishing the lower reaches of nearby Big Spring Creek one October afternoon years ago. My success with the pattern was good, very good. More than a dozen browns from 15 inches on up and a couple of 18-inch rainbows. Walking back to my Suburban, I noticed a man and his wife sitting on a boulder watching me. I saw that they had South Dakota plates – not necessarily a bad thing.

"You had yourself quite a time," the guy said. "What were you using if I may ask?"

"Woolly Buggers."

"So were we, but we didn't move a thing."

I asked to see their Buggers and he pulled one from the fleece on his vest. Emaciated, sparkly, thinly tied, pitiful. I showed him mine – the difference between an NFL lineman and a delicate wide receiver. He was unable to restrain himself and plucked the Cree Bugger from my hand, the point of the hook pricking my palm. His

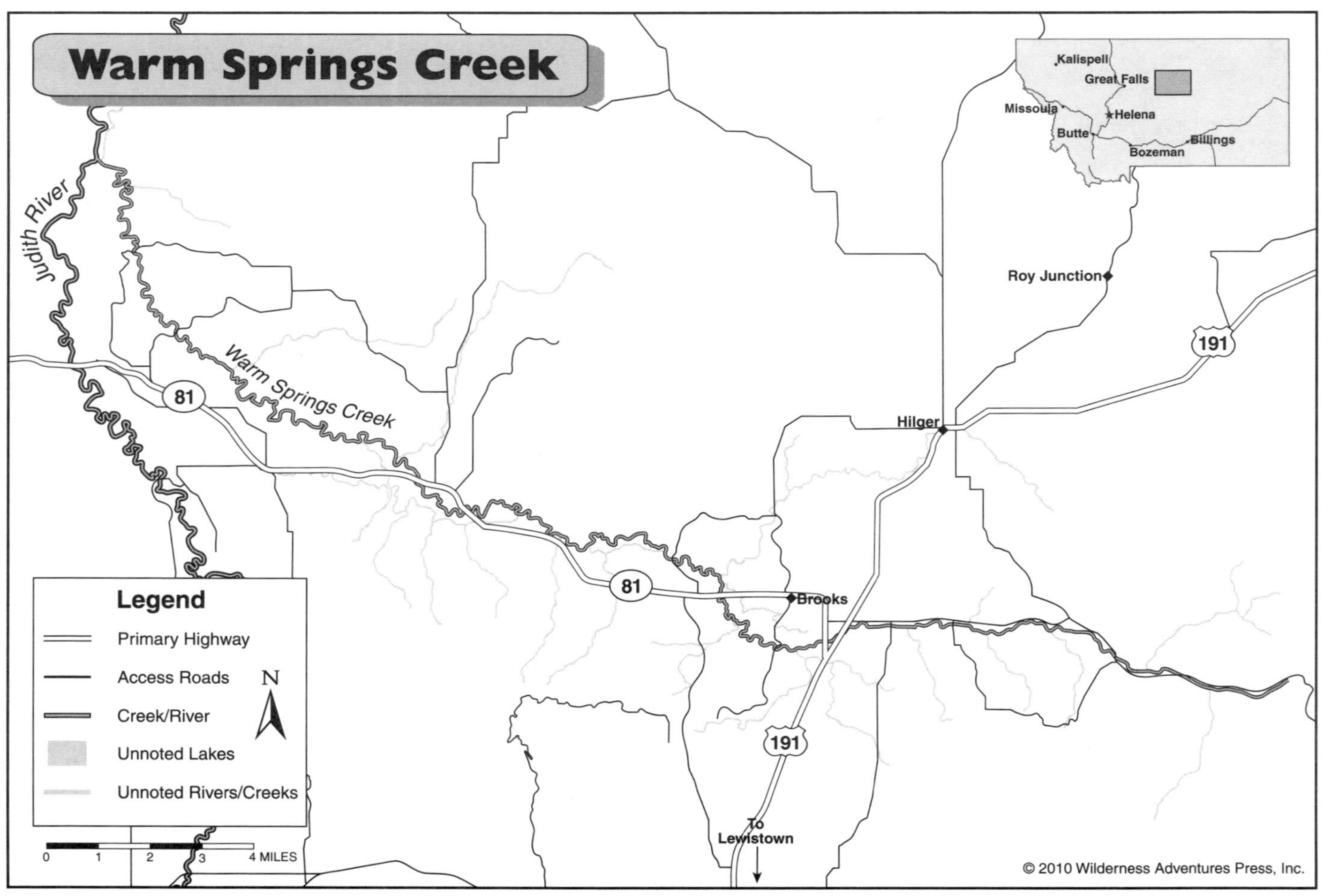
Warm Springs Creek
Kalispell
Great Falls
Missoula
Helena
Butte
Billings
Bozeman
Roy Junction
191
Judith River
81
Warm Springs Creek
Hilger
81
Brooks
191
To
Lewistown
Legend
Primary Highway
Access Roads
Creek/River
Unnoted Lakes
Unnoted Rivers/Creeks
N
0 1 2 3 4 MILES
© 2010 Wilderness Adventures Press, Inc.

wife smiled a little apologetically. A good woman in for a hard life with this man on the water. I laughed and gave him two more. We talked some about their hometown of Mobridge, but I could see that he was in a hurry to try them out.

"One thing," I offered. "They work best with a split shot crimped in at the head. It's ugly, but effective."

He nodded, the wife shrugged. I went off to build a tall, cold drink and smoke a large Honduran cigar.

Buggers are just that – Buggers. They are not delicate, crafted works of art. They are intended to imitate forage fish and large nymphs. And I think, more to the point, to look like a food source that triggers an atavistic, attacking response. My experience in Montana and on up through the Yukon and Northwest Territories is that the bushier, uglier the pattern the more likely a good-sized fish will strike. Strike, not rise and sedately sip a fly that imitates a small rising mayfly or caddis. And this has proven true over and over in the fast currents of Warm Springs where the water often rushes and crashes against banks as the stream makes a 90-degree turn or as the flow rips in powerful seams through waving fronds of plants. A large pattern that drops down near the streambed and attracts the smallmouth's attention is what's needed, even when a number of fish are taking caddis or mayflies on the surface. The best fish prefer larger food sources here.

Why I use Cree hackle I don't know. I remember finding a beautiful cape in a shop up in Rocky Mountain House, Alberta for about 20 bucks. A good one now is closer to 80. That winter when I tied up my Buggers, instead of using grizzly hackle (which I still employ to some extent), I worked in the blond-brown-barred Cree and the results the next year were very good. Larger trout and more of them, especially during the prime brown trout period from mid-October through mid-November. Maybe it is a case of my liking and having faith in this particular way of assembling a Bugger that leads me to fish the thing more thoroughly or maybe the Cree really makes a difference. Beats me, but I like the way the thing looks as it rests in my hand reflecting the sunlight and the way it pulses and shimmers in the water.

Life can be simple, productive, and fun at odd times. This tie works and I've learned not to question good fortune.

When I begin casting the Bugger along the edges and through channels in the dense aquatic weed growth or tight to the undercut banks, the bass came from everywhere and slammed the pattern often before I had an opportunity to do little more then make a slight twitch and short strip. Smallmouth from less than a half-pound to a little more than a pound that pulled and streaked in the fast-paced current. A bunch of fish in a couple of hours. And some rainbows in the 16-inch range hit the thing, too. They didn't put up as much of a fight, but their unique coloration more than made up for this. The overall coloration was rainbow-esque, but there was a slight suggestion of a golden-green hue throughout. Perhaps an adaptation that helps the fish blend into their surroundings to better avoid predation by raptors and wandering mammals.

I cast, quartering upstream and bank tight. Even in swift current I try to allow the fly time to sink down through the water column as much as possible, all the while mending and retrieving slack line. The strips are varied but usually no more than a foot. At the end of the drift I allow the Bugger to swing back and forth in the current, often pulling it upstream slightly. The smallmouths often hit at this time though the connection ratio because of the downstream location is low.

I'll always remember encountering a professional bass fisherman (something I've always dreamed of becoming, but life is filled with disappointment) along the reed beds of the Missouri River about 40 miles above the dam near Yankton, South Dakota one very hot, blue sky June day. We talked across the water for a bit and one thing he said has stayed with me all these years.

"Whenever you're chasing smallies, whatever you use, make damn sure it acts like it has a serious malfunction," he said with a honeyed southern accent endemic to his state. "Those bass go like hell for that."

So do browns, bull trout, northerns (though they'll hit about anything with any movement including the toe of my waders on one occasion) and even mountain whitefish make a determined effort to wrap their pursed lips around something that appears hurt or wounded. This has proved to be good advice from the southerner.

One evening, I spotted such a fish as it passed through a crease of light cast by the setting sun. I cast well ahead, allowed the Bugger to sink and began to retrieve it. Before five feet had been covered, my rod arced severely into the water and line spun from an old Hardy lightweight reel. The tip of the 4-weight seven-six Iron Feather (how I wish these were still in production) jerked up and down as the bass slammed its way upstream, quickly wrapping 3X tippet in the weeds and breaking off despite my laughable attempts to chase after the angry bass by slogging and high-stepping through accumulated mud in stream corners and through the plants that felt like anchors as they wrapped around my hip waders.

I saw the smallmouth only once for brief seconds in that slice of golden light, felt the creature's hard strength, watched line disappear at a spirited pace, felt the line snap and that was it. I've never been closer to a fish of that stature on Warm Springs, but that brief encounter stays with me, so whenever I find myself in the Lewistown area I always find time to fish the creek for at least an hour.

This spring day is windy, warm with large clouds moving northeast towards the Dakotas. Working up against the relatively warm current, the backside grasses all but blot out the sky and the sandy yellow and grey cutbanks. Hills covered with the muted green of new sage round off the horizon. The grass is over my head. The new green of small willow bushes clings thickly beside the moving water. The yellow-green of cottonwoods rises above me. The neon greens of aquatic grasses swing and wave in the current at my feet and as far ahead as I can see. I cast a large brown Elk Hair Caddis between the seams of grass because I see bugs that look like my fly rise off the surface – matching the hatch with technical subtlety.

Sizes 10 to 14 with 12 the most popular are the range I work with. Again, like the Buggers, I tie the Elk Hairs as bushy and buggy as possible, extending the hair over the eye of the hook. This makes threading the tippet a bit difficult, but my success rate has increased since I've begun tying the pattern this way. My skills are modest at best. I'm no Rene Harrop nor do I possess the skills of a number of my fly-tying

friends. But the way I assemble the Bugger and Elk Hair works, has worked for many years. I'm satisfied. I cast these three-quarters to directly upstream along foam lines, gaps in the aquatic weed growth or along the brushy, overgrown and often snaky (as in rattlesnakes) banks. A drag-free drift is all that's required. The Elk Hair imitates the caddis, hoppers and just looks like a food source.

I prefer a 4-weight rod of eight feet or less. My favorite is the aforementioned seven-foot-six Iron Feather, a rod no longer in production. This is pushing things a bit for launching the Woolly Buggers, but with some practice, the accuracy is acquired and casting distances are rarely over 25 to 30 feet. This rod works fine for the dries like the Elk Hairs and even working nymphs such as the Hare's Ear (gold-ribbed preferred). With the Buggers a leader of seven feet is maximum. For dries nine feet with maybe another 18-inches of tippet tapered to 4X or 5X. If I do use a nymph, I always place a split shot at the head to ensure the bug getting down in the rapid current. I've never liked bead heads. I have no logical reason for this other than the

split shot seems to give the nymph a bit more natural action. I also attach one or two shot at the head of the Buggers for the same reason. I usually wade this stream wet because of the relatively warm water temperatures, but hip or chest waders are acceptable, too.

As with any smallmouth fishing, dusk is an excellent time. The fish are out chasing less-than-wary forage fish like dace and sculpin. Size 6 to 8 streamers including the Bugger work well, cast slightly upstream and mended to maintain line contact as they drift across then below the angler, turning fish at times on nearly every cast. The smallmouth like to hammer a streamer as it swings out with perhaps a slight upstream pull that causes the pattern to splash on the surface.

As for the snakes, a note of minor caution. They are present in fair numbers but so are they along the likes of the Missouri, Prickly Pear, Bighorn, and many others. Watch where you place your hands and feet when walking on dry land or wading close to the banks. When you see a snake, give it plenty of room and pass on by quietly. Rattlesnakes are timid creatures and prefer to be left alone. While being bitten isn't high on my list of things to see and do in Montana, I consider the presence of the snakes to be a plus, a natural part of the Warm Springs riparian system.

On this delightful day the smallmouth are eager, unsophisticated or perhaps they're buzzed on the new season like I am. I catch a bunch of the bass in a couple of hours – none of them large, most of them small, 10 to 12 inches or so. They fight well. They are much stronger than trout inch for inch. A 12-inch bass smacks the Elk Hair then rips upstream, bending the rod, abruptly struggling like a two-pound cutthroat. The fish zips into the weeds, twists the line and with a shake of its head, snaps the tippet. I admire its tactical expertise. I can do this all afternoon and probably will, but for now, I edge over in the knee-deep water and sit on the bank in thick grass that surrounds me like a bower. The thick stems and wide leafy tops brush back and forth against my shirt, my face. I feel like I'm being caressed before realizing that I've been on the road alone a few days past healthy.

Quartering upstream and across the creek from me is a long spit of exposed sandy soil marked with serpentine strips of blue-green shading darker with black miniature slashes. One of the strips moves and coils. I think rattlesnake. I always think rattlesnake, even the one time I saw a red, white, and black milk snake alongside a game trail in the Missouri Breaks. My hands are shaking as I pull a small pair of binoculars from a pocket. Focusing in I see that there are seven or eight snakes enjoying the sun like bathers on a Riviera beach. I expect to hear strange French pop music coming from radios resting beside bottles of tanning potions. Perhaps this is a topless beach, I wonder. Way too far gone. It's back home tomorrow or maybe on to the Milk River. What's the difference at this point in the proceedings. The serpents reveal themselves to be common garter snakes out for a day at the beach. I relax, finish my sandwich and work up the creek through the watery plants swirling around my legs. I see a large smallmouth, maybe 15 inches, crash the surface as it crunches an early-season hopper. I change flies and close in.

TRIP INFORMATION

Timing: Because of its steady 68-degree temperature, Warm Springs Creek is open year round. The best times to fish are from the compression of the stream following spring runoff – often as late as the end of June – through mid-summer when the hoppers and caddis are in full force on into mid- to late October and that month's often glorious weather. September with its blue sky days can be delightful and productive.

Where: Warm Springs Creek is located 15 miles north of Lewistown on U.S. Highway 191. Paralleled by State Highway 81. Public access on state lands approximately six miles west off of 191 on 81. This one, like Big Spring Creek, sits dead center in the middle of the state.

Hub: Lewistown offers everything a traveling angler needs from motel rooms, a good selection of restaurants to sporting goods, clothing, hardware, anything at all, stores. The town is located on U.S. Highway 200 in the Judith Basin at the geographic center of the state, and about two hours east, southeast of Great Falls. Don's Western Outdoor Store, 800-879-8194. Don's is an excellent place to purchase anything you'll need for fishing and the outdoors and a prime location to acquire current local information on everything from stream conditions to guides to western clothing. We often stay at the B & B Motel, 520 E. Main Street, 406-535-5496. The Empire Café at 214 West Main is good for breakfast, and also the Rising Trout Coffee at 217 West Main Street – rolls and such. I'm always a sucker for any place called the Mint Bar & Grill for burgers, 113 4th Avenue South.

Appropriate Gear: Two- to 4-weight, eight-foot-six-inch fast-action rods, floating and as an option a five-foot sink-tip line (weighting the fly pattern is preferable), 7.5- to 9-foot leaders and tippet material to 5X, most often 4X. For nymphing or working large patterns like Buggers, some anglers may prefer a 5-weight, eight-six rod with slower action.

Favorite Patterns: Hare's Ear Nymph, Grey Elk Hair Caddis, Bird's Stonefly, Cree Woolly Bugger, Pheasant Tail, Marabou Muddler, Joe's Hopper, Royal Wulff, LaFontaine Double-Wing, Blue Winged Olive.

Special Regulations: Open entire year.

Cree Woolly Bugger

Hook: TMC 300 or
Mustad 79580, sizes
6-10

Thread: Black 6/0
Tail: Black marabou
Body: Medium, brown
chenille

Hackle: Cree (or
badger) hackle
palmered over the
body

Grey Elk Hair Caddis

Hook: TMC 100 or
Mustad 94845, sizes
10-16

Thread: Grey 6/0
prewaxed
Body: Grey rabbit or
Antron dubbing

Hackle: Grizzly
palmered over body
Wing: Dyed grey elk hair
or light natural

CHAPTER EIGHTEEN

Big Spring Creek

Fishing Big Spring Creek as it runs through a mostly agrarian valley below the state fish hatchery and the source of its remarkable waters is like stepping through contemporary time and wandering to a place that seems to be both of the past and a no-man's-land of tranquility. Where the stream has its beginnings is a peaceful place where thousands of rainbow trout are hatched and reared next to towering willows that offer some shade from a mean sun. Different strains of rainbow are raised here along with Yellowstone cutthroat, brown trout, and Kokanee salmon. No workers are seen, perhaps gone for lunch or laboring silently in one of the nearby buildings. A 25-foot diameter cement tank holds enormous trout that swim in circles and feed avidly on trout pellets. Some of them are 20 pounds, big burly beasts that have no idea that a much greater world lies a few yards from their confinement, a place that begins where springs bubble from the ground, and moss and aquatic plants grow thickly holding still more trout, some of them large, too. From here, Big Spring Creek pours in a rushing, white water chute as it madly escapes the darkness of the earth and moves towards open land where it winds through a corridor of hay fields, its banks guarded by willow, hawthorne, birch, some cottonwoods, and tall grass that drapes over the banks into the water as if in supplication to natural wonders, where long strands of this growth weave lazily in the current like a woman's hair flows in a summer breeze. There is a sensible pace to the stream here of riffle, run, pool repeating itself for miles as the water runs easily downhill into Lewistown. I've waded the cool water in the heat of a late July afternoon, the sound of a rancher cutting hay blending with the sound of gentle wind, grasshoppers clacking through the air, and the burbling of the creek while steadily taking trout on a dry fly. I felt like I was in another world, especially when juxtaposed with floating gridlock memories of the Bitterroot or Missouri at the same time of year in recent years.

The creek is really two streams in one. The classic spring creek above town with its enormous rainbows and the rougher edged, darker water below town that holds large browns; though both sections hold a mixture of each species along with a few brook trout, mountain whitefish, and good numbers of forage fish.

This is what the Department of Fish, Wildlife and Parks has to say about the stream, and the department says it quite well:

> *"Big Spring Creek, one of the largest spring-fed streams in Montana, originates nine miles southeast of Lewistown, near the state's Big Springs Trout Hatchery. It runs northwesterly 30 miles, mainly between the Big Snowy and Judith mountains, and enters the Judith River west of Brooks, Montana. Enclosing the large spring at the head of the creek, giant willows and cottonwoods shade a park and wildlife viewing area. From the spring, cold, high-quality water flows over green mats of water plants and down between a thick growth of bushes, trees and grass that seems tunnel-like in places. The creek continues its first 20 miles alongside hay and grazing fields and US 191, passing through Lewistown. Above the town, Big Spring Creek averages 38 feet wide, 18 inches deep, below to the mouth, 45 feet wide, 24 inches deep. Water quality degrades going downstream, due to erosion and pollution. In its last 10 miles, from the mouth of Cottonwood Creek to the Judith, the channel migrates. Its silty bottomland supports dense stands of cottonwoods, willows, birches, and hawthorne. Considered by anglers to be the most important trout stream in central Montana, Big Spring Creek attracts large numbers of wildlife, including waterfowl and furbearers. Agriculture, municipal and recreational uses, hunting, and home site development depend on or are associated with Big Spring Creek."*

That's a pretty good verbal photograph of the drainage, but I'll attempt to expand the image some as we roll along.

Working the upper stretch takes some patience but has never proven to be the mind-numbing finicky exercise that a person often finds on DePuy or Silver Creek. I like this since life has proven hard enough over the years. I like my pleasures pleasurable and not adventures in frustration and futility. Local anglers spend a good deal of time studying the water so that they may accurately mimic what is rising and attracting the trout's attentions. I've been completely happy using various sizes of Elk Hair Caddis say from #12 through #18, a Joe's Hopper when appropriate and Hare's Ear nymphs tan, black, and olive from #14 to 18. I don't use a Bugger up in these pools that are so clear, blue, and deep or along the dark rushes of current undercutting the banks. I don't need to, though I've been tempted. My Iron Feather 4-weight, seven-six with a 12-foot leader tapered to 5X handles the dry-fly portion of the extravaganza, while a nine-foot leader tapered to 4X does the submerged duty. My casts are rarely more than 30 feet and on a pleasant summer afternoon, I often take a dozen or more rainbows and, rarely, a brown that average 15 or 16 inches.

I once encountered a father and son who appeared new to flyfishing based on their rough-edged casting and noisy wading. We stopped and talked for awhile and I mentioned that the fishing was good with grey Elk Hairs but I'd been wading as

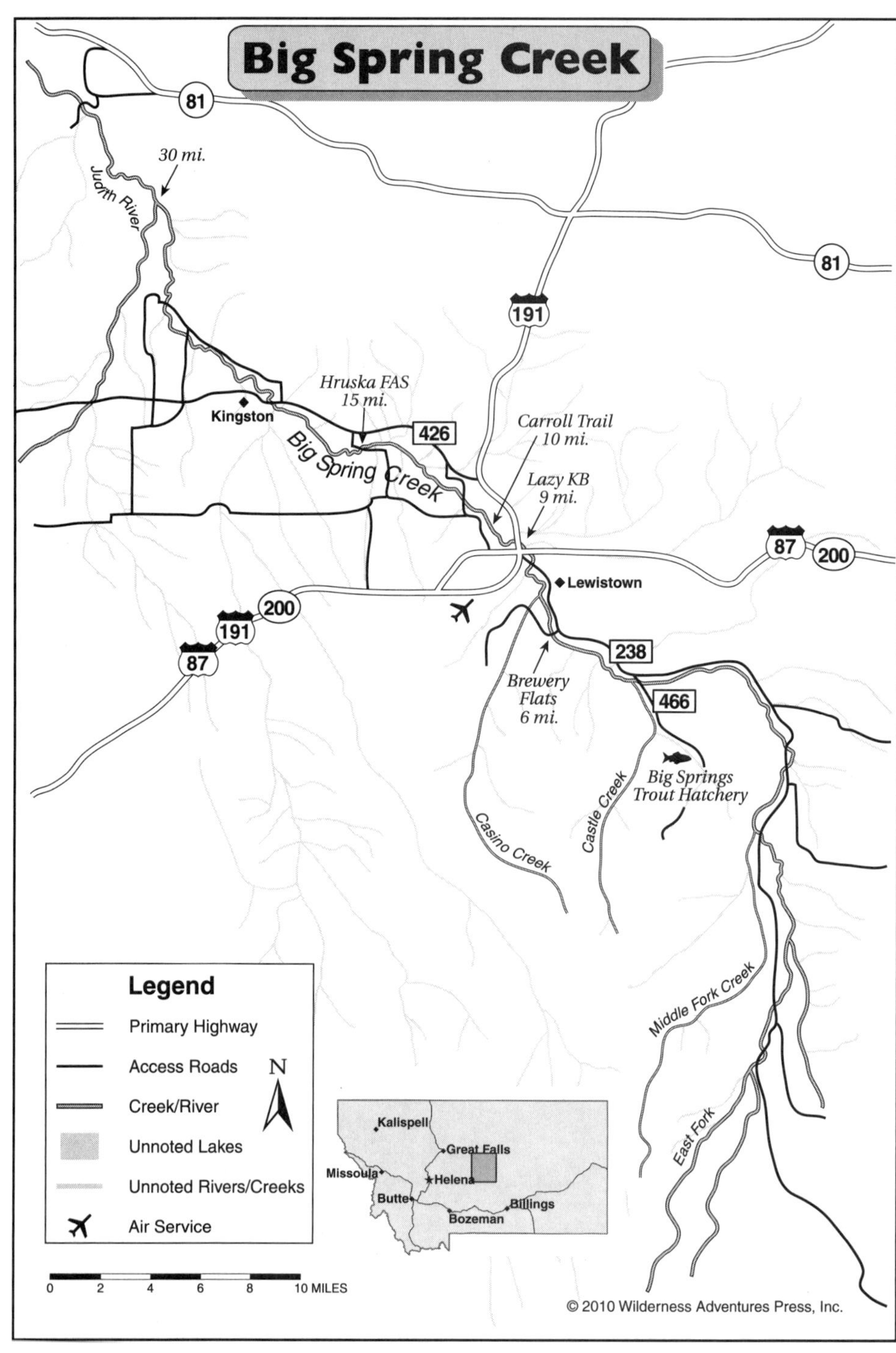
Big Spring Creek
81
30 mi.
Judith River
191
81
Hruska FAS
15 mi.
Kingston
426
Big Spring Creek
Carroll Trail
10 mi.
Lazy KB
9 mi.
87
200
200
191
87
Lewistown
238
Brewery
Flats
6 mi.
466
Big Springs
Trout Hatchery
Casino Creek
Castle Creek
Middle Fork Creek
East Fork
Legend
Primary Highway
Access Roads
N
Creek/River
Unnoted Lakes
Unnoted Rivers/Creeks
Air Service
Kalispell
Great Falls
Missoula
Helena
Butte
Billings
Bozeman
0   2   4   6   8   10 MILES
© 2010 Wilderness Adventures Press, Inc.

quietly as possible without splashing and really working on making my casts delicate and accurate (I wasn't kidding). The boy asked what an Elk Hair was and I opened a cracked fly box and dropped several in his hand sizes #12 to 14. He looked at them carefully and with a smile.

"Can we buy some of these in town?" the father asked. I handed him another half dozen, checked their tippets, adding on a couple of feet of 4X and handed him the spool. "That surgeon's knot works?"

I said, "Yes." We talked some more. The boy thanked me and the father thanked me, clapped me on the back and gave me a look that made me feel better than when I'd caught the rainbows earlier. That was fun and I felt good walking back from the stream.

From mid-summer on through September as the sun warms the air hoppers begin to shoot and arc out into the water. Casting a hopper pattern alongside banks, real close doesn't matter when the trout are excited, turns larger than average rainbows, a situation obviously not unique to Big Spring Creek. Quartering upstream I've had the fun of watching as the fish race up from the streambed or from the edges of cover and leap entirely free of the water as they nab my Joe's Hopper. Then they crash back into the stream before beginning a series of leaps up or across stream. Wading is easy, as moving from side to side for the best casting angle is accomplished by working over shallow riffles and along the grassy banks. Occasionally I'll go waist deep to reach a particularly promising spot.

Even during times of hopper abundance, I'll switch to a dark Hare's Ear, usually #14 when I encounter deeper, shaded runs. Cast upstream and slightly across, then dead drifting often turns lots of trout that otherwise would not be discovered since in these areas, most of the time, they are not interested in surface feeding. An Emergent Sparkle Pupa also works, but the nymphs turn more and larger fish on a more consistent basis. I rarely use an indicator and instead rely on the so-called sixth sense, where a take is detected before the line stops or moves away from me. This is merely a matter of stubborn preference on my part akin to my distaste for beadheads even though the weight I use in their place probably looks similar. Hardheaded is hardheaded.

There are enormous rainbows all through this stretch in the deeper and most difficult-to-reach holding spots. I've peeked through bushes down to pure water pouring over the edge of golden gravel drop-offs and observed rainbows that went over 10 pounds holding still with mouths opening and closing on various species of nymphs that float in their feeding line, but they've shown little interest in my efforts over the years. I did manage to have one engulf a #12 tan Hare's Ear but as soon as I lifted up on the rod the trout powered even farther under a rock shelf, shook its head violently, and popped the tippet like it was little more than diaphanous spider web. That's fine. One of these times I'll make a serious attempt to entice one of these big rainbows to take, maybe with a large Montana Nymph or a dead drifted Woolly Bugger on 1X or 0X tippet. Far and fine be damned. An 8-weight and a short, stout leader for a full-scale assault. Maybe next summer.

Spring runoff is over now. The billions of tons of ice and snow had melted and washed away to the Pacific. Big Spring Creek, while not a runoff madhouse like most Montana waters, is now in an easy going, summer mood, running with soft burbling sounds, afternoon sunlight bouncing off the riffles and lazy seams in its current. Steller's Jays squawk loudly among themselves over something important, maybe a dead field mouse, as they jump around in the pines and aspen. Several deer, fluffy white tails flicking, always flicking, graze lazily on the fresh green grass in the wide, open meadows above the river. The slightest, softest touch of warm breeze curls around the valley, drifting across the flats and slipping through the pines. The water pushes easily against my legs as I wade slowly across the gravel bottom, out to a position where I can reach a deep run along the far tree-lined, brushy bank, a stretch that is deeply undercut, water running in the darkness, swirling among clumps of exposed roots. Big browns hold here. Very big, but they are hard to move. It is difficult to get their attention with so much food – minnows, nymphs, crickets – floating right into their large jaws. A large pattern, in this case a #4 brown Woolly Bugger palmered with Cree feathers that are a mixture of golden brown, tan, and off-white, my favorite tie for this bug, is called for. I wrap the hook with 15 twists of thick fuse wire and place a pair of split shot at the head of the fly that is then attached to thick 0X tippet. Serious work at hand. Get the Bugger down deep to where the cannibal browns hang out and make sure the leader has the guts to horse the trout out (if it strikes) through the roots and determined current, out into the open where I'll have an honest chance at playing the fish, perhaps tiring it and bringing it to my feet. The water looks the same as it always does, like healthy, big-fish water full of promise and mystery, too. Wavering, ghostly images wander through the current from time to time leering at me like the faces from my crazy dreams. I move into position and begin working line out to cover the cast and the drift needed to sink the Bugger down under the bank, down to where the browns are hiding. The fly plops into a small eddy just above the bank and all its weight pulls it down into the darkness. I maintain in contact with the pattern by gently keeping a light tension on the line as the fly works way down near the bottom. I can feel it bouncing off rocks in gentle but slightly rough pings up through the line. It stops briefly as it runs into exposed, finger-like roots. Then I sense, before my eyes see, the line stopping. I pause a second to be sure of the take and then pull back quickly and firmly upstream parallel to the water. Next there is a throbbing that jumps up the line as the brown rattles its head and tries to pull even farther back into the tangle and undercut. I step back away from the bank steadily until I feel the branches of willow brushing my back, not yielding even an inch of line. The trout tries to hold its ground, powerful, like dragging a brick through thick cement. Then the pressure stops and her line curves up towards the surface. The huge fish rips clear of the river, shaking its broad flanks, standing on its tail. Wild. Angry. Water splashes on the grasses nearby and shimmers in a hundred spectral cascades. The brown slams back into the water before leaping and crashing downstream into the backing. I clatter along the bank and thrash through water knee deep chasing the fish, rod pointing directly at its fleeing form. Forty yards below me in a deep pool the trout stops, sounding in the depths of a large pool.

"Got you," I say to no one.

The brown will hold, then fly into the air and try to run again, but each attempt to break free becomes shorter, lesser in intensity until I finally pull the exhausted creature to my feet. Dropping down to my knees in the water as I always do when I want to touch a truly special fish, I gently slide my hands into the water and along the brown's belly, easily 24 inches. I've been fortunate to catch enough of them over the years to know their size pretty much to the inch by now. Heavy, solid, muscular. Golden, rich brown, copper, crimson and black spotting. Whites flashing pure along fin tips. Wicked rows of large, razor-sharp teeth. I twist the Bugger from the upper jaw and wonder at the powerful perfection of this fish. I watch for several seconds as the sunlight glows around the trout's body like an aura. The fish holds motionless, perhaps aware that its fate hangs in some strange, far off balance. I ease the brown back towards the depths of the river, slowly working it back and forth, gently, in the soft current, reviving the trout. Returning energy vibrates through the trout's body to the tail and up into my hands. I let go and watch as the fish slowly swims off to disappear in the darkness on the other side of the stream.

As they say with great self-importance in legal movies or on *Law & Order*, "Your honor, I'd like a sidebar", and the half-blasted, semi-comatose game & fish warden mumbles with surprising dignity, both anglers approach the bench. So here's a sidebar of brown-trout dimensions...

...After several delightful summers of severe drought, forest fires and smoke-clogged air with temperatures around 100 degrees, Montana is finally experiencing a season of reasonably wet proportions and non-hellish temperatures. Rains have been consistent from April into August. As I write this I've just returned from a day wading a nearby river for brown trout. Where in recent years, the grasses and brush have been dry, brown, stunted, dead, this time around featured lush, emerald growth above my head. Most importantly for anglers, ranchers have had abundant moisture this summer, so river levels are at or above normal. Fishing conditions resemble those of post runoff, those glorious days when rivers are clearing and compressing. I caught a half-dozen browns from 17 to 21 inches using early-season patterns like Hare's Ear nymphs and small Elk Hair Caddis. And even fooled a few Yellowstone cutts in the 15-inch range.

So what does any of this have to do with autumn fishing for browns? Plenty. The decent flow of cool water means that the spawning of this predatory fish will be pushed back a few weeks to mid- to late October and because of the fine stream flow conditions, the fish will be in excellent shape – well fed, hefty, and full of energy. Admittedly, the prime triggering aspects to spawning are the shortening of the days, the angle of the sunlight's incidence on the water as the northern hemisphere turns its back on our star, and decreasing water temperatures. But in over 40 years of chasing (seems like hunting to me, actually) browns out this way, I have observed that every year that features normal to above-normal stream flows equates to a delayed spawning season, one that offers more and larger browns that have always behaved more aggressively.

The classic rivers like the Missouri from Toston Dam on downstream, the Madison from a few miles below Slide Inn, the Bitterroot, the Beaverhead, and the Bighorn, to name a few, will all fish wonderfully from late September well into November. But I'd like to suggest a couple of slightly lesser-known waters – the brushy upper Clark Fork, and the Jefferson (yeah, I know, a lot of people have heard of this one). Each of these two rivers in their decidedly unique ways can hold their own when it comes to fall brown trout fishing, even with the big boys mentioned at the head of this graph.

The Jefferson, along with the Madison and Gallatin, is one of the three main headwater rivers that join at Three Forks to form the Missouri. While not nearly as famous or as heavily fished as the other two streams, the Jefferson consistently provides top-notch fishing with streamers in autumn for large browns. The water is accessible from Highway 41 from fishing access points, along the road, and by bridges. Wading is a productive way to work the undercuts, brushy banks, drop-offs from the gravel bars, and the deep glides. Some of my best success over the years has been in the area near the minute town of Silver Star. This is beautiful country with mountains and grassy benches providing the backdrop as the Jefferson wanders beneath stands of ancient cottonwoods that flare yellow-gold in October. Another great way to work this water is by floating. I would recommend contacting Tim Tollett at Frontier Anglers. He or his long-time guide Tim Mosolf know this part of Montana as well as anyone, and after five days of hard fishing with either of these guys, I guarantee you'll be a significantly better angler. Contact them at: Phone – 800-228-5263, email – frontieranglers@mcn.net, 680 North Montana Street, Dillon. Dillon offers plenty of food and lodging opportunities.

As for gear, I'd recommend 5- through 7-weight rods with plenty of backbone, stout seven-foot leaders tapered to at least 3X, a bunch of Woolly Buggers and other streamers like Marabou Muddlers. A five-foot sink-tip line isn't a bad idea either for the deeper glides – anything that looks fishy or will provoke the spawning territorial instincts of the browns. The weather may near 70 degrees and be sunny, but plan on windy, wet, cold and snow. Warm weather clothing, rain gear, along with chest and hip waders...

..."Ruling for the author", and the two wader-clad flyfishers trudge back to their drift boats.

Speaking of browns, Big Spring Creek below town is excellent water. Large fish are taken on every pattern imaginable, but as usual, I've had my best luck with my faithful companion the Cree Woolly Bugger. One day after taking several browns between 16 and 20 inches, Ginny and I were returning to our rig at the Hruska Access (some others include Brewery Flats a mile south of Lewistown, Reed & Bowles north of town, and Lazy KB on the edge of town on secondary Hwy 191) and parking area about six miles downstream from town, when we ran into a couple who'd had no luck at all (an encounter strangely similar to the one recalled in the Warm Springs Creek chapter). I asked what they were using and the husband showed me what he called a Woolly Bugger. His accent was deep south. He could not hide his frustration and disappointment. As in the aforementioned story, it was a skinny, pale looking thing and I smiled, opened a another cracked fly box (all of mine are cracked, crushed or dented if they are of the Wheatley variety) and dropped one of my bushy, mangy Buggers into his hand. Before I could offer any advice his fingers closed over the thing tightly, knuckles going white. His eyes bulged and sparkled as he headed down to the water without a word.

"He gets like that," his wife offered by way of apology for what she thought we'd interpret as boorish behavior.

I handed her a couple more Buggers and said that Ginny and I understood. We said "Good luck", and noticed at the parking area that their plates were Mississippi. Godspeed.

Even now as Big Spring Creek experiences increased pressure, the fishing remains very good. The stream is healthy, it's pure source of water and abundant nutrient base provides excellent habitat for aquatic plants, insects, and forage fish. The trout have excellent oxygen, cover, and food sources. The FWP and area residents take the welfare of the stream seriously. Big Spring Creek is in good hands and will be a joy to fish for years to come.

TRIP INFORMATION

Timing: Big Spring Creek is open all year and due to the nature of its water supply, the water is always well above freezing and ice free. There is little effect from spring snowmelt. Heavy rains cause some turbidity and level increase.

Where: Big Spring Creek flows through the heart of Lewistown. Highway 238 parallels the creek heading east and 426 follows the water to Spring Creek Junction west by northwest. Train tracks go along the stream for several more miles.

Hub: Lewistown offers everything a traveling angler needs from motel rooms, a good selection of restaurants to sporting goods, clothing, hardware, anything at all. The town is located on U.S. Highway 200 in the Judith Basin at the geographic center of the state, and about two hours east, southeast of Great Falls. Don's Western Outdoor Store, (800-879-8194). Don's is an excellent place to purchase anything you'll need for fishing and the outdoors and a prime location to acquire current local information on everything from stream conditions to guides to western clothing. We often stay at the B & B Motel, 520 East Main Street, Lewistown, 406-535-5496. The Empire Café at 214 West Main is good for breakfast, and also the Rising Trout Coffee at 217 West Main Street has rolls and such. I'm always a sucker for any place called the Mint Bar & Grill for burgers, 113 4th Avenue South.

Appropriate Gear: Any weight up to five and length to maybe nine-feet for nymphing. Chest waders preferred to hip waders. Mosquitoes are sometimes a problem, though not a major one.

Favorite Patterns: Pheasant Tail, Hare's Ear, gray and olive scuds, Prince Nymph, BWO, Griffith's Gnat, Black Ant, Sparkle Dun, hoppers, Woolly Bugger, Cranefly, Elk Hair Caddis.

Special Regulations: Entire creek – Open entire year. Upstream of US Highway 191 bridge, including East Fork Big Spring Creek downstream from the reservoir – catch-and-release only for all fish species. Fish consumption advisory in effect for this section of river.

Cranefly

Hook: Mustad C49S, Size 18
Thread: 8/0 rusty sun
Legs: Medium dun microfibbetts, knot approximately 3/8-inch from the tip
Abdomen: Cream-colored micro chenille
Wings: Med. dun hackle tips
Head: Tan CDC

CHAPTER NINETEEN

Bears Paw Mountains

Every year or so, I find myself back out here mired in this god-forsaken heat plodding beneath a sun so bright it has lost its circular identity and now holds white hot sway over the entire blasted-out sky. One-hundred degrees is a mirage shimmering within a realm of relative coolness. One-twenty-five seems about right and thankfully the sun is past its zenith. The heat of the day will eventually fade. Provided I don't do the same, I'll make it back to camp and the nearby refreshing cold-water spigots of a rarely used research station with its thick green grass, carpets of ponderosa needles, outhouse full of mouse droppings and chewed remains of years-old newspapers, trailers up on blocks and mostly boarded up, and weathered picnic table. My camp is only 100 yards from all of this luxury perched on a small promontory overlooking a pond surrounded with a dense shoreline of cattails. Vast fields of native grasses and sage surge casually towards the south.

The Bears Paw Mountains rise to the north. I've been captivated by these deeply eroded remnants of long-ago volcanic accumulations ever since I first drove around them on dusty, rough roads decades ago. These dusty flats that I'm moving along now are sitting on top of shonkinite lavas that hardened about the time the range above me formed. The terrain is flecked with spring-fed ponds, anomalous items in this place of dryness and sparse growth, explosions of deep green grasses and reeds and more cattails encircling aquamarine moisture that often holds fish – smallmouth, maybe sunfish, crappies, and perch or a rogue northern pike. Around sunrise and sunset, mule deer, coyotes, raccoon, sage grouse, once a black bear, and tracks of a mountain cat in the soft shoreline sands, have shown themselves as all of the animals come out from shadowed hidings to drink before and after the furnace blast of daytime. There are small spring-water inspired creeks that bubble here and there and they hold brookies and rainbows. I've tracked these waters from narrow wooden bridges far back into the hills and have found that there are some fish in the 15-inch range in them. Tight fishing with light, short rods but a lot of fun in light of the arid landscape that looks like something from outer Mongolia, which is nearly the same latitude.

Ranch ponds hold even larger trout. One just east of Road 300, about four miles north of its junction with 421, has some fat fish that take Sheep Creeks cast from a float tube, the pattern allowed to sink for a dozen seconds then twitched a few times, allowed to sink again and so on. The takes are fierce and 3X tippet is needed. Wind and flies are often problems, but what else is new out on the high plains?

The mountains stretch from west to east in a long string of rounded summits connected by easy saddles of pine, mostly ponderosa. The tops of these ancient volcanic structures remind me of a group of mildly crazed men gathered in some enormous free-form backyard for beers, shots of whiskey, and White Owl cigars. In this heat, I am sure that I can hear them murmur comments shaded with soft chuckles as they watch me push through the alkalai flats, my boots kicking up puffs of grey-white dust or skirting gardens of desiccated prickly pear. Level-headed clumps of juniper hold tight to ledges of yellow rock, the plants' fragrance like a never-made gin hangs in the stillness. A chance glance above and I see a pair of turkey vultures circling silently almost out of sight, waiting for a free meal that I may well provide. Baldy Mountain, Pegmatite Peak, and the rest of them are looking down, laughing with crinkled eyes formed from ragged ledges of garnet, sphene or wedged-shaped crystal, eudialyte, and other rare minerals. Perhaps this is an inside joke that I bring back to life with each visit here. Who can fathom the humor of the old ones? Not me, but I hear their voices drifting down the slopes against the rush of heated air, at once soft and powerful.

"Every year that damn fool comes here and, wouldn't you know it, he's always out stomping around when not even a snake or a scorpion is moving," says one of the guys.

"Mad dogs and Englishmen," says another with a bit of a feigned accent.

All of the mountainous boys have a good laugh at my expense while working on beers so cold they manage to pull what little moisture there is in this sun burnt air on to the metallic surfaces in a sensuous film of condensation.

What the hell. When you're 50 million years old like they are, you can do whatever you please. I know I'm heat-stroke nuts, but I've been here before and the pull to camp and icy liquids is doable. Trust me. I'm from the government and have your best interests at heart.

"You're wandering a bit there my boy," says Baldy and I check myself, manage to regain some semblance of composure and decorum. Appearances must be maintained, especially before this crowd. Still I say out loud, "Let them laugh. Mad dogs and Englishmen my ass." But I must admit that holding one of their chilled, moist cans in my hand sounds real good. One for each claw would be ecstasy.

I settle for surreptitiously viewing a rattlesnake passed out on a slab of sandstone. Four feet and not coiled in strike, but rather stretched out languidly, body lined in gentle curves, a series of barely discernible esses, the creature stoned from the sun. Its rattle hangs over the edge of the flat rock. Only the thinnest of quivers course through the reptile's muscles. They look like microscopic waves barely disturbing the buff, tan, and off-white scales. The inch-long rattle pays no attention to this slight activity.

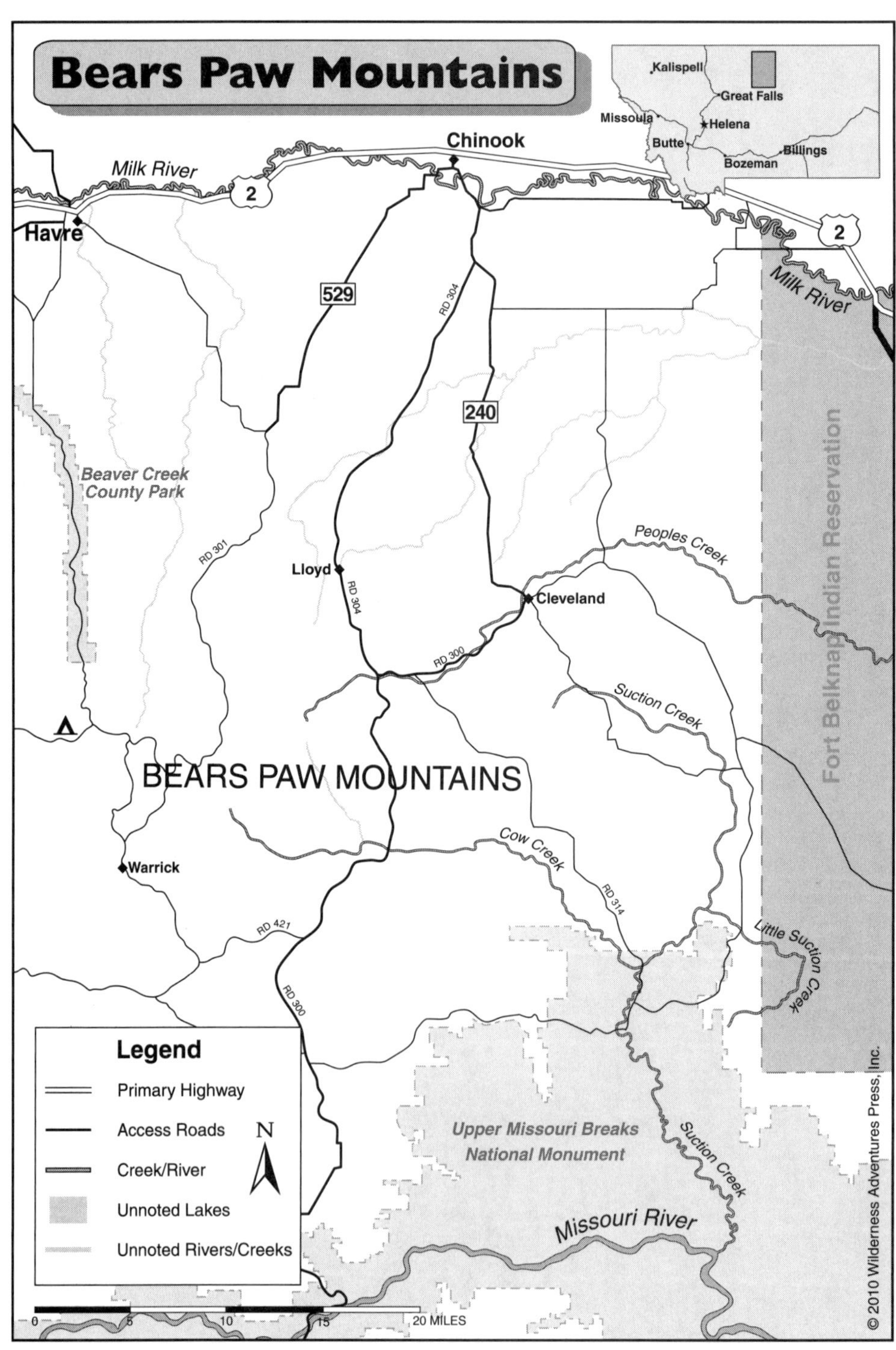
Bears Paw Mountains
Kalispell
Great Falls
Missoula
Helena
Butte
Billings
Bozeman
Milk River
Chinook
2
Havre
529
RD 304
240
Milk River
Fort Belknap Indian Reservation
Beaver Creek County Park
RD 301
Peoples Creek
Lloyd
RD 304
Cleveland
RD 300
Suction Creek
BEARS PAW MOUNTAINS
Warrick
Cow Creek
RD 314
RD 421
Little Suction Creek
RD 300
Legend
Primary Highway
Access Roads
N
Creek/River
Unnoted Lakes
Unnoted Rivers/Creeks
Upper Missouri Breaks
National Monument
Suction Creek
Missouri River
0   5   10   15   20 MILES
© 2010 Wilderness Adventures Press, Inc.

The only rancher from around these parts that I ever heard speak, and this was ten years or more back in time, told me from the shelter of his truck cab to be on the lookout for rattlers, especially "the old bastards that grow feathers and have hair on their blessed chins". I nodded and said "Thanks" while the man worked on a half-pint of something I clearly was not familiar with. Feathers? Hair? The mountains were laughing at me again. Was the guy real? Was any of this? Was I?

Looney Tunes once more with all-too-familiar feeling in the Bears Paws.

What draws me to country like this? There are no sparkling rivers filled with trout. A few trickles that may hold some brookies with names like Cow, Bullwhacker, and Suction. No deep blue lakes filled with more trout. A few ranch pond diversion items with stocked rainbows. That is the extent of the salmonid intrusion. The Bears Paw are not spectacular like the Beartooth Mountains with their well-above timberline snow and ice crowned peaks and heart-stopping canyon views like in the Rosebud and Stillwater drainages. Campsites are where I find them and what I make of them. The only people I encounter way out here are the odd (minor pun) rancher driving by to check me out with a quick glance at my 49 plate from Livingston. No smiles. Only rueful shakes of heads sulking beneath sweat-stained Stetsons or gimme ball caps before they turn their pickups around in the dusty orange-tan earth and motor back to the homestead, sounds of AM country fading on the breeze. Dwight Yokum. Ferlon Husky. Conway Twitty and his *Deck of Cards.*

All of this apparent nothing is what I live for. Death Valley. The Grand Erg Occidental south of anything remotely habitable in Algeria. The limitless lonesomeness of the Thunder Basin Grasslands in northeastern Wyoming. The isolation is restorative. I come to this Bears Paw landscape to get away from all of it – mortgage payments, traffic, television, grocery stores, bars – all of it. Setting up a dry camp on a wind-blasted ridge is basic – only the smallest of fires in my Little Smokey grill, tarp, pad and bag for bed, cooler and battered Coleman stove forming a kitchen and, if the need for luxury overcomes me, a canvas folding chair. Hell, I'm home. Some food. A drink or two. A cigar or two, usually my wife Ginny along for the ride. Nothing more is needed or desired.

I've spent a good deal of time exploring the ponds and impoundments in the region. One spring-fed oasis has proved to be packed with hefty largemouth bass that gorge on frogs, damsel and dragonflies, mayflies, grasshoppers that have filed erratic flight plans, and even mice that occasionally stray too close to shore. One bass of maybe three pounds, attracted by the minute scramblings of a rodent, waiting like motionless death right next to the bank, its back partially exposed above water. The mouse moved here and there, randomly searching for seeds, tiny flies, frog eggs. Then in what appeared to be an unconscious death wish, the little grey mouse moved to the water and washed its paws like a raccoon. As it bent over a final time the fish pounced in a ferocious splash and crunch then plowed down into the weeds with the hapless and doomed animal writhing in its jaws. I stopped fishing. The killing, while natural, was unsettling to one so gentle as myself.

Other ponds have proved lifeless. Still others are filled with stunted bass of two to four inches. Thousands of them that attack any streamer on the water as though their savior had arrived and was proffering deliverance from the liquid ghetto conditions. And I've caught rainbow-colored pumpkinseeds along with white and black crappie in a few larger ponds out on the flats but closer to the mountains. These species provide great sport as they slice their thin bodies this way and that through the water while connected to a very light fly rod. The fish, including the bass, are all members of the sunfish family, and their flesh tastes excellent when fried in a little peanut oil and served with lemon wedges, salt and pepper. Simple excellences.

The few ranch ponds with rainbows have proven to be a disappointment. Lots of bothersome flies that bother eyes, ears, and nose relentlessly, foul smelling mud, cow pies, and only a few fish resulting from hundreds of wind-blown casts. One plus is the surreal scenery. Dry, high plains. The Little Rockies holding like a purple mirage over east of Hays. The Missouri Breaks perhaps 20 miles south. Towers and down-sized buttes rising like still-life ghosts on the edges of stands of ponderosa. A sky full of drifting high clouds reminiscent of the Arctic. The streams are OK with sometimes a brook trout to 16 inches, but the best, deepest runs and holes are on private land and I'm not into a turf war over trout. Maybe someday.

The streams I've fished out here are rarely much in terms of cubic feet per second, but around bridge abutments and along oxbows the water piles up in places. These mini ponds often hold the largest trout. I fooled a 15-inch brook trout with a large hopper cast off a dirt slope and hustled across the calm surface. The fish came from some weed growth nearby, hit the bug and started to head back to cover. I pulled him to me. Fat, firm, and nicely colored though more silvery than he would be, come fall breeding time. I've turned fish in this pool and others like it each time I've fished them over the years, regardless of conditions. Hot, cold, bright sun, cloudy, windy, none of this seems to make any difference. There are probably not too many flyfishers out working the running water of the Bears Paw Mountains.

Below one reservoir where the water seemed more trickle than flow, I poked my head through prickly wild rose, dense alder and willow, all the while thinking "snake". About every 75 feet, some rocks or clumps of brush backed up the water creating a tiny impoundment and an even smaller pool below. I could see trout holding in each location as I struggled downstream. Sliding the rod through any negotiable opening in the bank side brush I dropped a #16 Adams on the water with nothing more than a nine-foot leader extended from the rod tip. It was frustrating trying to set the fly on the water without hanging up the leader or the fly and the drift, if I may be so bold as to describe the six-inch course the brave Adams would travel as such a thing, drove the trout crazy. A bunch of them would fight for the right to be hooked then, as I lightly lifted the rod, coupled with the lunatic leaps of the impaled trout, I would try and keep them from hanging up in the brush. In the largest of the holding spots, perhaps three feet by five, an enormous brookie of perhaps 13 inches took the Adams and dove to the bottom. I pulled back a little and the fish rocketed up free of the stream a foot or more in the air then started down, but the leader caught on a rose bush and the hapless trout wriggled in the hot light. I snapped the leader as near to the fly as I could and the trout dropped back into the water. My hand and forearm bled slightly – fin-thin streams (much like this creek) host thorns, perhaps a form of minor penance for my brook trout harassment. Most anglers sensibly ignore this sort of silly angling, but I love it. The ever-popular child-at-heart attachment running at full tilt.

Ginny and I have set up camps on grassy, wind-swept ridges out in this dryness and watched as the sun moved over and down in the west. The sky turned from light blue to blue to purple then black in an east-to-west progression as stars and planets began to show. Coyotes would bark and howl for hours. Nighthawks would boom. The distant lights of the tiny town of Hays, home to Gros Ventre and Assiniboine Indians on the Fort Belknap Reservation. The tribal land is located between the Milk River and the mine-ravaged Little Rockies island mountain range. The country is surreally gorgeous with a powerful vibe of lonesomeness and possible despair. Sitting in the dark in the middle of all this isolation is a powerful experience. One that forever resonates within.

So, in other words, the fishing is amusing to an extent, but not a destination attraction unless you're from someplace like Beirut or Kabul.

What does draw my persistent attention is the fact that this apparently dead, dried-out land is filled with mystery and life. Animals are everywhere once the sun nears the horizon. Deer come close to camp. One time I watched as a mother opossum scurried (I'm being generous here) past with six young clinging to her back, her tail looping back towards her head – short-lived marsupials marauding in the Montana badlands. The scent of not-so-distant skunk arrives on cooling air. Black bear scat is common around the lakes and pines. Claw marks scar the outhouse. Nighthawks boom and whiz above me gorging on bugs ranging from mayflies to dragonflies to mosquitoes. Bats arc and slide through the gathering dark searching for the same insects. American bullfrogs croak. Western toads peep like anemic chickens in the rushes below me. Fish break the surface chasing minnows. I hear all of this as stars appear and glide down around me covering all 360 degrees of the horizon. Meteors fizzle. Military jets and surveillance satellites pass overhead soundlessly, like they don't exist in my world. The fire, small as it is, crackles and sprinkles orange and yellow light in a perfect circle around camp.

The tops of the mountains glow with faintest of silver starlight. Old volcanoes gone to sleep.

Could do this forever. Space far into the universe. Glide into the Bears Paws. Blend with the dancing flames.

Modest perfection.

TRIP INFORMATION

Timing: Runoff is not really an issue in this country. When the warm weather comes on in mid-April, the country lights up in native grass greens and a glowing spectrum of wildflowers. Summer months are really hot, but from September into early November, the days are often autumn fine. When it rains, the roads are impassable and help is far away.

Where: The Bears Paw Mountains run from west to east and are located about 30 minutes south of Havre, which straddles US Hwy 2 along Montana's Hi-Line. County Roads 529 and 240 (takes you to the very small town of Cleveland) lead into the country where almost all of the fishing is located farther on along the south foothills and the open prairie that rolls off to the Missouri. There are a couple of reservoirs right by Cleveland with some trout, lots of mud, and cows. Peoples Creek is also right by town. Much of the ponds and streams are located on either/and/or BLM and state land. As always, access may be gained from bridges crossing streams, provided the angler stays below high-water marks. When in doubt up here, take the time to ask permission. Locals don't see a lot of outsiders up this way and tend to act accordingly.

Hub: Havre is a bustling town of around 10,000 and contains everything except a fly shop – grocery stores, restaurants, motels, the works. The Hi-Line Motel works – 406-265-5512, 20 2nd Street, Havre. Nalivka's Original Pizza Kitchen has good food – 1032 First Street North, 406-265-4050.

Appropriate Gear: Light, short rods up to seven-foot-nine for the creeks; 5- through 7-weight for the reservoirs due to the wind. A float tube is nice to have. Hip waders handle the creeks. Bring camping gear. There are countless places to pitch a dry camp. Watch any fires due to dry grasses and high winds.

Favorite Patterns: Muddlers, Buggers, small attractors for the creeks, Adams, Elk Hairs down to #16, Hare's Ear nymph, Sheep Creek Special.

Gold-ribbed Hare's Ear Nymph

Hook: Size 8 to 22, down-eye (regular or 2x shank)
Thread: Brown

Tail: Hare's mask guard hair
Body: Hare's ear fur
Rib: Fine gold tinsel

Thorax: Hare's ear fur
Wing case: Hen pheasant tail

CHAPTER TWENTY

Milk River

This stretch of the Milk River didn't look like much on the map, only some skinny blue lines running about on white background indicating a lack of trees or mountains or much else. These were the bends, turns, and out-of-the-way wanderings way out on the lonesome prairie north of Malta and Saco in northeastern Montana. I figured that this would be a pleasant cruise along an isolated stretch of a little-known river. Maybe there'd be a few fish, some mule deer, a few chattering coyotes, a thunderstorm with lots of pyrotechnics, some wind. I'm glad this proved wrong. Floating this water over a period of three days and two nights was heaven. Ginny and I felt like we'd dropped back a couple of centuries. Sure there were some cows, idle farm machinery, and a few miles of rusting barbed wire, but for the most part, our canoe and gear were the only man-made items we dealt with on a consistent basis. The river lazily worked its way through the dry northern high plains. Eroded bluffs exposing layers of sediments from ancient oceans gone by, defined the drainage. Native grasses blew golden, grey, and bronze in the September sunlight and warm afternoon breeze. We never saw another soul which roughly translated means, "I'm in paradise". We camped on gravel rises above the Milk, up in the wind to avoid the few flies and mosquitoes still hanging around this late in the season. Small fires built from bone dry limbs of cottonwood and willow, some with gnawed ends from beaver. No car, house, or ranch lights – only the intense glow of starlight bright enough to throw dark shadows on the silvery land.

Ginny guided the canoe easily along the gentle current while I cast a pattern called a Gapen's Spitfire tight to undercut banks, along riffles, and down deep in the occasional deep pool. The Spitfire is a black and brown little beauty that sports a red duck quill tail. I'm sure this wet fly was designed for the time-honored techniques associated with eastern brook trout, but I've learned that the fly tied large, #6 to #8, drives any predacious fish into a frenzy. So far on this jaunt I'd taken a few small – 24 inches – northerns, a pair of largemouth bass, lots of goldeye that fought like crazy using their narrow profiles to strategic advantage in the seams of current, and a few yellow perch that are now confined to the cooler for this evening's dining extravagance. They stopped flapping an hour ago. The ice cooled them out. The canoe has scared catfish – large ones – largemouth buffalo, and possibly freshwater drum. The fish thunder off leaving large, silty wakes in their flight. The wind blows wavelets across the river's surface erasing these tracks.

The fishing is good, catching a variety of species and never knowing what's next on the menu, but I'd do this river over and over again if only for the absolute sense of solitude and freedom. I've only experienced this sporadically in my travels, and the Milk holds its own with the Peel River in the Yukon or the unnamed streams of Iceland's interior in these respects or deep inside the Missouri Breaks, places like these, few in number and shrinking. Last night, the sky flashed into daylight in a series of silent explosions we thought were heat lightning before a final burst turned the land to complete daylight, illuminating a group of antelope that must have been stunned and an enormous beaver that probably weighed more than 60 pounds. Then we tracked the source as a meteor fizzled over the ridge behind us shedding rose-orange chunks of extra-terrestrial material in its wake.

What would tomorrow bring? Maybe that thunderstorm I mentioned earlier. I'd worry about that tomorrow. Right now I was heading down to the river with a lightweight spinning rod, some treble hooks and some aromatic chicken livers (sun-cured this very afternoon) in search of catfish fillets for breakfast. Breaded in cornmeal, fried in peanut oil, and served with lemon wedges along with coffee and orange juice. We'd survive.

More than 725 miles long from its headwaters along the Rocky Mountain Front on the western edge of the Blackfeet Reservation, the Milk River is a major tributary of the Missouri River. The north and south forks of the Milk River flow northeast through the Blackfeet Indian Reservation to merge just over the Canadian border. The main stem Milk River continues 171 miles through Alberta, re-entering Montana north of Rudyard. Fifty-three miles farther southeast the Milk River runs up against Fresno Dam, completed in 1939. The Milk River was given its name by Captain Meriwether Lewis, of the Lewis and Clark Expedition, who described the river in his journal:

> *"The water of this river possesses a peculiar whiteness, being about the colour of a cup of tea with the admixture of a tablespoonfull of milk. From the colour of its water we called it Milk River."*

This appearance results from rock flour suspended in its waters. These extremely fine-grained sediments are the result of glacial erosion at the Milk River's headwaters.

Above Fresno Reservoir, desert-like terrain, highly fluctuating flow caused in large part by irrigation drawdown, and near-blinding turbidity define the river. The channel is mostly shallow and braided. Turning due east below the dam, the river carries less sediment and runs within a single carved channel with vertical banks. From Fresno Dam down to Vandalia Diversion Dam, 318 miles, the river is fragmented by four diversion dams and one municipal water weir. East of Havre, the river bends and

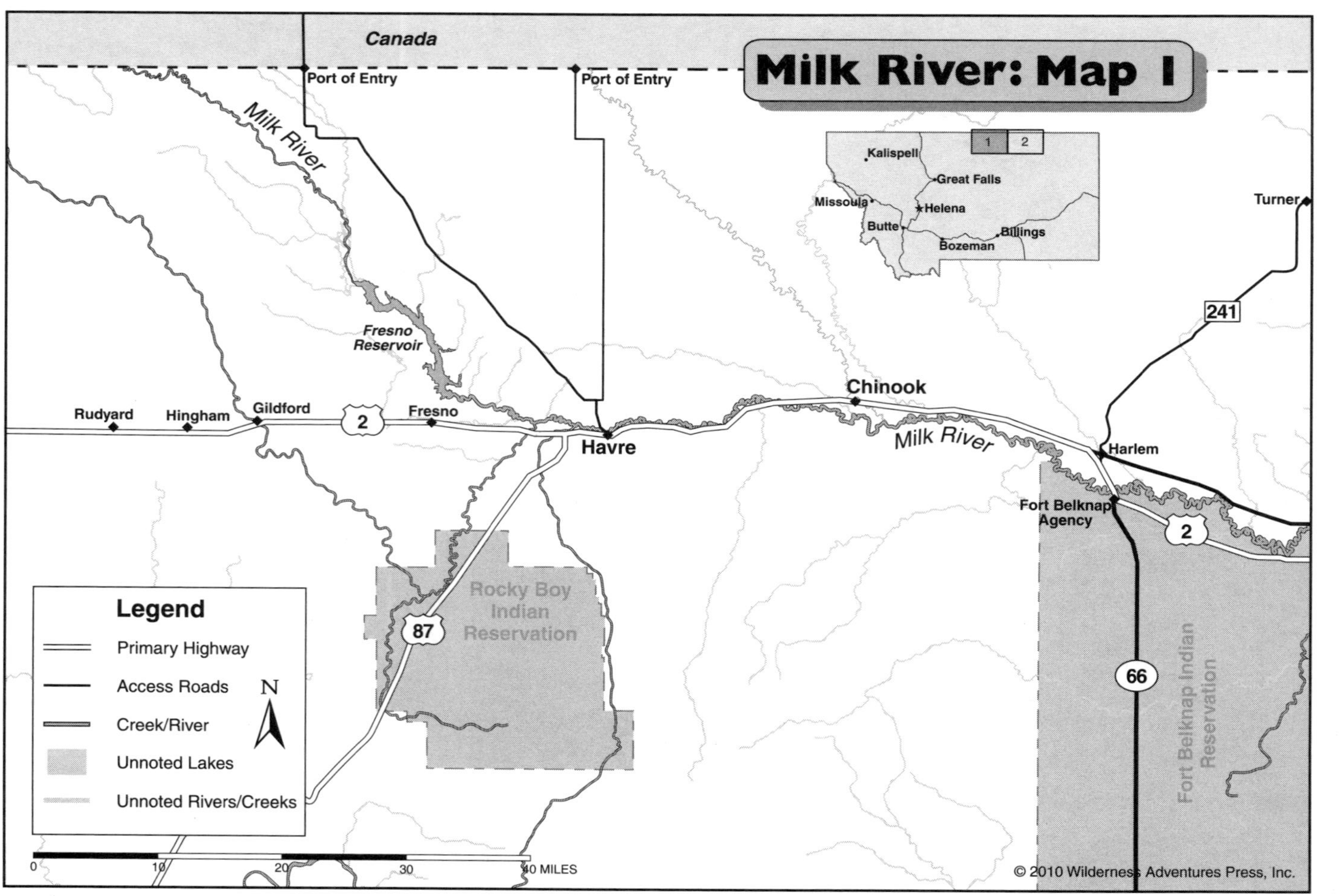
Milk River: Map I
Canada
Port of Entry
Port of Entry
Milk River
Fresno Reservoir
Kalispell
Great Falls
Missoula
Helena
Butte
Bozeman
Billings
1
2
Turner
241
Rudyard
Hingham
Gildford
2
Fresno
Chinook
Havre
Milk River
Harlem
Fort Belknap Agency
2
66
Fort Belknap Indian Reservation
Rocky Boy Indian Reservation
87
Legend
Primary Highway
Access Roads
Creek/River
Unnoted Lakes
Unnoted Rivers/Creeks
N
0   10   20   30   40 MILES
© 2010 Wilderness Adventures Press, Inc.

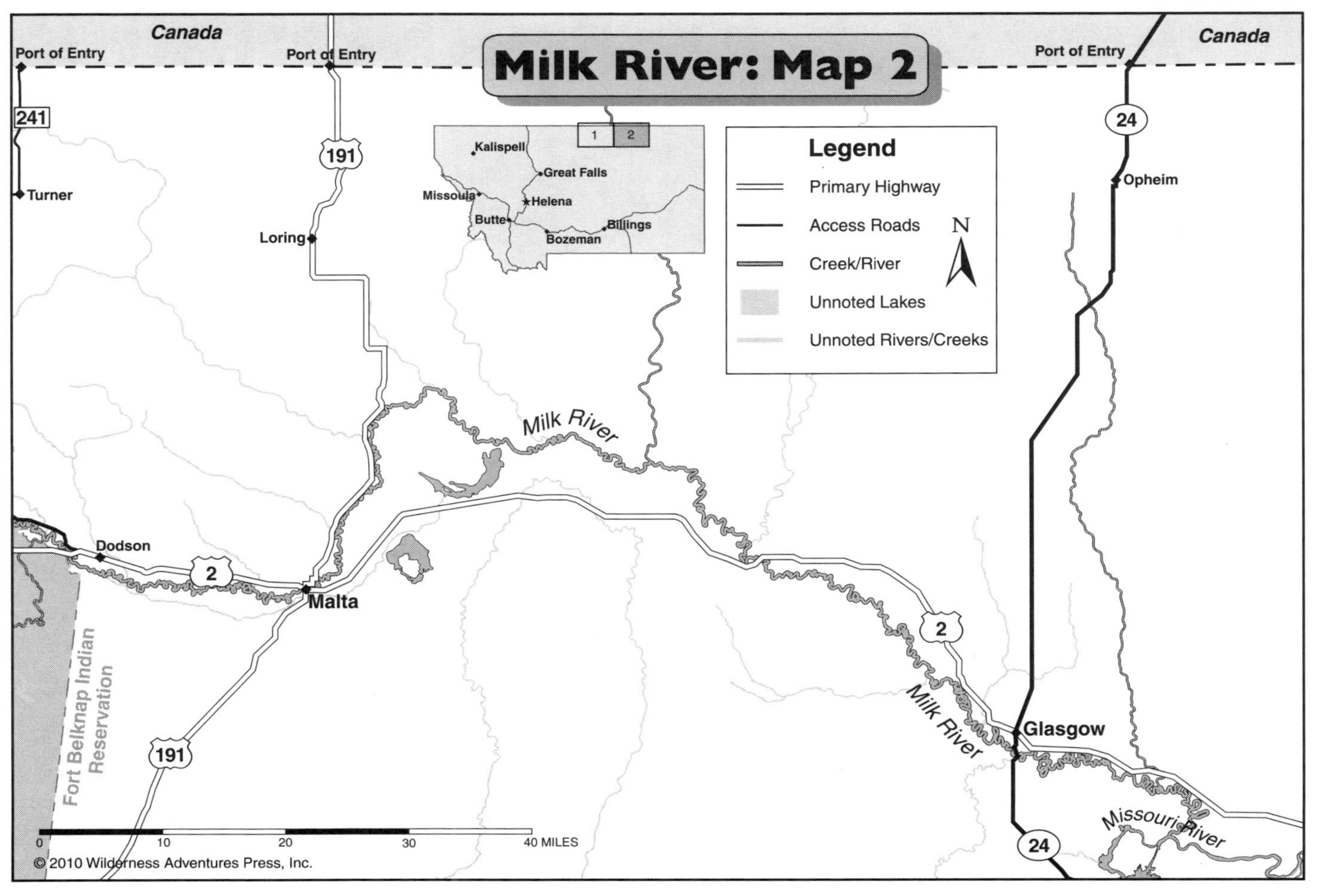
Milk River: Map 2
Canada
Port of Entry
Port of Entry
Port of Entry
Canada
241
191
24
Turner
Opheim
Loring
Kalispell
Great Falls
Missoula
Helena
Butte
Billings
Bozeman
1
2
Legend
Primary Highway
Access Roads
Creek/River
Unnoted Lakes
Unnoted Rivers/Creeks
N
Milk River
Dodson
2
Malta
2
Milk River
Glasgow
Fort Belknap Indian Reservation
191
24
Missouri River
0
10
20
30
40 MILES
© 2010 Wilderness Adventures Press, Inc.

twists through the pre-glacial-age valley of the Missouri, paralleled by U.S. Highway 2, and marking the northern boundary of the Fort Belknap Indian Reservation. Below Vandalia Diversion Dam, for its last 120 miles, although still a single-channel river, the Milk has well-developed riparian stands along its banks, deeper habitat, and rocky riffles. Today the Milk River results from a history of dams, channelization, flow modification, and expansion of land use, as well as natural development. Since the 1880s, the Milk River Basin has provided water for agricultural communities. The Milk River replenishes the wetlands and prairie habitats of the 16,000-acre Bowdoin National Wildlife Refuge where over 250 bird species and other wildlife families flourish. Perhaps the river's most important contribution to the area's fishery resource is its alliance with the Missouri River.

While trout angling purists turn their noses up at flows like the Milk, consider what this river offers in terms of fish species diversity. In its lowermost 73 miles, the Milk River provides critical spawning and rearing habitat for migratory and resident fishes, including native species of the Missouri River, such as blue sucker, channel catfish, freshwater drum, paddlefish, sauger, shorthead redhorse, and shovelnose sturgeon.

The list of fish swimming in the river according to the Montana Department of Fish, Wildlife and Parks is: bigmouth buffalo, black bullhead, black crappie, blue sucker, bluegill, brassy minnow, brook stickleback, brook trout, brown trout, burbot, channel catfish, cisco, common carp, creek chub, emerald shiner, fathead minnow, flathead chub, freshwater drum, goldeye, Iowa darter, lake chub, lake whitefish, largemouth bass, longnose dace, longnose sucker, mountain sucker, northern pike, northern redbelly dace, paddlefish, pallid sturgeon, pearl dace, plains minnow, rainbow trout, river carpsucker, sauger, sauger x walleye hybrid, shorthead redhorse, shortnose gar, smallmouth bass, smallmouth buffalo, spottail shiner, stonecat, walleye, western silvery minnow, western silvery/plains minnow, white crappie, white sucker, and yellow perch.

Nearly 50 species. Not bad for a river the self-absorbed, precious trout magazines could care less about.

Admittedly, the above list of fish is a good one, but there's always room for one more and I humbly offer this suggestion to those fun-loving boys at FWP – the legendary and regal zubatak. I first heard of this species years, hell, decades, ago when I was wandering about Yugoslavia in search of marble trout, which I never found; though I stumbled into some very primitive villages whose residents were most friendly and generous with a homemade distillation of grains, sugar beets, and grapes. A concoction that made moonshine seem like white wine. The liquor was so potent the only way to survive the next morning was to drink more of the stuff and we all know where that leads – no fish, no memory, no name.

Recently I came across information on the zubatak at a website operated by the Balkan Trout Restoration Group. Their website is quite interesting at www.balkan-trout.com/index.htm. I suggest that the FWP contact these knowledgeable individuals when they begin their *Zubatak in Montana Transplant Project* (you fisheries guys can use this name).

From balkan-trout.com:

> *Dentex trout (Salmo dentex), known as "zubatak" among the local people, is one of the last salmonids whose existence is still unclear. The fish was first described in the rivers Krka, Cetina and Neretva already in 1852 and confirmed in the Krka by in Gridelli (1936). Nowadays, this fish is reported to inhabit lower part of the river Neretva, Hutovo blato, the river Cetina, the Morana river basin in Montenegro, and possibly also the Aoos stream in Greece. The fish is, by its external appearance, somewhat similar to brown trout, softmouth trout and marble trout, all native to the dentex trout distribution range with the exception of the Aoos stream. That's why this fish has been sometimes considered a hybrid between these three groups. However, recent morphological analysis performed on museum specimen originating from the Neretva indicates that this fish might represent an independent trout lineage. Although the preliminary genetic data suggested the same, the recently performed genetic tests that included an extended molecular marker set and several samples of marmorated (veined or streaked like marble) trout from the Neretva River, indicated that dentex trout was genetically indistinct from Neretva marmorated trout. Dentex trout has been poorly studied due to lack of samples for detailed analyses, hybridization and diverse and multiple designation of the same trout in different areas of the region (e.g., in the upper Neretva, zubatak is a common name for brown trout, and glavatica for marmorated trout; in the lower part, some people call marmorated trout zubatak while S. dentex is known as zubara; others call S. dentex zubatak, and zubara is considered a "species" that has not yet been described.)*

Anglers from the region brave landmines from recent and ongoing wars. They are few, far between, and somewhat crazy, and they report that the zubatak is an excellent game fish and fine table fare. While I'm disappointed that the FWP never followed up on my cutting-edge suggestion of planting taimen in the Tongue River, I'm willing to let bygones be bygones if the department should, in what would historically be a rare act of creativity and courage, proceed with the implementation of my zubatak plan. Time will tell on this one. I have to admit that even though I'm an eternal optimist, my faith in the FWP participating in a vanguard operation such as this one is shaky at best. FWP employees for the most part are unwilling to rock the boat let alone take on a way-ahead-of-the-curve concept such as this one. Still, one can dream.

There are so many miles of this river to explore that a solid season would be needed to even fake familiarity with the Milk. And I've not paddled this water in the summer since an ugly time of mosquito frenzy along a grassy, willow- and cottonwood-lined stretch over by Malta. Even the wind failed to put down the bugs because the river was sheltered by steep 10- to 20-foot banks. Camping was a study in abject, earthly hell not visited by this fool since those fun-filled canoeing disasters on Ontario's Sand River in a hopeless search for brook trout over 2.56 inches while being devoured by black flies and mosquitoes when I was eleven, or camping along the MacKenzie River near Fort Providence in the Northwest Territories in late June where the mosquitoes were enormous, voracious, and relentless. The Milk River variety are quite obviously criminally insane. They don't land on exposed skin to suck blood with insect arrogance and righteousness. They power dive like marauding WWII German Stukas, sometimes coming in so hard and fast they bounce off flesh only to circle around for another run at a body's blood. Save the Milk for after the first frost, sometime in late August (or in spring before late May) or suffer the consequences.

We were heading west towards some northern pike fishing on Lodge Creek north of Chinook (population a shade over 1,500) in Hay Coulee (valley). Yesterday we'd escaped Livingston and all its near terminal permutations of cabin fever. Today is a cloudy, off-and-on wet late April situation as we drive back roads towards the stream. North then east then north some more on roads that are gravel and passable despite the precipitation. We work on mugs of coffee as we bounce along carefree in our renewal of freedom that is a pure rite of spring. We find a bridge crossing the water way up by the Canadian border. The bridge I've fished at many times. It's still corroded, still slightly sway backed and still full of bullet holes. Dirty, crusted snow is still packed into the cut banks of some of the oxbows. The water level at this point of Lodge Creek is low, but we crawl through an old fence and work our way upstream along a hill that looks down 40 feet to the stream. Just before noon, the wind drops and the sun comes out. The temperature jumps from the 30s to the upper 50s. Buttercups explode in the light. Looking down in a lake formed by beavers I see logs with fins that are cruising back and forth. April is the season of love for northerns and the males turn aggressive. Dropping down to the water, Ginny waits above with her camera, I tie on a streamer called the Widow Maker that looks like some type of missile, #2, 4X long-shaped minnow. A friend tied up several and mailed them to me from his ice-bound home on the shore of Great Slave Lake in Yellowknife. After working maybe 50 feet of line out I wing the pattern along a rock outcrop next to a steep hill. Stripping the streamer swiftly turns northerns from all over the place. A small one – about eight pounds – makes a grab and I move to slowly jerk the minnow away. The fish runs and thrashes while his large brethren follow him in a form of *esox lucius* support. The fish gives up the fight after a few minutes and I wrench the hook out of his bony, toothy mouth with a pair of needle-nosed pliers. I cast again towards a larger pike and he smashes the thing as it hits the water. More racehorse runs and then a release. The Widow Maker looks like it's gone through a nasty divorce.

Looking up I see Ginny zeroing in on me with a long lens. She gives a thumbs up while looking through the viewfinder.

There are more fish here, but I want to explore, so I edge my way along the edge of the hill on a narrow cow track past a narrow chute formed by shattered layers of copper-colored rock. Lodge Creek flows in a riffle for some distance and I take northerns of a few pounds along grassy banks, the grass dead-grey after fighting a Montana Hi-Line winter death trip. The creek squeezes in between the hills and twists away towards distant Havre before opening into an oxbow that resembles a cheap wine bota about to explode its contents of Paisano. There are northerns lying alongside downed limbs or swimming slowly in wide circles. This reminds me of musky water near Presque Isle, Wisconsin. Ginny is behind and slightly above me. A trio of mule deer, big ears twitching look down on both of us and maybe the fish. I make a shorter cast this time, about 40 feet, and the northerns see it coming. Three of them almost bang heads trying to attack the battered thing. The largest of the three wins and the race is on. Again this northern runs back and forth causing me to strip in line with the grace of a Rush Street drunk (don't ask) before the line burns through my fingers and off the reel when the pike zips away from me. The others follow along like they're watching some horribly bad (and aren't they all?) TV fishing show where the host drones on about the food, booze, and soft beds while doing battle with a quarter-pound crappie. When the thing tires, I pull it to me. This one is a dozen pounds easy. The hook has worked a hole on the jay and, barbless, it drops out of the fish's mouth and sinks to the sand that is speckled with bright flakes of iron pyrite (or possibly real gold).

"Do these fish stay here all winter?" asks Ginny.

I tell her I'm not sure. Some of the bends in the creek are deep enough and spring fed to avoid freeze out or oxygen depletion. And I imagine that northerns could move the many crooked miles up here from the Milk at Chinook. I really don't know. I guess I like to think they live in this nowhere nothing of a glorious creek.

I catch some more. Then Ginny tries here hand and a pair of pike in the next oxbow cooperate. She's very excited, but no more so than me. Hell, I've been in love with northern pike fishing since I used to chase them on the Mississauga River in Ontario a long, long time ago.

When I consider this fishing and the canoe trip over east by Saco and the hundreds of miles of water yet to explore, I realize that a river doesn't have to be a trout stream to be a special entity. The Milk River is as real a fishing experience as any in Montana and I'm glad the bugs bite viciously in the summer so all the fish can feed in relative privacy.

TRIP INFORMATION

Timing: Runoff comes thundering down from Glacier Park and makes the river unfishable often into mid-July. When the warm weather comes on in mid-April, the country lights up in native grass greens and a glowing spectrum of wildflowers. Summer months are really hot but from September into early November the days are often autumn fine. When it rains, the roads are impassable and help is far away.

Where: The Milk River flows for over 600 miles in Montana and more than 100 in Canada, though don't drift across the border if avoiding run-ins with angry border patrol guards is an issue. Highway 2 from west of Havre follows the river all the way to its confluence with the Missouri just south of Nashua. North of Havre, Highway 232 runs to the Alberta border. Dirt and gravel roads cut west to the river. On the Blackfeet Reservation, Radar Base Road heads off Highway 213 and accesses some intriguing water. On the rez, you're on your own, especially in this way out of the way neck of the arid high plains.

Hub: Havre is a bustling town of more than 10,000 and contains everything except a fly shop – grocery stores, restaurants, motels, the works. The Hi-Line Motel works – 406-265-5512, 20 2nd Street, Havre. Nalivka's Original Pizza Kitchen has good food – 1032 First Street North, 406-265-4050.

Appropriate Gear: Light, short rods up to seven-foot-nine all the way to nine feet, 5- through 7-weight (for the lower river due to the wind and river size). Canoes, rafts, drift boats are a decided plus. Chest waders. Bring camping gear. There are countless places to pitch a dry camp. Watch any fires due to dry grasses and high winds.

Favorite Patterns: The Widow Maker, Clouser Minnow, Muddler, Bugger, Gapen's Spitfire, Adams, Elk Hairs, Hare's Ear nymph, Joe's Hopper.

Gapen's Spitfire

Hook: Mustad 3906B
Tail: Red duck quill

Palmer rib: Brown hackle, folded
Body: Black chenille

Hackle: Guinea hen as collar

The Widow Maker

Hook: Mustad 34007 stainless saltwater, size 2

Eyes: Large prismatic dumbbell eyes

Thread: Common tying thread in matching colors

Head: Five-minute epoxy

Body: Super Hair or other moderately stiff synthetic fiber

CHAPTER TWENTY-ONE

Poplar River Drainage

When I first came to Montana a long time ago, I never thought that I'd ever fish for northerns, man. Hell, those fish are for Ontario or northern Saskatchewan I figured. But one does change over time. The years weather and wear a soul down to more honest dimensions. That's how I find myself doing the following.

Halfway through April and there's still snow on the ground. Old, dirty grey stuff packed and hardened into sheltered curves and crevices of the not yet green high plains here above Havre, not too far south of Saskatchewan. And there's several inches of newer, white snow that is melting rapidly under the intense spring sun. The land is more or less lifeless, not awake yet from a mild but long winter. The water I'm fishing is little more than a series of shallow, scummy oxbows connected by long stretches of mostly dry rock runs, slight trickles of brownish water seeping downstream from between the oxbows. I've been casting a large chartreuse barracuda streamer (a saltwater pattern) for hours, turning absolutely nothing. Casts to rock and brush piles and into dead-reed shallows fails to move a single northern pike. Everything is more or less dead up this way. Way too dead. And the fresh water of a new year's spring runoff hasn't arrived yet. The pike are probably dozens of miles away hanging out in their deep-water winter sanctuaries along the Milk River. At least I'm out here beneath the sun, out in the wind casting instead of reading another book, renting another predictable movie, or staring zombie-like at the never-ending forecast on the weather channel.

In the past few years, I've turned more and more to fishing for what are often termed either warmwater or trash species – catfish, goldeneye, smallmouth and largemouth bass, sunfish, bluegills and, most invigorating of all, the pike. So many of my favorite trout streams are clogged with wading and drifting flyfishers, that what was once a solitary exercise in escape from the day-to-day madness of living has turned into a competitive, unfriendly riparian land grab. That's why I find myself wandering the dry, lonely coulees and wind-swept flats of the eastern third of Montana casting to the lesser lights in the flyfishing panoply of gamefish.

Over by Plentywood, the area this chapter is really about – no offense to the fine people of Havre – I took pike after pike on nearly every cast in large bends in a creek that ran clear and tea-colored, small springs bubbling up through the clean sands and gravel. The northerns ran to a dozen pounds and hammered the bright green fly with a savagery uncommon to trout fishing. And around Havre and down near Chinook and so on the wind howls or the sun bakes or both, but over-dressed anglers are rare and the northerns have often never been cast to. Streams on the Fort Peck Indian Reservation in the northeast corner of the state are virtually ignored, virginal from a fishing perspective. For many years, I thought trout fishing was the epitome of flyfishing sophistication and joy. Now I have my doubts. I see things in the rapidly shifting light of relived experiences and the current, noisome commercialization of trout.

In the growing chill of this autumn day, I make a 70-foot cast into the wind, shooting the heavily weighted streamer to the deep water at the end of a grassy point. The pattern sinks swiftly and I begin a fast-paced, stripping retrieve. In seconds, a copper-green torpedo rockets from nowhere and, with a long mouth filled with millions of wicked curved teeth slashes the streamer in a raucous boil and splash. I yank back on the 8-weight and the northern pike goes ballistic, catapulting through the water in muscular undulations of its long, thick body. The pike then races straight downstream in the general direction of Glasgow and is into my backing in seconds. The rod isn't bowed from the fish's strength. I'm pointing the tip straight at the direction of its flight hoping to avoid a break off and a stress-induced explosion of over-wrought graphite. The pike sounds in ten feet of water that seems surprisingly deep in light of the fact that this little stream is narrow enough to leap across in places. I pull the pike towards me. Perhaps a mistake as the fish slams to the end of the oxbow and hurtles over a dozen feet of clean rock and gravel only just covered by the low October streamflow. The northern drops down into another dark pool and I reel in line as fast as possible as I fast-step it downstream. The pike makes a series of circling runs before I bring it to my hips where I'm standing in the water. The wind is stilled now, gone for the evening, the sun is setting in a golden-orange glow filled with deepening purple shadows that stretch out across the open prairie. Coyotes howl as the stars come out. Hereford cattle low and bellow from their grazing positions on distant benches. Ranch yard lights wink on and cast their eerie blue-white glow on the land. This pike is about 10 pounds and as solid as a well-trained athlete.

I return to camp, a simple setup as usual, of cooking area, sleeping bags arranged on the ground and chairs overlooking the stream as it winds its way through the swales, rises, and bluffs of this country. As I sip a cup of tea, I watch as a school of minnows leaps frantically from the water, some of them landing on the bank. A large pike makes a circling wake, dorsal fin breaking the surface, as it slashes its way through the terrified forage fish. Back and forth and then the pike is gone, returned to its deeper-water holding spot.

Simply put, I love this fishing. No matching the damn hatch with microscopic flies I can't see or remember the names of. No delicate tippets and artfully presented delicate casts. Just a gaudy, six-inch streamer, 60-pound big-game tippet and long,

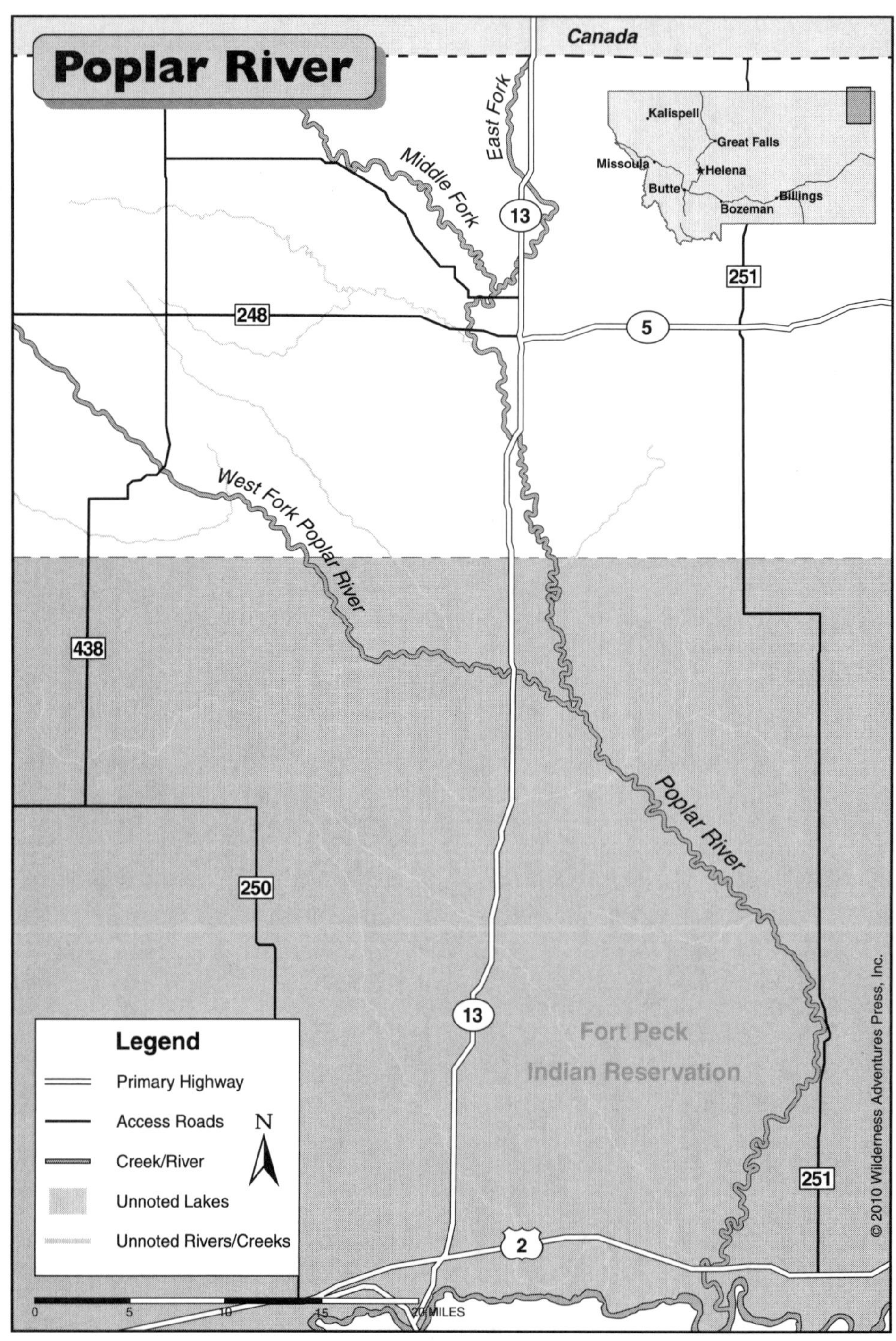
Poplar River
Canada
East Fork
Middle Fork
Kalispell
Great Falls
Missoula
Helena
Butte
Billings
Bozeman
13
251
248
5
West Fork Poplar River
438
Poplar River
250
13
Fort Peck
Indian Reservation
251
2
Legend
Primary Highway
Access Roads
N
Creek/River
Unnoted Lakes
Unnoted Rivers/Creeks
0   5   10   15   20 MILES
© 2010 Wilderness Adventures Press, Inc.

slamming casts. If the pike see the fly, they kill it in a burst of speed that probably goes from zero to 40 a hell of a lot faster than a Porsche.

I could do this forever. I used to say that about fishing the Madison or Rock Creek.

Just about every trout flyfisher turns his or her nose up at this fishing. Fine. Let them eat trout, except the blood part of my beloved blood sport is anathema to most of them. Catch-and-release gone mad in an elitist fashion. The northerns are native to Montana unlike rainbows, browns, or brook trout. They've been practicing their savage search-and-destroy trade for thousands of years in these isolated, little-known or unknown streams. The other day while talking with a Daniels County deputy sheriff (and for once it wasn't because a member of the law enforcement contingent thought I looked like a felony waiting to happen), he told me he'd taken an 18-pounder about a mile upstream of where I am holding the pike prior to release right now. And two friends of mine have caught a number of northerns of 20-plus pounds in slightly larger watery doings less than a dozen miles south of here on the reservation. In fact, one of the fish slashed one of my friend's waders with his rows of scythe-like teeth which in turn provoked a violent response from my friend.

"John when he bit me I had to stick 'em," he informed me over the phone. That was the trip where he also took out the driver's side window swinging on a turkey that chose to flee via the air waves instead of along the more conventional ground route. The copper-twos launched from my friend's 12-gauge ventilated his rig. A few days following the slightly manic phone call, I received a series of color prints showing man and pike, both bloodied, next to a small, nowhere stream, the wounded (not mortally) van whimpering in the background. The sporting life as it should be. May it always be so.

The next day in this country was more of the same for me. From early morning when the sun first topped the gently rising hills drifting off to the east, the star's hot rays lighting up the frost-cloaked landscape and turning the land into a motionless sea of glistening diamonds, emeralds, rubies, and sapphires, on through the relative heat of an autumn midday and on into another other-worldly sunset, I took northerns in water of a few inches deep in those grassy, reedy shallows where they held silently like freshwater sharks only to blast 30 feet or more in an instant to attack my streamers. And I took the pike in the deep depressions of the oxbows. Fish from a pound to more than a dozen. I lost streamers as the northern's shredded the thick leaders with their menacing teeth; and it was the most fun I'd had fishing in 20 years. I realized what I'd been missing since my youth when I used to hunt this species in the waters of the North Channel of Lake Huron in Ontario, and the pikes' cousin, muskies, in northern Wisconsin.

These are no bullshit fish. They live to kill and eat. Noisy presentations, large patterns, less than stealthy approaches mean nothing to these fish. Make the streamer – the bigger and gaudier the better – swim and undulate, hell, just make it move, and the pike explodes from out of nowhere in a murderous rush. Picky rainbows delicately sipping #22 *baetis*, I've had enough of that craziness. Finesse is not my style. The menacing voraciousness of the northerns is. I prefer the solitude, lonesomeness and straightforwardness of this fishing way out on the northern high plains. I'll take it any day (that is until I see 20-inch browns smashing wind-blown grasshoppers on a river near Livingston).

...Two days ago, around when we crossed the bridge over this nothing fork of the Poplar River, I looked down and was blown away. The water was clear, copper-tinted, running over a bright gravel and stone streambed. I'd expected a warm, turbid sluggish flow more suited to catfish. This looked like a trout stream. We kept on until we came to a wire gate that I opened, and we followed a two-track that led through grazed grass fields filled with huge platter-shaped dried cow pies that stretched off to the distant horizons. Long pieces of rusted, twisted barbed wire lay on the ground next to rotted posts. The grass was bright green and went on forever, past the banks of this stream, rolling across vast fields rippled with gentle swales like motionless waves and, farther on, hills and rounded bluffs rose several hundred feet above the valley and just kept going on to disappear in blue sky. Puffy white clouds drifted by riding a warm northwest wind. Because of the vast scale of this land, the river and hills gently winding out of sight to the north and south, the distant herds of cattle resembling grounded flocks of brown birds, because of all of this, the clouds appeared motionless and, if I kept staring at them, they never moved, but if I turned away to work at setting up camp and then turned back some minutes later, it was clear that the cumulous was moving away to the southwest, perhaps bound for Sidney or Glendive at a good clip.

This place was all but empty of the fast-paced confusion common to humans. No traffic noise, power lines, car alarms going off with machine-like futility, no police sirens, no frantic vibe of too many people doing too much of nothing on a too-tight, can't-make-it-fit, useless schedule. Cows were grazing on the slopes all around us. Large cylindrical bales of hay were stacked neatly here and there. Weathered-grey barns and sheds stood silently in small dips in the land, out of the wind. In the hour we'd been here organizing the cooking area, the coolers, rigging fly rods, only a pair of pickups had rattled by on the gravel county road, the dust the rigs raised disappearing lazily in the breeze. We were less than 20 feet from the stream that was burbling away as it cut into the dirt and gravel banks, squeezed through hard places in the ground or opened wide into mini-lakes. Red-tailed hawks worked in pairs along the crests of the hills. A red fox ran along the road then darted in the tall grass of the ditch when I looked at it. Nighthawks swooped and boomed in the afternoon light. Coyotes barked off and on from the distance of a couple of cottonwoods a mile or so downstream. A person could live peacefully here and I wondered what it would be like to live on the ranch that I could see clearly in the pure air, the one nestled into a wide groove in a bluff at least three miles away. I could see tall pines planted in neat rows as wind protection, more stacked hay, out buildings, tractors and so forth. Did the people that lived there realize the special nature of this place or did they only see a day-to-day never-ending grind involving their cows, cow shit, breaking machinery, heartless banks, constant wind, numbing cold and blistering heat? Did they fish this stream? Hunt the sharptails and sage grouse and pheasants? Or the deer and antelope? Or was this just home, a place that looked like anywhere else. Like Chicago looks to Chicagoans or the Himalayas looks to Tibetans. Pretty. Exciting. The same old, same old. Ugly because of familiarity. Barely noticed most of the time because of this familiarity.

The hell with this introspective jive. I notice the soft power of this country. If the ranchers don't see the place, well, that is their problem. I want to catch the trout this stream surely holds. Maybe browns. Or brookies. I'd know in a few minutes.

I didn't catch anything for a while. Each perfect, artfully presented cast into riffles, small eddies or beneath slight undercuts in the bank turned nothing. No trout. No bass. Not even a whitefish, though I did see several carp. Ten pounders sunning themselves in the shallows. I was fishing what looked like ideal holding water for browns or brookies and seeing nothing when it dawned on me with a flash of

obviously nascent insight that I was here for northern pike and they, being the insane predators that they are, keep to different water than do trout.

To examine a pike is to experience evolution in the predatory sense at its finest. The fish are designed to kill their prey quickly, efficiently, with little wasted motion. The long, muscular body propels a barracuda-shaped head that is filled with rows of wicked teeth towards unsuspecting prey at astounding velocities, 30 miles per hour or more. I tripped back to the youthful days spent catching the species in the reedy shallows of the North Channel of Lake Huron in Ontario. Back then I used spinning gear to launch Johnson Silver Minnow spoons, red and white Dardevles, wooden minnows, Lazy Ikes and anything else that even vaguely resembled food. The lure would arc through the air, plop into the water among the tall reeds and as soon as I began reeling in, the pike would zoom in out of their nowhere invisibility making v-shape wakes and slamming the lures in a voracious splash. I still have several mangled wooden plugs riddled with teeth marks from those days.

With that in mind, I began casting to similar water, especially in the slow, wide bends of the stream, in tight to snake grass, grama grass banks, and mossy shallows. Throwing the large, bright green saltwater fly 70 feet (the slow water here grew to widths of well over 100 feet despite the small volume of flow) in the constant wind with a 6-weight fly rod was entertaining and occasionally painful when the weighted pattern would slam into my head or back. The vicissitudes of angling, I guess. The second cast brought a familiar response. A mottled green, cream, and tan shape rocketed from several inches of water and drilled the streamer. The fight wasn't much and the northern was only two pounds, but now I knew the fish were here, and I began casting to all likely-looking water with lunatic vigor, laughing and talking to myself.

"Great cast, Holt," as I unhooked the fly from my shirt.

"Son-of-a-bitch," as a six-pound pike boiled and snapped my 20-pound leader when it pounced from just off a small point in a bay-like bow in the river. I switched to 60-pound big-game tippet to try and offset the knife-like effects of the pikes' teeth.

"Damn, this is outrageous," I yelled as a 10-pound pike slammed the chartreuse pattern in the same spot just off the point. The pike ran and churned up the surface as I followed it downstream in knee-deep water. The rod was bent well more than double, and vibrating intensely with the energy from the northern. The fish pulled into the backing, then abruptly gave up. I reeled it in. "Amazing. What a fish in this little thing (the stream)." Close to 30 inches. Deep shades of green. Cream, square spotting. Coppery tints along the back. White belly. Rich brown fins streaked with black. And hundreds of mean, curved teeth in jaws that slowly opened and closed. The pike had crushed the six-inch streamer in its middle to break its back, kill it. As I twisted the hook free of its tough mouth with a pair of pliers, the fish shook itself and those teeth raked my thumb and forefinger. Crimson blood dropped onto the fish's flanks and into the water. The price of pike. I continued taking northerns everywhere along the flats and in the wide bends until well into dark. I couldn't stop. The crazed, full-blown nature of these animals hooked me and made me realize what I'd been missing with my obsession for trout at the exclusion of species like this. Straight-ahead, no bullshit killers. No half-assed #22 BWOs on 7X tippets ever-so-lightly cast in fear of spooking neurotic trout who have seen it all too many times from a flyfishing perspective. Throw the weighted chartreuse barracuda fly with authority and strip the thing back. Northerns are insane, marauding killers and this color seems to bring out their better nature. The pike aren't scared by the splash and noise. They're attracted to it. I was totally addicted one more time to this passion of hunting, finding fish in out-of-the-way, unexpected locations.

I used to fish to catch fish. That was the only reason. Now I fish to find out what's in a river, stream, lake, pond, reservoir, drainage ditch. Standing in the water and casting and discovering these pike, or ranch pond bluegills, or large brook trout in a high plains lake or diminutive rainbows in a crystalline stream sparkling like cut crystal flowing out in the desert of southeastern Montana or catching catfish in a little stream on a late May night in even drier country; all of this connects me to the land and tells me that the natural system is intact.

This fork of the Poplar River, as well as the other branches of the drainage, was alive with fish, tons of them lying in wait to eat smaller fish or cruising the shallow eddies at night chasing forage fish in a quicksilver flash and splash of spraying water and terrified leaping minnows. When I'm sunk this deep in one of my true passions, I see everything. Nighthawks flitting overhead. Caddis coming off the water. Flickers and bands of crisp orange light tracking the setting sun, slight darkening of clouds indicating night showers, the taste of sweetgrass on a cool evening breeze, the long-distant cry of a coyote or, out of the corner of my eye a quarter-mile away, the steep dive of a falcon powering down to hammer some small rodent. The fishing becomes automatic. I know where the pike are and more than this, I know I will catch them on nearly every cast. That's the way all of this becomes when I lose the Holt crap and the living in town crap and submit to all of this. Chattering away like a truly free madman, casting like a chaotically-designed machine with no governor, the streamer landing exactly where I want it to without thinking or calculation, the northern rushing out of skin-thin water, white toothy jaws wide open, the murderous take and above all this, the sharp cry of two red-tailed hawks signaling each other as they stalk jackrabbits over on a low ridge and the soft sound of this water flowing out of the bend and over a coppery gravel run. Lose the dominant ego and I'm connected in this plane, making congruent ripples that echo back and forth from me to the pike to the coyote to the light to the dark to the wind all at once and outside the limitations of linear time. No thought. Just the feel of the cold water, the cut of the pike's teeth as they tear my skin, the predator coldness of the fish's eye as it bores through me, the pull of the line on my backcast and the rare, insane joy of being alive without thinking about it.

That's what I fish for any more. Not numbers. Not species life lists. Not showing off fancy, over-priced equipment. Not geographic checklists.

Only this little river cruising through this wide open, stoned country and these predacious, wild northerns. I could do this forever and will as long as I can...

TRIP INFORMATION

Timing: Late April through June and then September into October are best, though July and August will work as well.

Where: In the far northeastern corner of the state west of Plentywood (population less than 2,000), ride along Highway 5, then 248 towards Opheim and you'll cross the water. Highway 13 runs north-south and crosses the Poplar on the Fort Peck Indian Reservation.

Hub: Plentywood is the main town in this sparsely-populated area just below Saskatchewan. The Gold Dollar has good food for dining in or take-out, 120 S Main Street, 406-765-2730. Sherwood Inn is located 17 miles from the Canadian Border at 515 West 1st Avenue on the west side of Plentywood, 406-763-2810. Hi-Line Sports, also on the west side of town on the highway, has most things you might require.

Appropriate Gear: I prefer a stout 6-weight or my old Orvis travel 8-weight. Eight-foot-six to nine feet for cheating the wind on longer casts in the oxbows of the streams. Short leaders of five to six feet tipped with 60-pound test or even wire to minimize the effects of the northerns' teeth. Hip waders for the cooler days.

Favorite Patterns: Anything large like Sculpins, Matukas, Buggers, red-and-white color combinations work well much like Dardevle lures with muskies and northerns. My favorite pattern is a chartreuse barracuda fly. The seemingly ludicrous notion of using this garish pattern in Montana has a certain appeal to a slightly-warped aesthetic.

Special Regulations: All non-Fort Peck Tribal members fishing within the boundaries of the reservation must possess a tribal fishing license. Fishing is open year round from February 28 to March 1. Tags – Montana resident: $10 per stamp and tag. Out of State: $20 per stamp and tag.

Chartreuse Barracuda Fly

Hook: Standard saltwater sizes 1/0 to 4/0

Thread: Chartreuse

Body: Krystal flash or body braid, color same as thread

Tail: Super hair in chartreuse braided and tied off with thread (glue the thread)

Eyes: Stick-on eyes in silver

Wing: Bucktail to match tail, on top of and underneath hook

Head: Five- or 30-minute epoxy coating